1 MONTH OF
FREE
READING

at

www.ForgottenBooks.com

By purchasing this book you are eligible for one month membership to ForgottenBooks.com, giving you unlimited access to our entire collection of over 1,000,000 titles via our web site and mobile apps.

To claim your free month visit:

www.forgottenbooks.com/free821214

ISBN 978-0-365-29939-4
PIBN 10821214

For support please visit www.forgottenbooks.com

INTO THE

LIFE and *WRITINGS*

OF

HOMER.

By *Thomas Blackwell*, J. U. D.
Late Principal of *Marifhal* College in the
Univerfity of *Aberdeen.*

The THIRD EDITION,

TAYTHI.

Gravelot, inv.

G. Scotin, fculp.

LONDON:

Printed for E. DILLY, at the Rofe and Crown in the
Poultry, near the Manfion-Houfe. MDCCLVII.

INUS

MY LORD,

IT is the good-natured Advice of an admired *Ancient,* To think over the feveral Virtues and Excellencies of our Acquaintance, when we have a mind to indulge ourfelves, and be chearful. His Friends, it wou'd feem, were fincere and conftant, or found it their Intereft to appear fo; elfe the Remembrance of good or great Qualities, never to be employed in his Service, cou'd not have proved fo entertaining.

B

'T IS

Sect. I.   'Tis however certain, That the Pleasures of
Friendship and mutual Confidence, are pursu-
ed in one shape or other by Men of all Characters: Neither Business, nor Diversions, nor
Learning, can exempt us from the Power of
this agreeable Passion.   Even a fancied Presence
affects our Minds, and raises our Spirits both in
Thought and Action.   The Moralist's Direction
extends its Influence to every part of Life; and
at this moment I put it in practice, while I endeavour to enliven a few Thoughts, upon no
mean Subject, *by addressing them to your Lordship.*

It is HOMER, *My Lord*, and a Question
concerning him which has been looked upon as
hitherto unresolved : " *By what Fate or Dif-*
" *position of things it has happened, that None*
" *have equalled him in* Epic-Poetry *for two*
" *thousand seven hundred Years, the Time since*
" *he wrote ; Nor any, that we know, ever sur-*
" *passed him before.*" For this is the *Man*,
whose Works for many Ages were the Delight
of Princes [a], and the Support of Priests, as well
as the Wonder of the Learned, which they
still continue to be.

How unsafe soever it might have been, to
have said so of old at *Smyrna* [b], where *Homer*
was

a Πτολεμαῖ۞ ὁ φιλοπάτωρ, κατασκευάσας Ὁμήρω Νεών, αὐτὸν
μὲν καλᾶς ἐκάθιτε, κύκλω δὲ τὰς πόλεις σεείσωση τὸ ἀγάλματ۞
ὅσαι ἀντιποιενται τὸ Ὁμήρε.   Ἀιλιαν.

b *Strabo*, speaking of *Smyrna*, says, Ἐσὶ ἢ κỳ βιβλιοθήκη; κỳ τὸ
Ὁμηρεῖον· τοὰ τετράγωνο۞ ἔχεσα Νεών Ὁμήρε κỳ ξύανον· ἀνποιενν-
ται

was deïfied, or at *Chios* among his Pofterity [c], Sect. 1.
I believe it wou'd be difficult to perfuade your
Lordfhip, " That there was a *Miracle* in the
cafe. *That*, indeed, wou'd quickly put an end
to the Queftion: For were we really of the
fame Opinion as the Ancients, that *Homer*
was infpired from *Heaven*; that he fung, and
wrote as the *Prophet* and *Interpreter* of the
Gods [d], we fhould hardly be apt to wonder:
Nor wou'd it furprize us much, to find a Book
of an heavenly Origin without an Equal among
human Compofitions: To find the Subject of
it equally ufeful and great, the Stile juft, and
yet fublime, the Order both fimple and exqui-
fite; to find the Sentiments natural without low-
nefs, the Manners real, and withal fo extenfive,
as to include even the *Varieties* of the chief Characters of Mankind; We fhou'd expect no lefs,
confidering whence it came: And *That* I take
to have been the Reafon, why none of the Ancients have attempted to account for this Pro-
digy. They acquiefced, it is probable, in the
Pretenfions, which the Poet conftantly makes
to celeftial Inftruction, and feem to have been
of *Tacitus*'s Opinion, " That it is more pious

B 2

and

ται ὃ ἢ ἔτοι διαφερόντως τὸ Πο.ητῷ. Καὶ δὴ ἢ Νομίσμα ἡ χαλκῷ
παρ᾿ αὐτοῖς Ὁμήρειον λέγεται. Στραβ. Βιβ. ιδ. This ſtatue
was built by *Lyſimachus*, one of *Alexander*'s Succeſſors.
　[c] Ἀμφισβητῶσι δὲ ἢ Ὁμήρι ΧΓΟΙ, μαρτύειον μὲν τὰ ΟΜΗ-
ΡΙΔΑΣ καλνμένες, ἀπὸ ἢ τὰ γίνες τεκμαιζόμ.
Στραβ. Βιβ. ιδ.
　[d] Ὡς φησιν ὁ ΘΕΟΣ, ἢ Θεῖος ΠΡΟΦΗΤΗΣ.
　　　　　　　　　Πλάτων. Ἀλκιβιαδ. β.

" and refpectful to believe, than to enquire " into the Works of the Gods [e]."

But the happy Change that has been fince wrought upon the face of religious Affairs, leaves us at liberty to be of the contrary Opinion: Tho' in ancient times it might have gone near to banifh us from *Smyrna* or *Colophon*, yet at prefent it is become perfectly harmlefs; and we may any where affert, " That *Homer*'s Poems " are of *human Compofition*; infpired by no " other Power than his own natural Faculties, " affifted by the Chances of his Education: " In a word, That a *Concourfe* of *natural* " Caufes confpired to produce and cultivate " that mighty Genius, and gave him the no- " bleft Field to exercife it in, that ever fell to " the fhare of a Poet."

Here, *My Lord*, there feems to be occa- fion for a little Philofophy, to put us, if poffi- ble, upon the *Track* of this fingular Phenome- non: It has fhone for upwards of two thoufand Years in the *Poetic* World; and fo dazzled Mens Eyes, that they have hitherto been more employed in gazing at it, than in enquiring *What formed it, or How it came there?* And very fortunately, the Author of all Antiquity, who feems to have made the happieft union of the *Courtier* and the *Scholar*, has determined a Point that might have given us fome trouble. He has laid it down as a Principle, " That " the greateft Genius cannot excel without

[e] *De Moribus Germanorum.* " *Culture;*

" *Culture*; nor the fineſt Education produce Sect. 1.
" any thing *Noble* without *natural Endow-*
" *ments* [f]." Taking this for granted, We may
aſſure ourſelves that *Homer* hath been happy in
them both; and muſt now follow the dark
Hints afforded us by Antiquity, to find out *How
a blind ſtroling Bard could come by them.*

   I DO not chuſe to entertain your Lordſhip
with the *Accidents* about his Birth [g]; though
ſome Naturaliſts would look upon them as the
Beginnings of his good Fortune. I incline rather to obſerve, That he is generally reputed to
have been a Native of *Aſia the leſs*; a Tract of
Ground that for the Temperature of the *Climate*,
and Qualities of the *Soil*, may vie with any in
Europe [h]. It is not ſo fat and fruitful as the
Plains of *Babylon* or Banks of the *Nile*, to effeminate the Inhabitants, and beget Lazineſs and
Inactivity : But the Purity and Benignity of the
Air, the Varieties of the Fruits and Fields, the
Beauty and Number of the Rivers, and the conſtant Gales from the happy Iſles of the weſtern
Sea, *all conſpire* to bring its Productions of every
kind to the higheſt Perfection : They inſpire
that Mildneſs of Temper, and Flow of Fancy,
        B 3   which

[f] Horat. De Arte Poet.

[g] Σμιέβη τὴν παίδα (μητέρα Ὁμήρȣ) μιγᾶπαν ἀνδεὶ λαθεαίας,
ἐν γαςεὶ χεῖν.   Ἡρόδοτ. βίῳ Ὁμήρȣ.

[h] *Mimnermus*, a Man of a delicate Taſte, who knew the Country well, calls it, ἱμερτὴν Ἀσίην, *the lovely Aſia* : And *Herodotus*,
who was acquainted with it, and moſt of the fine Countries then
known, affirms, ὅτι μὲν Ἴονες ἔτοι, ᾗ ᷎ τὸ Πανιώνιον ἐςὶ, τῷ μὲν
Ὀυεανῷ ᷎ τῶν Ὡρέων ἐν τῷ καλλίςῳ ἐτύγχανον ἱδρυσάμȣνοι πόλιας
πάντων ἀνθρώπων τῶν ἡμεῖς ἴδμȣν.   Ἡρόδοτ. Κλείω.

Sect. 1. which favour the moſt extenſive Views, and give the fineſt Conceptions of *Nature* and *Truth.*

In the Diviſion commonly made of Climates, the Rough and Cold are obſerved to produce the ſtrongeſt Bodies, and moſt martial Spirits; the hotter, lazy Bodies with cunning and obſtinate Paſſions; but the *temperate Regions*, lying under the benign Influences of a genial Sky, have the beſt Chance for a fine Perception, and a proportioned Eloquence.[i] Good Senſe

[i] Leſt it be thought that theſe Conſequences are ſtrained, it may be worth while to ſet down the Opinion at length of the Great *Hippocrates*, in his Treatiſe of Air, Water, and Situation : Βέλομαι δὲ χὶ πεδὶ τ̃ Ἀσίης χὶ τ̃ Εὐρώπης δεῖξαι, ὁκόσον διαφέρουσιν ἀλλήλων ἐς τὰ πάντα.——τὴν ΑΣΙ'ΗΝ πλεῖσον διαφέρειν φημὶ τ̃ ΕΥΡΩ'ΠΗΣ ἐς τὰς φύσιας τ̃ ξυμπάντων, τ̃ τε ἐκ γῆς φυομένων, χὶ τ̃ ἀνθρώπων. πολὺ γὰ καλλίονα χὶ μείζονα πάντα γίνεται ἐν τῇ Ἀσίῃ ἥ τε χώρη τ̃ χώρης ἡμερωτέρη, χὶ τὰ Ἤθεα τ̃ ἀνθρώπων ἠπιώτερα χὶ εὐοργότερα. Τὸ δὲ αἴτιον τουτέων, ἥ τε κρᾶσις τ̃ Ὡρέων, ὅτι τοῦ ἡλίε ἐν μέσῳ τ̃ ἀνατολέων κεῖται πρὸς τὴν ἠῶ, τοῦ τε ψυχροῦ πορρωτέρω. Τὴν δὲ αὔξησιν χὶ ἡμερότητα παρέχει πλεῖςην ἁπάντων, ὁκόταν μηδὲν ᾖ ἐπικρατέων βιαίως, ἀλλὰ πάντ@ ἰσομοιρίην δυναςεύῃ. Ἔχει δὲ κατὰ τὴν Ἀσίην ξ πανταχῇ ὁμοίως· ἀλλ᾽ ὅσα μὲν τ̃ χώρης ἐν μέσῳ κεῖται τοῦ θερμοῦ χὶ τοῦ ψυχροῦ, αὕτη μὲν εὐκαρποτάτη ἐςί, χὶ εὐδενδροτάτη, χὶ εὐδιεςράτη, χὶ ὕδασι μάλιςα κέχρηται, τοῖσί τε οὐρανίοισι χὶ τοῖσι ἐκ τ̃ γῆς. Οὔτε γὰ ἐκ τοῦ θερμοῦ ἐκκέκαυται λίαν· Οὔτε ὑπὸ αὐχμῶν χὶ ἀνυδρίης ἀναξηραίνεται· Οὔτε ὑπὸ ψύχε@ πέπηγυται· Νοτίη τε διάβροχός ἐςι, ὑπό τε ὄμβρων πολλῶν χὶ χιόν@. Τά τε ὡραῖα αὐτόθι πολλὰ ἐοικὸς γίνεσθαι, ὁκόσα τε ἀπὸ σπερμάτων, καὶ ὁκόσα αὐτὴ ἡ γῆ ἀναδιδοῖ φυτά, ὧν τοῖσι καρποῖσι χρέονται ἄνθρωποι, ἡμερῦντες ἐξ ἀγρίων, καὶ ἐς ἐπιτήδειον μεταφυτέοντες. Τά τε ἐκτρεφόμενα κτήνεα εὐθενεῖν εἰκὸς καὶ μάλιςα, τίκτειν τε πυκνότατα, καὶ ἐκτρέφειν κάλλιςα. Τούς τε Ἀνθρώπους εὐτραφεῖς εἶναι, καὶ τὸ εἴδεα καλλίςους, καὶ μεγέθη μεγίςους, καὶ ἥκιςα διαφόρους ἐς τε τὰ εἴδεα αὐτῶν καὶ τὰ μεγέθεα. Εἰκός τε τὴν χώρην ταύτην προσεγγίζειν τε εἶναι τῷ κατὰ τὴν φύσιν καὶ τὴν μετριότητα τ̃ Ὡρέων. Τὸ δὲ ἀνδρεῖον, καὶ τὸ ταλαίπωρον, καὶ τὸ ἔμπονον, καὶ τὸ θυμοειδὲς, οὐκ ἂν δύναιτο ἐν τοιαύτῃ φύσει ἐγγίνεσθαι, μήτε ὁμοφύλου, μήτε ἀλλοφύλου, ἀλλὰ τὴν ἡδονὴν κρατέειν. Ἱπποκράτης πεδὶ τόπων, &c.

To the ſame Purpoſe the Philoſopher, Ἡ Θεὸς (Ἀθηνᾶ) προτέρους ὑμᾶς κατῴκισεν, ἐκλεξαμένη τ̃ τόπον ἐν ᾧ γεγένησθε, τὴν Εὐκρασίαν τ̃ Ὡρῶν ἐν αὐτῷ κατιδοῦσα, ὅτι ΦΡΟΝΙΜΩΤΑΤΟΥΣ ἄνδρας οἴσοι. Πλάτων@ Τίμαι@.

3

Senfe is indeed faid to be the Product of every Sect. I.
Country, and I believe it is; but the richeft
Growths, and faireft Shoots of it, fpring, like
other Plants, from the happieft Expofition and
moft friendly Soil[k].

THE purfuing a Thought thro' its remoteft
Confequences, is fo familiar to your Lordfhip,
that I need hardly mention the later Hiftory
of this Tract of Land. It has never failed to
fhew its Virtue, when *Accidents from abroad*
did not ftand in the way. In the early
Times of Liberty, the firft, and greateft
Number of *Philofophers* [l], *Hiftorians* [m], and
Poets

[k] *Ingenia Hominum ubique locorum fitus format.* Q. Curtius,
Lib. viii. The Proof of this Affertion is attempted in form in a
Treatife of *Galen*'s; *That the Manners of Mankind depend upon the
Conftitution of their Bodies.*

[l] *Thales* of *Miletus*, contemporary, with *Cyrus*: *Anaximander,
Anaximenes*, his Scholars, of the fame Place. *Pythagoras* of *Samos. Heraclitus* of *Ephefus*; and *Hermagoras*, who was banifhed
that City for his too great Sobriety. *Chryfippus* was of *Solis, Zeno*
of *Cyprus, Anaxagoras* of *Clazomene. Xenophanes*, the Naturalift,
was of *Colophon. Cleanthes*, the Stoic, of *Affus*, where *Ariftotle* ftaid for many Years. *Metrodorus*, the great Friend of *Epicurus*, was of *Lampfacus*; where this Philofopher too dwelt fo long
that he may almoft pafs for a Native. *Theophraftus*, and his Companion *Phanias*, were of *Ereffus*, and his Succeffor *Neleus*, the Heir
of *Ariftotle*'s Library, was of *Scepfis*. Thefe, and *Xenocrates* the
Platonic, *Arcefilas* the Academic, *Protarchus* the Epicurean,
and *Eudoxus* the Mathematician, *Plato*'s Friend (all great Names
in Philofophy) drew their firft Breath on the fame Coaft: As did
likewife *Hippocrates, Simus, Erafiftratus, Afklepiades, Apollonius*,
the greateft Mafters of Medicine. It is alfo obfervable, that of the
feven early Sages, called the *wife Men* of *Greece*, FOUR belonged
to this Climate: *Pittacus* of *Mitylene, Bias* of *Priene, Cleobulus* the
Lindian, and the abovementioned *Milefian Thales.*

[m] *Hecataeus* and *Pherecydes*, the two oldeft Hiftorians the *Greeks*
had, was the one of *Miletus*, and the other of the little Ifland
Syros. Hellanicus was of *Lefbus, Theopompus* of *Chios*: Old *Scylax*
was of *Caryanda. Ephorus*, the great Hiftorian, was of *Cumae*;

Ctefias,

Sect. 1. *Poets* [n], were Natives of the *Asiatic* Coast, and adjacent Islands. And, after an Interval of Slavery, when the Influences of the *Roman* Freedom, and of their mild Government, had reached that happy Country, it repaid them, not only with the Delicacies of their Fields and Gardens, but with the more valuable Productions of Men of Virtue and Learning [o]; and in such Numbers, as to fill their Schools,

Ctesias, Physician to *Artaxerxes* King of *Persia,* and a great Writer of Wonders, was of *Gnidus:* To whom if you join the inimitable *Herodotus,* you will have the Names of the chief Historians among the *Greeks,* excepting the two *Athenians, Thucydides* and *Xenophon.*

[n] *Hesiod,* near *Homer*'s own Days, was of *Cumæ* ; *Mimnermus* of *Colophon, Archilochus* of *Paros, Tyrtæus* of *Miletus* ; *Thales,* the Poet and Law-giver, and *Epimenides,* the Charmer, were of *Crete. Anacreon* was a *Teian, Simonides* a *Cean, Arion* and *Terpander* were *Lesbians :* And not to mention the particular Places of every one's Birth, The admired *Sappho,* her Lover *Alcæus, Bachyllides, Chærilus* (not *Alexander*'s,) *Phocylides, Bion, Simmias, Philetas, Ion* the Tragedian, *Philemon Menander*'s Rival, *Hegemon Epaminondas*'s Panegyrist, and the Astronomic Poet *Aratus,* were all born in this *Poetical* Region. It had also the Honour of producing the *Erythræan Sibyl,* and another inspired Lady, *Athenais,* under *Alexander.* But what is by far the most remarkable upon this Article is, That the famous FIVE, who distinguished themselves in *Epic-Poetry,* were *all* Natives of this very Climate, and the *two greatest* born in the two neighbouring Towns, *Cumæ* and *Smyrna.* Hear the Testimony of the learned *Tzetzes:* Γεγόνασι δὲ τέτων τ̂ Ποιητῶν ('Επικῶν) ἄνδρες ὀνομασοὶ πέντε· 'Ομηρος ὁ παλαιός, 'Αντίμαχ Θ· ὁ Κολοφώνι Θ·, Πανύασις, ΠείσανδρΘ· ὁ Καμιρεὺς, καὶ ἔτΘ· ὁ 'ΗσιωδΘ·. 'Ιωαν. Τζέτζης εἰς 'Ησιοδόν. *Pisander* was of *Rhodes,* and of great Reputation. ΠείσανδρΘ· ὁ διασημότατΘ· Ποιητὴς, Κοριεφεὺς ἦν. Στεφαν. περὶ πλεῶν. *Antimachus* wrote the *Theban* War ; and *Panyasis* the Labours of *Hercules :* He was of *Halicarnassus.* *Suidas* says of him, Σϐισϑέισαν τὴν Ποιητικὴν ἐπανήγαγε, *He retrieved Poetry when it was almost extinguished.*

[o] *Panætius, Stratocles, Andronicus* the Peripatetic, *Leonidas* the Stoic. and before them *Praxiphanes, Eudemus,* and *Hieronymus,* were all of *Rhodes. Posidonius* was of *Apamea* in *Syria,* but lived, governed, and taught in the same Island. *Charon* the Historian, *Adeiman-*

Schools, and the Houses of the Great; to be Sect. I. Companions for their Princes[p], and to leave some noble Monuments for Posterity.

IT will probably be thought too great a Refinement to observe, that *Homer* must have been

-ius, and *Anaximenes* the *Rhetor*, were of *Lampsacus*. *Agatharchides* the Aristotelic, of *Gnidus*. *Erastus* and *Caryscus*, of the Socratic School, were Natives of *Scepsis* near *Troy*. That little Place was formerly famous for the Birth of *Demetrius*, the celebrated Critic, contemporary with *Aristarchus*; and of *Metrodorus*, a Man of high Spirit and Eloquence, the unhappy Favourite of the great *Mithridates*. *Hegesias*, *Xenocles*, and *Menippus*, were the Authors and greatest Ornaments of the *Asiatic* Eloquence: And in general, the Teachers of Oratory and Philosophy came from the same Coast: *Diophanes*; *Potamon* and *Lesbocles*, great Men and Rivals, from *Mitylene*; *Crinagoras*, *Dionysius Atticus*, *Diodorus Sardianus*, *Diotrephes*, *Alexander* surnamed *Lychnus*, *Dionysocles*, and *Damasus* called *Scombrus*; *Apollonius Nysæus*, *Menecrates*, *Apollonius Malacus*, *Nicias* of *Cos*, who grew ambitious and turned Tyrant; *Theodorus Cronus* the Dialectic, *Archidamus*, *Antipater*, *Nestor*, Stoics; with many others, whom see in *Seneca* the Father, his *Controver. & Suasor.* Lib. where he relates the Sentences of the *Grecian* Masters.

[p] *Theophanes* the Historian, *Pompey*'s great Friend and Counsellor, was of *Mitylene*: His Son was afterwards Prefect of *Asia*. *Aristodemus* of *Nysa* had been *Pompey*'s Master; and his Cousin-german of the same Name, was entrusted with the Education of the Children of that great Man. *Pompey*'s younger Son, *Sextus*, when he was Lord of the Seas, had *Dionysius* the *Halicarnassean* among his Friends, the celebrated Historian and Critic. *Theopompus* of *Gnidus*, and his Son, were both Favourites of *Julius Cæsar*; and the Father had a great hand in his short Administration. *Apollonius Molo* was *Cicero*'s Master. *Pompey* going to his Eastern Expedition, paid *Posidonius* a Visit in his School at *Rhodes*, and humbled his *Fasces* at the Gate, as they used to do to a Superior: When he was about to take leave, he asked his Commands, and this courtly Philosopher bid him, in a line of *Homer*,

Ἀιὲν ἀριστεύειν καὶ ὑπείροχον ἔμμεναι ἄλλων;

Always excell and shine above the rest;—the thing in the World he most wanted to do. *Hybreas*, the finest Speaker in his time, was in high Favour with *Marc Antony*; and the Care of *Augustus*'s Manners was committed, by *Cæsar* his Uncle, to *Apollodore* the *Pergamenian*. The elder *Athenodore* needs no other Proof of his Virtue and Merit, than that he lived and died with *Marcus Cato*. The *younger* held

been the firſt or ſecond Generation after the Tranſplantation, or rather the final Settlement of this Colony, from the rocky *Morea* to theſe happy, Lands: A Situation, in which Nature is obſerved to make the moſt vigorous Efforts, and to be moſt profuſe of her genial Treaſure. The Curious in Horſes are concerned to have a mixed Breed, a Remove or two from the foreign Parent; and what Influence it might have here, will belong to the Curious in *Mankind* to determine.

I f *Homer* then came into the World in *ſuch* a Country, and under ſo *propitious* an Aſpect of Nature, We muſt next enquire, "What "Reception he met with upon his Arrival; in "what Condition he found things, and what "Diſpoſitions they muſt produce in an exalted "Genius, and comprehenſive Mind." This is a difficult Speculation, and I ſhou'd be under ſome Apprehenſions how to get thro' it, if I did not know that Men moving, like your Lordſhip, in the higher Spheres of Life, are well acquainted with the Effects of *Culture* and *Education.* They know the Changes they are able to produce; and are not ſurprized to find them, as it were, new-moulding human Creatures, and transforming them more than *Ur-ganda*

held a high Place in *Auguſtus*'s Favour, grew dearer to him the longer he lived, got great Honour; and, when weary of the Court, returned with abſolute Power from the Prince to reform and govern his native City. He was ſucceeded in Favour and Honour by *Neſtor* the Academic, who was charged with the Education of the noble *Marcellus, Octavia*'s Son, and apparent Heir of the Empire.

ganda or Circe. The Influence of Example and Sect. I. Difcipline is, in effect, fo extenfive, that fome very acute Writers have miftaken it for the only Source of our Morals [a]: tho' their Root lies deeper, and is more interwoven with our *Original* Frame. However, as we have at prefent only to do with *Homer*, in his Poetical Capacity, we need give ourfelves no further Trouble in confidering the Tenour of his Life, than as it ferved to raife him, To be the *Prince* of his Profeffion.

IN this Search, we muft remember that *young Minds* are apt to receive fuch ftrong Impreffions from the Circumftances of the Country where they are born and bred, that they contract a mutual kind of *Likenefs* to thofe Circumftances, and bear the Marks of the Courfe of Life thro' which they have paffed. A Man who has had great Misfortunes, is eafily diftinguifhed from one who has lived all his Days in high Profperity; and a Perfon bred to Bufinefs, has a very different Appearance from another brought up in Sloth and Pleafure: Both our Underftanding and Behaviour receive a Stamp from our Station and Adventures; and as a liberal Education forms a Gentleman, and the contrary a Clown, in the fame manner, if we take things a little deeper, are our Minds and Manners influenced by the Strain of our Lives. In this view, the Circumftances that may reafonably be thought to have the greateft Effect upon us, may perhaps be reduced to thefe following:

[a] Monf. *Mothe le Vayer,* &c.   FIRST,

Sect. 1.   FIRST, The *State of the Country* where a
Perfon is born and bred; in which I include the
common *Manners* of the Inhabitants; their
Conftitution civil and religious, with its *Caufes*
and *Confequences:* —— Their *Manners* are feen
in the *ordinary* way of Living, as it happens to
be polite or barbarous, luxurious or fimple.

.. NEXT, the *Manners* of the *Times*, or the
prevalent Humours or Profeffions in vogue: ——
Thefe two are publick, and have a common
effect on the whole Generation. Of a more
confined Nature is, firft, *Private Education* ;
and after that, *the particular Way* of Life we
chufe and purfue, with our *Fortunes* in it.

FROM thefe Accidents Men in every Country may be juftly faid to draw their Character,
and derive their Manners. They make us *what
we are*, in fo far as they reach our Sentiments,
and give us a peculiar Turn and Appearance :
A Change in any one of *them* makes an Alteration upon *Us*; and taken together, we muft
confider them as the Moulds that form us into
thofe Habits and Difpofitions, which fway our
Conduct, and diftinguifh our Actions.

SECT.

Gravelot. del.   Scotin. sculp.

SECT. II.

THERE are some Things, *My Lord*, which, tho' they happen in all Ages, are yet very hard to describe. Few People are capable of observing them; and therefore Terms have not been contrived to express Perceptions which are taken from the widest Views of Human Affairs. Of this kind is a Circumstance which attends the Fate of every Nation. It may be called a *Progression of Manners*; and

depends

Sect.2. depends for the moft part upon our Fortunes:
As they flourifh or decline, fo we live and are
affected; and the greateft Revolutions in them
produce the moft confpicuous Alterations in the
other: For the Manners of a People feldom ftand
ftill, but are either polifhing or fpoiling. In
Nations, where for many Years no confiderable
Changes of Fortune happen, the various Rifes
and Falls in their moral Character are the lefs
obferved: But when, by an Invafion and Con-
queft, the Face of things is wholly changed; or
when the original Planters of a Country, from
a State of Ignorance and Barbarity, advance, by
Policy and Order, to Wealth and Power, it is
then, that the Steps of the Progreffion become
obfervable: We can fee every thing on the growing Hand, and the very *Soul* and *Genius* of the
People rifing to higher Attempts, and a more
liberal Manner.

FROM the Accounts left us of the State of
ancient Greece, by the moft accurate of their
Hiftorians [a], we may perceive *three Periods* in
their Affairs. The *firft*, from the dark Ages,
of which they had little or no Knowledge [b], to
the time of the *Trojan* War. The *fecond*, from
the taking of *Troy*, to the *Perfian* Invafion, under *Xerxes*. The *third*, from that time, to the
lofs of their Liberty, firft by the *Macedonians*,
.. and

---

[a] *Thucydides*, Lib. i.
[b] Cur fupera Bellum Thebanum & Funera Trojæ,
Non alias alii quoque res cecinêre Poetæ?
Quo tot facta Virûm toties cecidêre? Nec ufquam,
Æternis famæ Monumentis infita florent?   T. Lucre

and then by the *Romans.* *Greece* was *peopled* in Sect. 2.
the First; she grew, and the *Constitution* was settled in the Second; *she enjoyed it* in the Third,
and was in all her Glory. From the two *first*
Periods *Homer* drew his *Imagery* and *Manners,*
learned his *Language,* and took his *Subject,*
which makes it necessary for us to review them.

WHAT is properly called *Greece,* is but a
rough Country: It boasts Indeed, as well it may
in such an Extent, many a fine Vale, and delicious Field; but taking it together, the Soil is
not rich or inviting. It was anciently but thin-
ly inhabited; and these Inhabitants were exposed to the greatest Hardships: They had no
constant nor fixed Possessions; but there were
frequent Removes, one Nation or Tribe expelling another, and possessing themselves of
their Seats [c]: This was then look'd upon to be
a Calamity, but not near so grievous as we
imagine it now, or indeed as they themselves
thought it afterwards: For there being no Traffick among them, or secure Intercourse, they
had but the bare Necessaries of Life: They
planted no Lands, acquired no Superfluities, and
built only Shelters from the Weather [d]: Experience

[c] ἡ Ἑλλας ἐ παλαὶ βεβαίως ὀικηθῆναι, ἀλλὰ μεταναϛάσεις τε τὰ πρότερα.
                          Θυκυδ. β. α.

[d] Nec robustus erat curvi Moderator Aratri
  Quisquam; nec scibat ferro mollirier Arva;
  Nec nova defodere in terram Virgulta; nec altis
  Arboribus, veteres decidere falcibu' ramos.
  Quod Sol atque Imbres dederant, quod Terra creârat
  Sponte suâ, satis id placabat Pectora donum.
  Glandiferas inter curabant Corpora Quercus.
                    T. Lucret. Lib. 5to.

Sect. 2. rience made them sensible of the Uncertainty of their Possessions; and as they knew not how soon a superior Force might spoil them of their Lands, so they were sure of finding such a scanty Subsistence as they then enjoyed, in any Country where they happened to wander; and therefore, without making much Opposition, they quitted their sorry Dwellings, and made room for an Invader.

OF a piece with this way of living at Land, was their Manner *at Sea*, as soon as they began to build Ships, and ventured to visit distant Coasts: They turned themselves wholly to Piracy; and were so far from thinking it *base*, that the living by Plunder gave a Reputation for Spirit and Bravery. This Practice continued long in *Greece*, not among the meaner sort of People only; but the most powerful of the Tribe sailed out with those under their Command, took what Ships they met; and, if they thought their Numbers sufficient, they often fell upon the Villages along the Coast, killed the Men, and carried the Women and Goods to their Ship [e]. *Thucydides* says, that even in his time there were several uncivilized Countries in *Greece*, whose Inhabitants lived both by Sea and Land after the old barbarous manner [f].

THESE

---

[e] Πορθνται γ ησαν δι Ελληνες, και επιθυμηται τ αλλοτελας, κατα σπανιν γης. Strabo Geograph. Lib. xvii.

[f] Thucydides, Lib. i. Και μεχρι τϋδι πολλα τ Ελλαδ τω παλαιω τρόπω νεμεται. περι τε Λοκρυς τος Οζολας και Αιτωλυς, και Ακαρνανας, και την ταυτη Ηπειρον. See also Plutarch, in the Life of T. Q. Flaminius.

THESE then were the *Manners* in *Homer's* Sect. 2.
Days; and *such* we find them in his Writings.
Ulysses returning in difguife to his own Country,
was received by his Servant *Eumæus,* as a poor
old Man, into his Cottage; and being que-
ftioned *who* and *whence* he was, tells this plau-
fible Tale; " That he was of *Crete,* a natural
" Son of the renowned *Caftor,* and much be-
" loved by his Father while he lived; but at
" his Death, his Brothers had drove him out
" of the Houfe, and defrauded him of his
" fhare of the Patrimony: That neverthelefs
" his Worth and Bravery had procured him a
" rich and honourable Match:" He then bids
him judge of the Ear by the Stalk; expatiates a
little upon his own martial Charaĉter, and adds,

ΤΟΙΟΣ Ε᾽ ΕΝ ΠΟΛΕΜΩ ΕΡΓΟΝ ΔΕ᾽ ΜΟΙ ΟΥ
ΦΙΛΟΝ ΕΣΚΕΝ.

Such in the War; I fcorned Country Toils
And Houfhold Cares, and bringing up of Chil-
    dren:
But Ships with Sails and Oars rejoic'd my Soul;
Battles, and burnifh'd Arms, and glitt'ring Spears,
Things that to others Terror bring, and Dread,
Were my Delights; fo God had form'd my Heart.

HERE is a Man who plainly *profeffes* Piracy; and accordingly he tells, that in nine feveral Courfes he gained fo much Wealth, that
C

he

Sect. 2. he was held in great Esteem among his Countrymen,

———ΑΙΨΑ Δ' ΟΙΚΟΣ ΟΦΕΛΛΕΤΟ, *&c.*

My House was soon advanc'd; and afterwards
I Reverence had, and Awe among the Cretans.

And when *Ulysses*, in his turn, comes to enquire into the Fortunes of *Eumæus*, he chuses
this Supposition, as the most natural he could
make :

But come, and tell me truly what I ask;
Whether the spacious Town was pillaged,
In which thy Father, and thy Mother liv'd?
Or whether Men came unawares upon thee,
Left single with the Oxen, or the Sheep,
And dragging thee aboard, sail'd over hither
To this Man's Dwelling? —— ᵍ

These being the Manners of the Times, we
need not wonder at *Homer's* representing the
good *Nestor*, as entertaining *Telemachus* and his
Company very honourably in his House, and after the Repast, asking them, *Whether they were*
Merchants——Η ΜΑΨΙΔΙΩΣ ΑΛΑΛΗΣΘΕ, ΟΙΑ
ΤΕ ΔΗΙΣΤΗΡΕΣ *;*

——Or do you rove uncertain,
As being Robbers?——

No r was *Homer's* own Country behind-hand
with the rest of the *Greeks*. We learn from

ᵍ *'Οδυσ. σ.*   Hero-

Herodotus, that *Latona's* Oracle in *Boutoo* had Sect.2.
affured *Pfammetichus* (one of the twelve Kings,
when *Egypt* was broken into petty Governments) That *brazen Men* would come to his
Affiftance : They were no other, fays the Hiftorian, than 'ΙΩΝΕΣ τε ᾧ ΚΑΡΕΣ ἄνδρες ᾳτὰ
λnίlω ἐκπλώσανῖες, *Ionian* and *Carian* Crews,
who had failed out on Piracy, and were forced
by Storm to land in *Egypt*.

BUT as every Misfortune forces Men to
think of a Remedy, the Calamities to which
this barbarousWay of living was expofed, taught
the *Greeks*, in procefs of time, the Neceffity
of *walling* their Towns; which, in its turn,
procured them Security and Wealth, and firft
enriched the Cities upon the Sea : Thefe who
lay moft expofed to Infults before, were now
moft open to Trade; and the *Phænician* and
Egyptian Merchants quickly taught them the
Methods of Gain : By this means *Chalcis*, *Corinth*, and *Mycenæ* were the firft opulent Cities after the Ifles. Riches foon produced *Sub-
ordination*; the lefs powerful being contented
with the Protection of the Rich and Brave; and
thefe, on the other hand, were glad of Numbers for carrying on their Affairs [h].

POVERTY was ftill prevalent in the Country,
when *Pelops* came from *Afia*, with a Flood of
Wealth

[h] Condere cœperunt tum Urbeis, Arcemque locare
Præfidium Reges ipfi fibi, perfugiumque;
Et Pecudes & Agros divifêre; atque dedêre
Prô facie cujufque, & viribus, ingenioque.
T. Lucret. Lib. v.

Sect. 2. Wealth 'till then unknown to *Greece*; and by that, and his Skill in the neceſſary Arts of Life, he gained ſuch Power among the rude Inhabitants, that he gave his Name to a great Part of the Country [i].

His Deſcendants *Atreus* and *Thyeſtes* added to their hereditary Dominions; and Fortune made a Preſent of a new Kingdom to the elder Brother. *Euryſtheus* his Nephew, King of *Mycenæ*, of the Line of *Perſeus*, going againſt the *Heraclides*, or Poſterity of *Hercules*, entruſted him with the Government during his Abſence. The Expedition proved fatal to *Euryſtheus*; and the Inhabitants of *Mycenæ* being afraid of a victorious Tribe, and having proof of the Ability of their Governor *Atreus*, unanimouſly offer'd him the Kingdom.   Thus the Family of *Pelops* got the poſſeſſion of two Kingdoms, and became ſuperior in Wealth and Power to the *Perſëids* their Rivals.

·This *Atreus* ſeems to have been the *firſt*, who, after the Days of *Minos*, had fitted out a Fleet; for beſides a large and flouriſhing Kingdom on the Continent, he left to *Agamemnon* the Sovereignty of many of the *Iſlands*, which cou'd never be held in ſubjection without a naval Force. They had been early enriched, as hath been obſerved above, by Commerce with *Syria*, *Phœnicia*, and *Egypt*, the firſt civilized Countries.

AGA-

---

[i] *Peloponnesus* or *Pelop's Iſland.*

AGAMEMNON poffeffed of this wide Do- Sect. 2.
minion and great Wealth, as things then went,
was more in a condition, than by the Oaths
fworn to ·*Tyndarus*, to refent his Brother's
Wrongs, and to put himfelf at the Head of the
firft Expedition which *Greece* made in common againft a foreign Enemy [k]. But the length
of the War, e'er *Troy* was taken, and the Mif-
fortunes the *Greeks* met with in their Return,
brought new Diforders upon the victorious Nation. Many of the Princes [l] being killed, and
fome of them loft by the way, *Parties* ftarted
up in the Cities, and the *Greeks* fell to their old
Trade of one Tribe's expelling another, as formerly.

BUT now the Contentions were longer and
more obftinate, and more Blood was fpilt before either Side wou'd fubmit. Their Cities
were better worth fighting for, and were not
eafily given up by People grown expert in War.
Nor did the Tribe that was worfted wander up
and down, as before, to feek new diftant Habitations; but they *fortified* their new Cities, to
fecure themfelves and their Pofterity againft the
like Calamities. Thus for fome Ages after the
taking of *Troy*, *Greece* was indeed increafing in
Wealth, and Numbers of Inhabitants; but was
continually engaged in Wars; Taking of Towns,

Battles

---

[k] Πρὸ ᵹὃ τ̃ Τρωïκῶν ἐδὲν φαίνεται πρότερον κοινῇ ἐργασαμθρὴ
ἡ Ἑλλάς.   Θυκιδ. α.
[l] Τῶν ἡγμόνων οἱ Βοιωτὰς ἐς Θεϐλαν ἤραγον μᵉγ᷅Θ ἀνέρεϛᴅσιν
οἴκαδὲ ἡ ἈυτᴅΘ.   Παυσ. Βοιωτ. βιϐ. α.

Sect. 2. Battles of Tribes, Piracy, and Incursions, were
common Adventures [m].

IN the second or third Age of this Period
was HOMER born; that is, "at a *Time* when
" he might, as he grew up, be a Spectator of
" all the various Situations of human Race;
" might observe them in great Calamities, and
" in high Felicity; but more generally they
" were increasing in Wealth and Discipline."
For I cannot help observing, that from these
hard Beginnings, and jarring Interests, the *Greeks*
became early Masters of the *military* Art, and
by degrees, of all others that tend to enrich or
adorn a City, and raise a Commonwealth: Ship-
ping and Commerce, domestic Order, and foreign Influence, with every subservient Art of
Policy and Government, were invented, or improved; and some of them brought to a very
great degree of Perfection.

AND truly it cou'd not be otherwise, while
each City was *independent*, rivalling its Neighbour, and trying its Genius in Peace, and its
Strength in War [n]. Upon good or bad Success,
the Citizens, all concerned in the Administration, made a careful Enquiry into the Cause of
it;

---

[m] Μάλιϛα μὲν οὖν κατὰ τὰ Τρωϊκὰ, καὶ μετ᾽ ταῦτα, γενέϛς τὰς
ἐφόδυς καὶ τας μεταναϛάϛεις συνέβη τῶ τε βαρβάρων ἅμα καὶ τῶ
Ἑλλήνων, ὁρμῇ τινι χρησαμένων πρὸς τὴν τῆς ἀλλοτείας κατάϛησιν.
Ἀλλὰ καὶ περὶ τῶ Τρωϊκῶν ἦν ταῦτα· τό τε γὰρ Πελασγῶν ἦν φῦλον,
καὶ τῶ Καυκώνων, καὶ Λελέγων. Εἴρηται δ᾽ ὅτι πολλαχῆ τῆς Ευρώ-
πης ἐτύγχανε τὸ παλαιὸν πλανώμενα ἅπερ ποιῶ τῆς Τρωσὶ συμμα-
χῦντα ὁ Ποιητὴς ἐκ ἐκ τῆς περαίας.   Στραβων. Μυσία. βιβ. ιϚ.

[n] Πᾶσα γὸ ἡ Ἑλλὰς ἐσιδηροφορεῖ διὰ τὰς ἀφράϛυς τε οἰκήσεις
καὶ ἐκ ἀσφαλεῖς παρ᾽ ἀλλήλυς ἐφόδυς.   Θυκιδίδε ξυγγρ. α.

it; What Fault in their Conduct had procured the one, or what Excellency in their Constitu- tion the other? This Liberty produced Hardi- ness and Discipline; which at length arose to that height, that ten thousand *Greeks* were an Overmatch for the *Persian* Monarch, with all the Power of the *Asiatic* Plains.

Th is indeed happened long after; but the Struggle was *fresh* in *Homer*'s Days: Arms were in Repute, and *Force* decided *Possession* ⁹. He saw Towns taken and plundered, the Men put to the Sword, and the Women made Slaves: He beheld their despairing Faces, and suppliant Postures; heard their Moanings o'er their mur- dered Husbands, and Prayers for their Infants to the Victor.

On the other hand, he might view Cities blessed with Peace, spirited by Liberty, flou- rishing in Trade, and increasing in Wealth. He was not engaged in Affairs himself, to draw off his Attention; but he wander'd through the various Scenes, and observed them at leisure. Nor was it the least instructive Sight, to see a *Colony* led out, a City founded, the Founda- tions of Order and Policy laid, with all the Pro- visions for the Security of the People: Such Scenes afford *extended* Views, and natural ones

C 4 too,

too, as they are the immediate Effect of the great Parent of Invention, *Neceſſity*, in its young and untaught Eſſays.

THE Importance of this good Fortune will beſt appear, if we reflect on the Pleaſure which ariſes from a Repreſentation of *natural* and *ſimple Manners:* It is irreſiſtible and inchanting; they beſt ſhew human Wants and Feelings; they give us back the Emotions of an *artleſs* Mind, and the plain Methods we fall upon to indulge them: Goodneſs and Honeſty have their Share in the Delight; for we begin to love the Men, and wou'd rather have to do with them, than with more refined but *double* Characters. Thus the various Works neceſſary for building a Houſe, or a Ship; for planting a Field, or forging a Weapon, if deſcribed with an Eye to the Sentiments and Attention of the Man ſo employed, give us great Pleaſure, *becauſe we feel the ſame.* Innocence, we ſay, is beautiful; and the Sketches of it, wherever they are truly hit off, never fail to charm: Witneſs the few Strokes of that nature in Mr. *Dryden's Conqueſt* of *Mexico,* and the *Inchanted Iſland.*

ACCORDINGLY, we find *Homer* deſcribing very minutely the Houſes, Tables, and Way of Living of the Ancients; and we read theſe Deſcriptions with pleaſure. But on the contrary, when we conſider our own Cuſtoms, we find that our firſt Buſineſs, when we ſit down

down to poetize in the higher Strains, is to Sect. 2.
unlearn our daily way of Life; to forget our ∿
manner of Sleeping, Eating, and Diverfions:
We are obliged to adopt a Set of *more natural*
Manners, which however are foreign to us;
and muſt be like Plants raiſed up in Hot-Beds
or Green-Houſes, in compariſon of thoſe which
grow in Soils fitted by Nature for ſuch Productions. Nay, ſo far are we from enriching Poetry with *new* Images drawn from Nature, that
we find it difficult to underſtand the *old.* We
live within Doors, cover'd, as it were, from
Nature's Face; and paſſing our Days ſupinely
ignorant of her Beauties. We are apt to think
the Similies taken from her *low,* and the ancient
Manners *mean,* or abſurd. But let us be ingenuous, *My Lord,* and confeſs, that while the
Moderns admire nothing but Pomp, and can
think nothing *Great* or *Beautiful,* but what
is the Produce of Wealth, they exclude themſelves from the pleaſanteſt and moſt natural
Images that adorned the old Poetry. *State* and
Form difguiſe Man; and Wealth and Luxury
difguiſe Nature. Their Effects in Writing are
anſwerable: A Lord-Mayor's Show, or grand
Proceſſion of any kind, is not very delicious
Reading, if deſcribed minutely, and at length;
and great Ceremony is at leaſt equally tireſome
in a Poem, as in ordinary Converſation.

    I T has been an old Complaint, that we love
to difguiſe every thing, and moſt of all *Our-*
ſelves.

Sect. 2. *felves.* All our Titles and Diftinctions have been reprefented as Coverings, and Additions of Grandeur to what Nature gave us [p]: Happy indeed for the beft of Ends, I mean the pub. lick Tranquillity and good Order; but incapable of giving delight in Fiction or Poetry.

By this time, your Lordfhip fees I am in the cafe of a noble Hiftorian; who having related the conftant Superiority his *Greeks* had over the Inhabitants of the *Affyrian* Vales, concludes " That it has not been given by the " Gods, to one and the fame Country, to pro- " duce rich Crops and warlike Men [q]:" Neither indeed does it feem to be given to one and the fame Kingdom, to be throughly civilized, and afford proper Subjects for Poetry.

The *Marvellous* and *Wonderful* is the Nerve of the Epic Strain: But what marvellous Things happen in a well-ordered State? We can hardly be furprized; We know the Springs and Method of acting; Every thing happens in *Order*, and according to Cuftom or Law. But in a wide uncultivated Country, not under a regular Government, or fplit into many, whofe Inhabitants live fcattered, and ignorant of Laws and Difcipline; In fuch a Country, the Manners are *fimple,*

---

[p] Quel fuon faftofo e vano,
Quel inutil Sogetto
Di Lufinghe, di Titole e d' Inganno;
Ch' *Honor* dal volgo infano
Indegnamente è detto,
Non era ancor' degli Animi Tiranno.
                    Paftor Fido, Choro dell' Atto 4to

[q] *Herodotus.*

fimple, and Accidents will happen every Day : Sect. 2.
Expofition and Lofs of Infants ; Encounters ;
Efcapes ; Refcues ; and every other thing that
can inflame the human Paffions while acting,
·or awake them when defcribed, and recalled by
Imitation.

THESE are not to be found in a well-go-
verned State, except it be during the Time of
a *Civil War,* when it ceafes to be fo : and yet,
with all the Diforder and Mifery that attends
that laft of Ills, the Period while it rages is a
fitter Subject for an Epic Poem, than the moft
glorious Campaign that ever was made in *Flan-
ders.* Even the Things that give the greateft
Luftre in a regular Government ; the greateft
Honours and higheft Trufts, will fcarcely bear
Poetry : The *Mufe* refufes to beftow her Embel-
lifhments on a *Duke's* Patent, or a *General's*
Commiffion. They can neither raife our Wonder, nor gain our Heart : For Peace, Harmony
and good Order, which make the Happinefs of
a People, are the *Bane* of a Poem that fubfifts
by Wonder and Surprize.

To BE convinced of this, we need only fuppofe that the *Greeks,* at the time of the *Trojan*
War, had been a Nation eminent for Loyalty
and Difcipline : that Commiffions in due Form
had been iffued out, Regiments raifed, Arms
and Horfes bought up, and a compleat Army
fet on foot. Let us fuppofe that all Succefs had
attended them in their Expedition ; that every
Officer

Sect. 2. Officer had vied with another in Bravery againſt the Foe, and in Submiſſion to his General: That in conſequence of theſe Preparations, and of this good Order, they had at firſt Onſet routed the *Trojans*, and driven them into the Town: Suppoſe this, and think,——What will become of the glorious *Iliad?* The Wrath of *Achilles*, the Wiſdom of *Neſtor*, the Bravery of *Diomedes*, and the Craft of *Ulyſſes* will vaniſh in a moment. But Matters are managed quite otherwiſe;

Seditione, Dolis, Scelere atque Libidine & Irâ,
Iliacos intrâ Muros peccatur, & extrâ.

It is thus that a People's Felicity clips the Wings of their Verſe: It affords few Materials for Admiration or Pity; and tho' the Pleaſure ariſing from the ſublimer kinds of Writing, may make us regret the Silence of the Muſes, yet I am perſuaded your Lordſhip will join in the Wiſh, *That we may never be a proper Subject of an* Heroic Poem.

But now that I have ventured ſo far, I begin to apprehend that I ſhall be deſerted. The Habit of reconciling Extremes when a publick Concern calls for Attention, is become ſo natural to your *Lordſhip*, that it muſt incline you to wiſh our Epic Affairs not ſo deſperate; and your Knowledge of the Poetical Privilege will immediately ſuggeſt, " That *Our private Manners*,
" ners,

" *ners*, it is poffible, admit not fuch Repre- Sect. 2.
" fentation : nor will our mercenary Wars,
" and State Intrigues, receive the Stamp of
" *Simplicity* and *Heroifm :*" But why may
not a Poet *feign?* Can't he counterfeit Manners, and contrive Accidents, as he fees good ?
Is he not intituled to fhift Scenes, and introduce
Perfons and Characters at pleafure ? Let him
but exercife his Prerogative, and all will be well :
Our Manners need be no Impediment ; he may
give his new-raifed Generation what *Turn* and
Caft he pleafes.

THo' this feems to promife fair, yet in the
end, I am afraid, it will not hold good. Your
Lordfhip will judge whether my Fears are juft,
when relying on that Penetration which attends your Opinions, I venture to affirm, " That
" a Poet defcribes nothing fo happily, as what
" he has feen ; nor talks mafterly, but in his
" native Language, and proper Idiom ; nor mi-
" micks truly other Manners, than thofe whofe
" Originals he has practifed and known *r*."

THis Maxim will, no doubt, appear fevere ; and yet, I believe, upon enquiry it will
hold true *in fact.* If we caft an Eye backward
upon Antiquity, it will be found that none of
the great *original* Writers have excelled, but
where they fpoke of the Things they were
moft converfant with, and in the Language and
Dialect

---

e See the Note, pag. 33.

Sect. 2. Dialect they conftantly ufed[f]. The fatyrical buf-
foonifh Temper of *Archilochus* is well known ;
nor is it a Secret, that he indulged his Paffions,
which were neither weak nor few. The *Sen-
tentious* Writings of *Euripides*, and *Menander*'s
polite Pictures of Life, reprefented their daily
Converfation. *Plato*'s admired Dialogues are
but corrected Tranfcripts of what paffed in the
Academy: And *Lucilius*, preferred by fome *Romans* to all that ever wrote[t], wrote himfelf
juft as he fpoke. *Herodotus*'s Hiftory fhows.
the *Traveller*, *Thucydides*'s the *Politician*, *Dionyfius*'s the *Scholar*, *Xenophon*'s the *Captain* and
the *Philofopher*, as truly as they acted thofe
Characters in their Lives: Nor cou'd thefe
Heroes have excelled each in his different Way,
had they done otherwife.

But the Truth of this Maxim will beft appear, if we obferve its Influence in Converfation and Behaviour. *He* who affects no other
than his natural Manners, has a better chance to
excel, than if he fhou'd attempt to copy another
Man's Way, tho' perhaps preferable both in
Language and Gefture to his own. It is a fmall
Circle of Acquaintance, which does not afford
fome diverting Proofs of this common Miftake:
And if it was not a difagreeable Occupation, to
blame

---

[f] As for the Poets in particular, fays *Cervantes*, En refolucion,
todos los Poetas antiguos efcrivierón en la Lengua que mamaron en
la Leche; y no fueron a bufcar las eftrangeras para declarar la al-
teza de fus Conceptos. *Don Quixote*, Parte II. lib. 5. c.16.

[t] *Lucilius* quofdam ita deditos fibi habet Amatores, ut eum om-
nibus Poetis præferre non dubitent. Quintil. de Satyr.

blame and find fault, it were eafy to produce many Inftances of the fame mifcarriage in *Writing*.
I will only put your Lordfhip in mind of two
great Men, who, with every thing befides to recommend them, have fplit upon this fingle
Rock; and for that reafon, as well as their being dead near two hundred Years ago, they may
be mentioned with lefs Reluctancy. The Perfons I mean, are both *Italians*, who had the
happinefs to fee the golden Age of Learning in
that Country, the *Pontificat* of *Leo* X.

PIETRO BEMBO was of a noble Family in *Ve-
nice*; his early Merit recommended him to *Leo*,
who loved to fill his Court with learned Men,
and had a true Judgment in fuch things himfelf. *Bembo* was made Secretary for the *Apo-
ftolic Briefs*; and, after two Succeffions to the
Pontificat, was raifed to the Dignity of the
Purple, chiefly for his Reputation in Literature:
And indeed his Learning and Abilities are unqueftionable. But at the fame time, this great
Man, admiring only the *Roman* Eloquence and
Manners, wrote a Hiftory of his own Country,
fo much upon the Model of a *Latin Annal*, that
not only the general Turn and Caft of the Work
is fervilely copied, but the Peculiarities of their
Stile, their Computation of Miles and Time,
and the *Forms* of their Religion and Government, are with infinite labour wrought into a
Venetian Story. The effect of it is, to enervate
and deaden his Work, which a Writer of half
his

Sect. 2. his Knowledge and Accomplishments, would have told better without his *Affectation*.

A LITTLE younger than the Cardinal was *Giovanni Giorgio Trissino*, a Native of *Vicenza*. He was look'd upon as one of the greatest Masters of ancient Learning, both *Greek* and *Roman*, of his Age; and, which rarely happens, was blest at the same time with a Flow of *Tuscan* Eloquence. A Man so qualified, easily saw the Faults of his contemporary Writers; and thought it not impossible, with his Talents and Judgment, *To produce such a Poem in* Italian, *as* Homer *had done in* Greek.

HE set about it, and placed this great Model before his Eyes: He abandoned the use of Rhyme, followed the natural Run of Speech in his Verse; and endeavoured to adapt his Inventions to the State and Temper of his Age and Nation. He took *Italy* for the Subject of his Poem, as *Homer* had taken *Greece:* He has Champions of the same Country, as *Homer* has *Grecian* Heroes: He uses *Angels* for his Divinities, and supplies the ancient *Furies* with modern *Devils:* In his Geography, as *Homer* described *Greece,* and chiefly *Thessaly; Trissino* describes *Italy,* and dwells on *Lombardy.* He has even attempted *Fable;* and interwoven allegorical Stories of Life and Morals, with the Body of the Narration. But after all, the *native Italian* Manners are lost; and the high Spirit and secret Force which bewitches a Reader, and dazzles his Eyes, that

he

he can fee no Faults in *Dante* and *Ariofto*, is Sect. 2.
here crufh'd by Imitation. Its Fate has been
anfwerable: The *Italia Liberata* (for fo he called his Poem) being no more read or known,
than *Chapelain's Pucelle* wou'd be without *Boi-*
leau, or Sir *R* * * *'s *A* * **d* without the
D * * *. *Triffino* owes his Fame to his *Sopho-*
nifba, a Tragedy, and to his *Mifcellanies*; and
the *Cardinal* is preferved from Oblivion by his
Letters and *Love-Verfes*; and there too, the
fame Inclination *to copy* has made him check
his natural Fire, that he might attain *Cicero's*
Elegance in the one, and *Petrarcha's* Purity
and Softnefs in the other.

To fay the Truth, *My Lord*, we are born
but with narrow Capacities: Our Minds are
not able to mafter two Sets of Manners, or
comprehend with facility different *Ways* of
Life [u]. Our Company, Education, and Circumftances make deep Impreffions, and form
us into a *Character*, of which we can hardly
diveft ourfelves afterwards. The Manners not
only of the Age and Nation in which we live,
but of our City and Family, ftick clofely to
us, and betray us at every turn, when we try
to diffemble, and wou'd pafs for Foreigners.
Thefe we underftand, and can paint to perfection; and there is no one fo undifcerning,

as

[u] Καὶ ἔτι γε τετῶν, φαίνεταί μοι, ἐς μικρότερα καὶ ἀκριβέςε-
ρα τᾶ ἀνθρώπε φύσις, ἄςε ἀδύνατ ἢ εἶναι πολλὰ καλῶς μιμεῖσθαι, ἢ
αὐτὰ ἐκεῖνα πράπειν, ὧν δὴ καὶ τὰ μιμήματά ἐςι ἀφομοιώματα.
Πλάτων. περὶ Πολιτ. γ.

D

Sect.2. as not to see, how happy we have been in de-
scribing those Parts of *modern* Life we have undertaken.   Was there ever a more natural Picture than the *Way of the World?* Or can any
thing in its kind surpass the *Rape of the Lock?*
The Authors, doubtless, perfectly knew the Life
and Manners they were painting, and have succeeded accordingly.

HERE THEN was *Homer's* first Happiness: He took his plain natural Images from
Life; He saw *Warriors*, and *Shepherds*, and
Peasants, such as he drew; and was daily
conversant among *such* People as he intended
to represent: The Manners used in the *Trojan*
Times were not disused in his own: The same
way of living in private, and the same Pursuits
in publick were still prevalent, and gave him a
Model for his Design, which wou'd not allow
him to exceed the Truth in his Draught.   By
frequently and freely looking it over, he cou'd
discern what Parts of it were fit to be represented, and what to be passed over [x].

FOR so unaffected and simple were the Manners of those Times, that the Folds and Wind-
dings of the human Breast lay open to the
Eye; People were not as yet taught to be
ashamed of themselves and their natural Appetites, nor consequently to dissemble them: They
made no scruple of owning the *Inclinations* of
their Heart, and openly indulged their Passions,
which

[x] ————————————Et quæ
Desperat tractata *nitescere* posse, relinquit.   Horat.

which were entirely void of Art and Defign *y*. Sect. 2.
This was *Homer*'s Happinefs, with refpect to
Mankind, and the living Part of his Poetry:
As for the other Parts, and what a Painter wou'd
call *Still-Life*, he cou'd have little Advantage
over the Moderns: For we are not to imagine,
that he cou'd difcover the entertaining Profpects,
or rare Productions of a Country better than we
can. *That* is a Subject ftill remaining to us, if
we will quit our Towns, and look upon it:
We find it, accordingly, nobly executed by many of the Moderns, and the moft illuftrious Inftance of it, within thefe few Years, doing Honour to the *Britifh* Poetry *z*.

IN SHORT, it may be faid of *Homer*, and of
every *Poet* who has wrote well, " That *what* he
" felt and faw, *that* he defcribed ; and that
" *Homer* had the good Fortune to fee and learn
" the *Grecian* Manners, at their true Pitch and
" happieft Temper for Verfe :" Had he been
born much fooner, he could have feen nothing
but Nakednefs and Barbarity : Had he come
much later, he had fallen either in *Times of
Peace*, when a wide and fettled Policy prevailed
over *Greece* ; or in *General Wars*, regularly carried on by civilized States, when private Paffions are buried in the common Order, and
eftablifhed Difcipline.

D 2   S E C T.

y. Bold *Homer* durft not fo great Virtue feign
    In his beft Pattern: Of *Patroclus* flain,
    With fuch Amazement as weak Mothers ufe,
    And frantick Gefture, he receives the News.   WALLER.

z The SEASONS, by Mr. *Thomfon*.

SECT. III.

Sect. 3. WHOEVER reflects upon the Rise and
Fall of States, will find, that along with
their Manners, their *Language* too accompanies them both in their Growth and Decay.
Language is the Conveyance of our Thoughts;
and as they are noble, free, and undisturbed, our
Discourse will keep pace with them both in its
Cast and Materials. By this means a Convention of Men of Spirit and Understanding, who
have the Business of a City or State to manage (if they are not to receive their Orders
in silence from a Superior) will naturally produce

duce Speakers and Eloquence. The same Men, Sect. 3.
when they quit their Town, and look abroad, will
speak of the Objects presented to them by Nature's Face, with the same Freedom and Happiness of Expression: And if, in a wide Country, there are many such Societies, speaking the
same Tongue, but in different Dialects; the
Language will reap the Benefit, and be enriched
with new Words, Phrases, and Metaphors, according to the Temper and Genius of the several People: While at the same time, each approve their own, because it is used by their Go-
vernors in their own *independent* State.

I T is a little surprizing to observe, what a
contemptible Figure the Beginnings of the human Race make in the Pictures drawn of them
by the Ancients:

Cum prorepserunt primis Animalia Terris,
Mutum & turpe Pecus, glandem atque cubilia
   propter,
Unguibus & Pugnis, dein Fustibus, atque ita porro
Pugnabant Armis, quæ pòst fabricaverat Usus;
Donec Verba, quibus voces sensusque notarent,
Nominaque *invenêre.*——[a]

They thought, it would seem, that *Language* was
the first Tamer of Men [b], and took its Origin to
D 3   have

---

[a] Horat. Sat. iii. Lib. i.

[b] 'Εfγενομένων δ' ἡμῶν τῶ πρῶθεν ἀλλήλων, καὶ ὁκλῶν πρὸς ἡ-
μᾶς ἀυτὲς ὅτι ἂν ἐν βουληθώμψ, ἢ μόνον τῶ ΘΗΡΙΩΔῶΣ ΖΗ͂Ν
ἀπηλλάγημψ, ἀλλὰ καὶ συνελθόν[ες πόλεις ᾠκίσαμψ, καὶ νόμους
ἐθέμεθα, καὶ τέχνας εὑράμψ· καὶ σχεδὸν ἅπανlα τὰ δι' ἡμῶν με-
μηχανημένα ΛΟΓΟΣ ἡμῖν ἐςὶν ὁ καlασκευάσας.

'Ισοκράl. πρὸς Νικοκλ.

Sect. 3. have been certain rude accidental Sounds, which that naked Company of scrambling Mortals emitted by chance [c].

UPON this Supposition, it will follow, that at first they uttered these Sounds in a much higher Note than we do our Words now; occasioned, perhaps, by their falling on them under some *Passion*, Fear, Wonder, or Pain [d]; and then using the same Sound, either when the Object or Accident recurred, or when they wanted to describe it by what they felt from its Presence : Neither the Syllables, nor the Tone could be ascertained ; but when, prompted by the Return of the Passions, under which they invented them, they extended their Throats and put several of these *vocal* Marks together, they wou'd then seem *to sing.* Hence ΑΥΔΑΕΙΝ signified at first simply *to speak* or utter the Voice, which now, with a small Abbreviation (ΑΔΕΙΝ) signifies to sing : And hence came the ancient Opinion , which appears so strange to us, " That Poetry was before " Prose."

THE Geographer *Strabo,* a wise Man, and well acquainted with Antiquity, tells us, that

Cadmus,

[c] Τὰς δ' ἐξ ἀρχῆς γεννηθέντας τ̄ ἀνθρώπων, φασὶ τ̄ ἐν ἀτάκτῳ κỳ θηριώδει βίῳ καθεστῶτας, σποράδην ἐπὶ τὰς νομὰς ἐ ξιέναι, κỳ προσφέρεσ δ τε βοτάνης τὴν προσηνεστάτ lω, κỳ τὰς αυτμάτες ἀπὸ τ̄ δένδρων καρπὰς. Καὶ πολεμκμῷόες ὑϕ ὑπὸ τ̄ ε ηρείων, ἀλλήλοις βοηθεῖν, ὑπὸ τὰ συμφέρονϑ διδασκομένες,——τ̄ Τῆς φωνῆς δ' ΑΣΗΜΟΥ κỳ ΣΥΓΚΕΧΥΜΕΝΗΣ ἔσης ἐκ τῦ κα τ̄ ὀλίγον ΔΙΑΡΘΡΟΥΝ τὰς λέξεις. Διοδὼρ. Σικελ. βιβλίοϑ. α.

[d] Καὶ γὸ εἰκὸς ἀνθρώπες ΕΝ ΧΡΕΙΑ λόγε τὸ πρῶτον κỳ φωνῆς ἐνάρθρε γενέσϑ, τάς τε πράξεις κỳ τὰς πράττοντας ἅ η τας, κỳ τὰ ΠΑΘΗ κỳ τὰς ΠΑΣΧΟΝΤΑΣ ἀλλήλοις διασαφῶν : κỳ ἀποσημαίνειν, βελομένες. Πλουταρχ. Πλατωνι ὦρ. ζητημα ηιν.

Cadmus, *Pherecydes*, and *Hecataeus* firſt took the Sect. 3. Numbers, and the Meaſure from Speech, and re- ~~ duced that to Proſe which had always been Po- etry before. And the admired Judge of the Sub- lime, in the Fragment of a Treatiſe we have un- happily loſt, has this remarkable Sentence :

    " MEASURE, ſays he, belongs properly to
" Poetry, as it perſonates the various *Paſſions*
" and their Language ; uſes Fiction and Fables,
" which naturally produce Numbers and Har-
" mony : 'Twas for this reaſon, that the An-
" cients in their *ordinary Diſcourſe* delivered
" themſelves rather in Verſe than Proſe e ".

    HAD I to do with ſome others, I ſhould be at the pains to ſhew the Connexion of the firſt and laſt Part of this Opinion ; but your Lord- ſhip will eaſily ſee, That he thought the Life of the Ancients was more expoſed to *Accidents* and Dangers, than when Cities were built, and Men were protected by Society and a *Publick* ; and of conſequence that their Diſcourſe muſt be more paſſionate and metaphorical. Give me leave only to add, that the Compoſition of the Names of TRAGEDY and COMEDY, which were Repre- ſentations of *ancient* Life (Τραγῳδία, Κωμῳδία) undoubtedly prove that they were originally *ſung* when acted, and not repeated, as they are now. Nor do I in the leaſt queſtion, but that the firſt

D 4   things

---

e Μᾶλλον δὲ πϱόσεσι τὸ μέτϱον τῷ ποιητικῷ, πάϑεσι πλείσοις χϱωμένῳ ϰ̓ λέξει· Καὶ δὴ, ϰ̓ μύϑοις ϰ̓ πλάσμασι, δὶ ὧν ἁϱμο- νία ϰατασϰυάζεται. Ταῦτ᾽ ἄϱα ϰ̓ ὅι Παλαιοὶ ἐμμέτϱως μᾶλλον τὰς οἰϰείας ἐποίυν λόγυς ἢ πεζύς. Λογγίνυ πεϱὶ ΜΕΤΡΟΥ, ἀπο σπασματ.

Sect. 3. things which were committed to Writing in *Greece*, as Oracles, Laws, Spells, Prophecies, were in Verse; and yet they got the simple Name of ʼΕΠΕΑ, Words or Sayings[f]; as the first *Romans*, for the same reason, called them FATA, from a Verb signifying to *utter the Voice* or to *speak* [*]. But however these things be, it is certain, that the

primitive

[f] Some Vestiges of this Poetic Turn remain in the Pictures of Eastern Manners, that are preserved in the oldest Accounts of the *Moors* and *Spaniards*; where the *Romanzes* occur every other Page, and the Conversations upon passionate Subjects run into a loose kind of Verse: For Example,

> Abenamar! Abenamar!
> Moro de la Moreria!
> El dia que tu naciste,
> Grandes Señales avia:
> Estava la Mar en Calma,
> La Luna estava crecida;
> Moro que en tal Signo nace
> No deve dezir Mentira.

And in the same Spirit,

> Reduan! Si se te acuerda
>   que me diste la Palabra,
> Que me darias a Jaen
>   en una noche ganada:
> Reduan! Si tu lo cumples
>   darete paga doblada:
> Y si tu no lo cumpliesses
>   desterrarte hé de Granada.

Histor. de las Guerras Civiles de Granada.

These *Romanzes* are so old, that they are brought by the *Arabs* as the Proofs of their Histories.

[*] FARI: the Word derived from it was not used single at first; but they commonly called those things FATA JOVIS, I believe from the old Oracle in *Dodona*, sacred to *Jupiter*. So *Virgil*, the great Imitator of ancient Language, *Et sic Fata Jovis poscunt.* Æneïd. vi. Tho' afterwards, from the Import of the Subject, it came to bear the present Signification. The *Greeks*, when they begun to affect Accuracy, made a Compound of the single Word ΦΑΤΑ, and called it Θέσφαΐα; not only Sayings, but Sayings of the God, Θεός Φάτη.

primitive Parts of the Languages repúted *Ori-* Sect. 3.
ginal, are many of them rough, undeclined,
imperfonal Monofyllables; expreffive commonly
of the *higheft Paffions,* and moft *ftriking Objects*
that prefent themfelves in *folitary favage Life*[h].

FROM THIS Deduction, it is plain that any
Language, formed as above defcribed, muft be
full of Metaphor ; and that Metaphor of the
boldeft,

[h] As this way of tracing a Language places it in an uncommon
Light, it will be proper to illuftrate it by a few fuch Examples, as
are moft connected with ordinary Life. The two ufual Words in
Hebrew for Meat and Food, *Lechom,* and *Tereph,* fignify at the
fame time, the one *Fighting,* and the other *Rapine* or *Plunder. Gur*
fignifies to *go abroad,* to *travel* ; and the Adjunct of it to *dread,*
to *be in fear* : And *Ger* or *Gur,* a *Stranger* and a young *Lion.* The
old Word for *Wealth* in *Greek,* Λεία, means nothing originally
but *Spoil,* the Product of War and Piracy ; and comes from Λάω
Abigo, whence the Word in ufe ἐλαύνω, forms its Tenfes : And the
great variety of Words they have to fignify *Good* and *Better,*
take their Origin from *Strength* and *Violence.* This Collufion of
different Significations to the fame Word, which is obfervable
throughout the original Languages, muft be very convincing to fuch
as are acquainted with their Idiom and Propriety. The conftant
Reafon of them is, the Connexion which thefe various Meanings
had in the *Manners* then prevalent. Some of thefe Connexions are
vaniſhed in a civilized Life and Change of Manners : Others of
them ftill remain ; fuch as *Zonah,* Caupona, Hofpita ; and *Zonah* Scor-
tum, Meretrix. *Hbaſhar, to grow rich* ; and *Hbaſar, to receive
Tythes, to be a Prieſt* ; with a hundred more of the fame kind.
But it gives us an Idea of a difmal Way of Living, to find the
Word *Karab,* that fignifies *to draw near to one, to approach,* fig-
nifying at the fame time, *to fight, to make War* ; and thence the
Word *Kerab,* a *Battle.* It puts me in mind of the horrible Image
given us by *Orpheus.*

Ἦν χρόνῳ ἡνίκα φῶτες ἀπ' ἀλλήλων βίον εἴχον
Σαρκοδακῆ κρείασαν δὲ τ' ἥττονα φῶτα δαίζε.

Σέξτ. Ἐμπειεικῦ πεϱὶ Μαθημ. βιβ. β.

Father *Ricci* in his *Chriſtian Expedition* to *China,* fays expreſly,
That their Language confifts wholly in Monofyllables : The
fame feems to have been the Cafe of the ancient *Ægyptian* ; and,
as we may obferve ourfelves, of the greateft Part of the Northern
Tongues.

Sect. 3. boldeſt, daring, and moſt natural kind: For Words taken wholly from rough Nature, and invented under ſome Paſſion, as Terror, Rage, or Want (which readily extort Sounds from Men [i]) would be expreſſive of that Fanaticiſm and Dread, which is incident to Creatures living wild and defenceleſs [k]: We muſt imagine their Speech to be broken, unequal, and boiſterous; one Word or Sound, according to its Analogy to different Ideas, wou'd ſtand for them all; a Quality we often miſtake for Strength and Expreſſion, while it is a real Defect.

But let us take another Step, and ſuppoſe the Affairs of the rude Community to be a little advanced; that they begin to underſtand their own *Gibberiſh*, live in tolerable Security, and are at liberty to look around them: In that caſe, *Admiration* and *Wonder* will ſucceed. Wonder is the proper Paſſion of raw and unexperienced Mortals, when rid of Fear. The great Critic among the Ancients has aſſigned it to *young Men*: A witty Modern of the laſt Age gives it to the *Ladies*; and one of the fineſt Pieces written in our Language confines it to *Fools*.

'Tis

---

[i] At varios Linguæ ſonitus *Natura* ſubegit
    Mittere; Et *Utilitas* expreſſit Nomina rerum.   Lucret.

[k] Nam fuit quoddam tempus, cum in agris Homines paſſim Beſtiarum more vagabantūr, & ſibi victu ferino Vitam propagabant; Nec ratione Animi quicquam, ſed pleraque Viribus Corporis adminiſtrabant. Nondūm divinæ Religionis, non humani Officii ratio colebatur: Nemo legitimas viderat Nuptias; non certos quiſquam inſpexerat Liberos: Non jus æquabile, quid utilitatis haberet, acceperat. Ita propter errorem atque inſcitiam, cæca ac temeraria dominatrix Animi Cupiditas, ad ſe explendam viribus Corporis abutebatur, pernicioſiſſimis Satellitibus.
                    M. T. Ciceronis de Inventione Lib. i.

'T I s certain, that in the Infancy of States, Sect. 3.
the Men generally refemble the *publick Confti-*
tution : They have only that Turn which the
rough Culture of Accidents, perhaps difmal
enough, thro' which they have paffed, could
give them : They are ignorant and undefigning,
governed by Fear, and Superftition its Companion : There is a vaft *Void* in their Minds; they
know not what will happen, nor according to
what Tenour things will take their Courfe : Every new Object finds them unprepared; they gaze
and ftare, like Infants taking in their firft Ideas
of Light[1]: Their Words exprefs thefe Feelings;
And as there is a mighty Diftance from this
Starting-place of *Ignorance* and *Wonder*, to the
Condition of a wife experienc'd Man, whom few
things furprize; who is acquainted with the
Fates of Nations, and the Laws and Limits of
our Situation, the *Language* is tinctured in proportion, and bears the Marks of the intermedi-
ate Stages.

I T W E R E eafy to prove thefe Affertions by
abundance of Grammatical Examples, but they
can only be underftood by Men, who, like your
Lordfhip, have it in their power to recollect
them at pleafure. I will only obferve, that the
Turks, Arabs, Indians, and in general moft of
the

---

[1] Οἱ πρῶτα μὲν βλέπον]ες, ἔζλεπον μάτίω·
Κλύον]ες ἐκ ἤκουον· ἀλλ' ὀνειρᾴτων
Ἀλίζκιοι μορφαῖσι, τὸν μακρὸν χρόνον
Ἔφυρον εἰκῆ πά:]α.   ΑΙχυλ. ΠΡΟΜΗΘΕΥΣ.
This Account of the *firft Mortals* is confirmed by the learned and
fagacious Philofopher, Ἐικός τε τὰς πρώτας, ἔιτι γηγνᾶς ἤσαν, ἔιτ'
ἐκ φθορᾶς τιν⊙ ἐσώθησαν, ὁμοίας ἄναι· ἢ τὰς τυχόντας ἢ τὰς
ἀνοήτυς, ὥσπερ ἢ λέγεται κατὰ τ γηγνᾶν.   Ἀριστοτ ἢ Πολιτικ β.

Sect. 3. the Inhabitants of the *East*, are a solitary kind of People: They speak but seldom, and never long without Emotion: But when, in their own Phrase, they *open* their *Mouth*, and give a loose to a fiery Imagination, they are poetical, and full of Metaphor. *Speaking*, among such People, is a matter of some Moment, as we may gather from their usual Introductions; for before they begin to deliver their Thoughts, they give notice, *that they will open their Mouth; that they will unloose their Tongue; that they will utter their Voice, and pronounce with their Lips*[m]. These Preambles bear a great Resemblance to the old Forms of Introduction in *Homer*, *Hesiod*, and *Orpheus*, in which they are sometimes followed by *Virgil*.

IF THERE is then an inviolable and necessary Connexion between the Dispositions of a Nation and their Speech, we must believe that there will be an *Alloy* of Simplicity and Wonder in the Beginnings of every Language; and likewise that the Dialect will improve with the Affairs and Genius of the People. Upon a nearer View of that which *Homer* spoke, we find it not *original*, but derived from others more ancient: Yet it seems to have begun upon a very small Stock, which the *Pelasgi* spoke [n], and the
old

---

[m] See the *Arabian* Nights Entertainments; a Translation from the *Arabick*.

[n] Τῦ γηγενοῦς ἰὰρ εἰμ᾽ ἰγὼ παλαίχθον@
῎Ινις ΠΕΛΑΣΓΟΥ, τῆς δὲ γῆς ἀρχηγέτης.
Ἐμῦ δ᾽ ᾿Ανακl@ εὐλόγως ἐπώνυμον
Γένο@ ΠΕΛΑΣΓΩΝ τὴν δὲ καρποῦται χθόνα
Καὶ πᾶσαν ᾿Α.αν ἧς δ᾽ ᾿Αλγ@ ἔρχεται
Στρυμόν τε πρὸς δύνοντ@ ἥλιυ κρατῷ.
ΑΙΧΥΛ. ᾿ΙΚΕΤΙΔΕΣ.

old Inhabitants of the Northern Parts of *Greece*. Sect. 3.
The greater Part of its Acquisitions it drew
from *Asia, Phœnicia,* and *Egypt,* by the way of
Cyprus and *Crete* °: Thefe, with the other
Iflands, poffeffed chiefly by the *Carians,* were
firft peopled and inftructed in the Arts of Life:
They lie moft conveniently for Merchants failing from the above-named Countries; and it
was either *Trading* People, or Perfons under a
Neceffity of travelling abroad for fome bold Actions at home ᵖ, who were the firft Inftructors
of the ancient *Greeks* ᑫ.

THESE Adventures came to a Climate which
inclines not Men to Solitude, and forbids Idle-
nefs: The Neceffity of Labour and Contrivance;
a growing Commerce, and, more than any thing
befides, the Number of independent Governments, and rival Cities, foon raifed a nobler Language than any of the Originals. It was at firft
fimple, unconfined, and *free,* as was their Life:
The *Politick* Stile grew with their *Conftitution;*
and was at its *height* when they had moft Affairs of that kind, and of the *greateft confequence*
to manage: And when a rough warlike People
had ftripp'd them of their Liberty, they had recourfe

° (Κρήτη νῆσΘ) πᾶσιν ἐπίκειται τῇ Θαλάσση, χεδὸν Ƭ ΕΛΛΗ-
ΝΩΝ ἱδρυμβῴων περὶ Ƭ Θάλασσαν πάντων. Ἀριστοτέλ. Πολιτιχ β.
ᵖ *Danaus, Cadmus,* &c. See the *Marmora Arundel.* Epoch. 9.
concerning the ΠεντηκόντορΘ: and the following Note.
ᑫ Τὸν μὲν ἐπέκεινα χρόνον, οἱ δυστυχοῦντες ὸν τοῖς βαρβάροις,
Ƭ ἑλληνίδων πόλεων ἠξίων ἄρχειν. Καὶ Δαναὸς μὲν ἐξ Αἰγύπτε
φεύγων, ἌργΘ κατέχι. ΚάδμΘ δὲ ὁ ΣιδώνιΘ Θηβῶν ἐβασίλευσε.
Κᾶρες ᶃ τὰς Νήσυς κατῴχισν. Πελοπόννησον ᶃ συμπάσης ὁ Ταντά-
λυ Πέλοψ ἐκράτησε.　Ἰσοκράτ. Ἑλένης Ἐγκώμιον.

courfe to *Philofophy* and *Learning*. The Coun‑
cils of a free State are managed by *Speaking*,
which quickly introduces Eloquence, and the
Arts of Perfuafion: When *thefe* turn ufelefs, or
dangerous in Publick, Men betake themfelves to
lefs obnoxious Subjects.

THESE were the Stages through which the
Greek Language paffed. It went thro' them
flowly, and had time to receive the Impreffion
of each: It lafted long, and far out-lived the
Latin, as it had begun before: The reafon was,
that amidft all the Broils of *Greece*, they had
ftill Liberty and Employment enough, either in
Bufinefs or Literature, to keep alive fomething
of their Spirit and Language: *That* will always
follow our Fortunes, and be fitted to our Affairs
and Condition ᵣ. For, in fact, what elfe do we
talk of? For this reafon, a flourifhing, happy
Nation, not over-difciplined at the Beginning,
that after a long Struggle, and much Trial, comes
to excel in every Art of Peace and War; fuch
a Nation muft fpeak the nobleft Language;
which, in its turn, becaufe of the Inftability of
human Affairs, has no Security for its Duration.

AFTER fuch a Deduction, your Lordfhip is
no doubt in Expectation, what is at length to
be made of it? It is this, *My Lord,* " That
" when by the Progreffion above-mentioned,
" the *Greek* Language was brought to exprefs
" all the beft and braveft of the human Feelings,
" and

ᵣ Format enim Natura prius nos intùs ad omnem
Fortunarum Habitum ――――   Horat. ad Pifon.

" and retained a fufficient Quantity of its *Ori-* Sect. 3.
" *ginal, amazing, metaphoric* Tincture; *at*
" *that Point of Time did* Homer *write."*

I KNOW nothing more proper to convince us
of the Truth of this happy Circumftance, than
the Confideration of the *Machines* which he em-
ploys : The greater Part of them are *natural*;
and except the *Egyptian* and *Orphic* Allegories
(which he ufually puts in the Mouths of his
Gods ᶠ) they are told in the *prevailing Language* of the Country. It is given as a Rule in
Poetry ᵗ, " To ftrip the common Accidents of
" Life of their plain Drefs, and afcribe them
" to fome fuperior Power, in order to keep up
" their Dignity ; as for inanimate things, we
" muft give them Life, cloath them with a
" Perfon, and proper Attributes :" But few People imagine that the *ordinary* Language wore
this metaphorical Habit at that time. Yet it
wou'd be inexcufable elfe, to put Poetical Expreffions in the Mouth of any other than the
Poet himfelf : 'Twou'd be really *falfe Writing*,
and is a common Fault in many excellent Performances. *Homer's* grand Copier, who has
wrought one wonderful Poem out of the other's
two, feems to a very candid Judge, to have come
fhort of his Original in this particular : It is the
ingenious Monf. *De la Motte* I fpeak of, who
thinks *Eneas* by far too great a Poet ; and owns,

that

ᶠ When the Poet mentions them in his own Perfon, he commonly introduces them with φασὶ, *They fay.*
ᵗ See *Boileau's* Art of Poetry.

Sect. 3. that he could not help feeling that Impropriety thro' the whole of the fecond and third Books of the *Eneid*; where the Hero is not lefs florid and figurative in his Narration, than the Poet himfelf is in the reft [u].

VIRGIL's writing fo long after *Eneas*'s Expedition, and in a Language too refin'd for the Manners then in ufe, makes this Incongruity the more perceptible: But in the *Trojan* Times, their Speech, as well as their Manners retained much of the *Eaftern* Caft; their Theology was a *Fable*, and their moral Inftructions an allegorical *Tale*. When *Priam* came to beg the Body of his flaughter'd Son, *Achilles* comforts him with a parabolical Story concerning the two Veffels, out of which *Jupiter* difpenfes to every Man his Proportion of Good and Evil [x]; and *Glaucus* tells *Diomedes*, " That like the Leaves " of the Trees, firft fpreading, and then decay- " ing, fo are the Generations of mortal Men [y]".

[u] Difcours fur l'Ode : & Reponfe a la XI Reflection de Monf. Defpreaux fur Longin.
          [x] Iliad *ω*.   [y] Iliad *ζ*.

S E C T.

gravelot inv.   *G. Vander Gucht. Sculp.*

S E C T. IV.

N EX T to the Originals from which a Language is derived, the common Manners
under which it is formed, and the critical Period of its Duration, it is chiefly affected by
the *Religion* of a Country, and the Manners of
the *Times*. These might have been included
under the *Common Manners* of the Nation; but
their Influence is great enough, particularly upon
the *Turn* and *Genius* of the Language, to deserve a separate Confideration.

E

I

Sect.4.   I SHALL foon have occafion to make a ftricter Enquiry into the Origin both of the *Grecian Religion* and *Learning*. At prefent it is fufficient to fay, that they came from the great Parent of *Sacred* and *Civil* Inftitutions, the Kingdom of *Egypt*. That wife People feem to have early obferved the Curbs of the human Paffions, and the Methods of governing a large Society. They faw the general Bent of Mankind, *to admire what they do not underftand*, and to ftand in awe of unknown Powers, which they fancy capable to do them great good or ill: They adapted their religious Belief and folemn Ceremonies, to this Difpofition ; made their Rites *myfterious*, and delivered their allegorical Doctrines under great Ties of profound and pious Secrecy.

Ω ΤΕΚΝΟΝ ! ΣΥ ΔΕ ΤΟΙΣΙ ΝΟΟΙΣΙ ΠΕΛΑΖΕΟ, ΓΛΩΣΣΗΝ ΕΥ ΜΑΛ' ΕΠΙΚΡΑΤΕΩΝ ΣΤΕΡΝΟΙΣΙ Δ' ΕΝΘΕΟ ΦΗΜΗΝ [a].

Now, thou my Son! approach with Mind intent,
And careful keep thy Tongue: But in thy Breaft
Revolve thefe awful Sounds.——

HENCE the Number of monftrous Stories concerning their Gods, which the firft *Grecian* Sages that travell'd into *Egypt* certainly underftood, and explained to their Adepts [b], among whom,

---

[a] Ὀρφεὺς πρὸς Μυσαίον· In Fragment. Ὀρφικῶν Ἐπῶν.
[b] *Diodorus* the *Sicilian*, after having explained the natural Signification of the Allegory of *Bacchus*'s being the Son of *Jupiter* and *Ceres*, or Wine's being the Production of the *Earth* and *Moifture*, adds thefe remarkable Words, σύμφωνα δὲ τύτοις εἶναι τά τε δηλύμψια, διὰ τ͞ ΟΡΦΙΚΩΝ ΠΟΙΗΜΑΤΩΝ, ᾗ τὰ παρεισαγόμψια κατὰ τὰς Τελετὰς, πεὶ ὧν ὐ θέμις τῆς ἀμυήτοις ἱςορῶ τὰ κατὰ μέρ⊙. βιϚ. γ. Which plainly fhews the Nature and Tendency of the *Orphic* Rites.

whom, after fome Defcents, I reckon *Hefiod* Sect. 4.
and *Homer:* But falling afterwards into the
hands of Men of warm Fancies, who thought
they might *invent* as well as their Mafters, there
were many traditional Stories tacked to the former ; fometimes untowardly enough, and fometimes fo as to make a tolerable Piece of the *literal* Relation, but confounding when applied
to the *Allegory.* Thefe are all the ιροι λογοι
(*facred Traditions*) mentioned fo often by *Herodotus,* with a Declaration that he will not
venture to publifh them ; and of the fame kind
is the θειος λογος (*the divine Tradition*) recommended by *Orpheus* to his favourite Scholar, and quoted by a primitive Father for another purpofe [c].

THIS Allegorical Religion having been tranf-
planted into *Greece,* found it a very proper Soil
for fuch a Plantation. It took deep root in the
Minds of the *Greeks,* who were grofly ignorant, and prepoffeffed with no rival Opinions:
They made Additions to it of their own, and
in a few Ages it was incorporated with their
Manners, mixed itfelf with their Language, and
gained *univerfal Belief.* " Such was its Con-
" dition when *Homer* made his Appearance in
" the World: It had attained its Vigour, and
" had not loft the Grace of *Novelty* and *Youth* :"
This is the Crifis, when every body affects to

talk

---

[c] 'Εις δ ΘΕΙΟΝ ΛΟΓΟΝ βλέψας, τέτω προσέχων.
Juftin Martyr. Λόγος παραινετικὸς πρὸς 'Ελληνας.

Sect.4. talk in the prevailing Stile ; which joined with the early metaphorical *Caft* of the Language, is one great Reafon of the conftant Allegory in the ancient Writings.

WE HAVE frequent Examples, how much the firm Belief of any Sect makes Men fpeak and write in the *approved Idiom :* They introduce it into their *Bufinefs*, allude to it in their *Plea-fures*, and abftain from it in no Part of Life ; efpecially while the Doctrine flourifhes, and appears in Bloom: For your Lordfhip knows, that thefe things, among the Ancients, had their *Spring* and *Summer* as well as natural Growths ; and after a certain time, like a fuperannuated Plant, they turned fcrubby and lifelefs, were difregarded by degrees, and at laft vanifhed.

WHAT FURTHER Advantages *Poetry* might reap from a Religion fo framed, will appear afterwards [d]: Let us now confider the *Manners of the Times*; by which I underftand the Profeffions and Studies that are *in vogue*, and bring moft Honour to thofe who poffefs them in an eminent degree.

THEY likewife follow the *Fortunes* of a Nation : In the *Progreffion* above-mentioned, the Arts of the greateft *Ufe* in Life, I mean thofe that fupply our natural Wants, and fecure our Perfons and Properties, are the *firft* that ennoble their Inventers ; and in procefs of time, when Wealth has made its Entrance, the
Refiners

[d] See Pag. 142. 192. 277.

Refiners of Pleasure, and Contrivers of Magni-Sect. *c.*
ficence draw our Attention.

FROM THE Accounts already given of the
State of *Greece,* it is eafy to conclude, " that
" the *firft* muft be ftill prevalent when *Homer*
" lived;" a piece of good Fortune that exempted him from the *two Vices,* to whofe charge
the admired *Longinus* lays the Fall of Poetry :
An infatiable Defire of Riches, and what he
calls (ἀ᾿Ͷνέςατον Πάθος) *a mean difpiriting Paffion,* the Love of Pleafure [e].

IN effect, *Arms* at that time was the honoured Profeffion, and a *publick Spirit* the
courted Character : There was a Neceffity for
them both. The *Man* who had bravely defen-
ded his City, enlarged its Dominion, or died
in its Caufe, was revered like a God: Love of
Liberty, and Contempt of Death, with their
nobleft Confequences, Honour, Probity, and
Temperance, were *Realities.* There was, as I
faid, a *Neceffity* for thofe Virtues [f]: No Safety
to Life or Fortune without them : For while
every State, that is to fay, almoft every City
was envied by its warlike and encroaching

E 3 Neighbour,

[e] Περὶ Ὑ᾿ψῦς. Τμῆμα μδ'. ζήτημα λαμπρὸν·

[f] Ὁ γὸ δὴ χρόνΘ ἐκεῖνΘ, (the Age of *Thefeus,* a little before the
Trojan War) ἤνεγκεν ἀνθρώπες, χειρῶν μὲ ἔργοις, ἢ ποδῶν τάχει,
καὶ σωμάτων ῥώμαις (ὡς ἔοικεν) ὑπερφυεῖς καὶ ἀκαμάτες· πρὸς
ἐδὲν δὲ τῇ φύσει χρωμένες ἐπιεικὲς, ἐδὲ ὠφέλιμον· ἀλλ᾿ ὕβρει τε
χαίρονίας ὑπερηφάνῳ, καὶ ἀπολαύονίας τ᾿ δυνάμεως ὠμότητι καὶ
πικρίᾳ, ἐπὶ τῷ κρατεῖν, βιάζεῶς τε, καὶ διαφθείρειν τὸ προσπίπτον·
Ἀιδῶ δὲ καὶ δικαιοσύνην, καὶ τὸ ἴσον, καὶ τὸ φιλάνθρωπον, ὡς
ἀτολμίᾳ τῷ ἀδικεῖν, ἢ φόβῳ τῷ ἀδικεῖσθαι, τὲς πολλὲς ἐπαινῦντας,
ἐδὲν οἰομένες προσήκειν τοῖς πλέω ἔχειν δυναμένοις.
ΠΛΥΤΑΡΧ· ΘΗΣΕΥΣ.

Sect. 4. Neighbour, there was no choice, but either resolutely to defend itself by dint of Arms, or shamefully submit to Oppression and Slavery.

" And no wonder if the Man who learns these
" Virtues from *Necessity*, and the Things them-
" selves, knows them better than Schools and
" Systems can instruct him ; and that the *Re-*
" *presentations* of such genuine Characters bear
" the Marks of *Truth*, and far outshine those
" taken from counterfeit Worth, or fainter
" Patterns."

THUS WE find, that the *Fortunes*, the *Manners*, and the *Language* of a People are all linked together, and necessarily influence one another. Men take their Sentiments from their Fortunes; if they are low, it is their constant Concern *how to mend them* ; if they are easy, *how to enjoy them :* And according to this Bent, they turn both their Conduct and their Conversation ; and assume the Language, Air, and Garb peculiar to the *Manner* of the different Characters.

In most of the *Greek* Cities, *Policy* and *Laws* were but just a forming, when *Homer* came into the World g. The first Sketches of them were extremely *simple* h ; taking their Rise from the Exigencies

---

g They had no well-digested Body of Laws, or Plan of a Civil Constitution, before *Onomacritus.* So *Aristotle*, Ὀνομακριτῦ γινομδύε πρῶτε δέωε περὶ Νομοθεσίαν.   Πολιτ. α.

h Τὰς γὸ ἀρχαίες Νόμες λίαν ἁπλῶς εἶναι ἢ βαρβαρικὲς. Ἐσιδηροφορῦντο γὸ οἱ Ἕλληνες, καὶ τὰς γυναῖκας ἐωνῦντο παρ' ἀλλήλων. Ὅσα τε λοιπὰ τ ἀρχαίων ἐσὶ που Νομίμων, εὐήθη πάμπαν ἐσὶ.   Ἀριστοτ. Πολιτ. β.

Exigencies of the rude Way of Life then pre-Sect. 4. vailing. The great Law of *Hospitality* made the chief Part of the Inftitution : To violate a Stranger, who had taken Sanctuary under your *Roof*, had participated of your *Table*, or fat down by your *Fire*, was made the higheft, and moft deteftable Impiety. The reft were of a piece; generally Prohibitions from Violence, or fuch Regulations of Manners as we fhould think unneceffary or barbarous. The Tribes were but beginning to live fecure within the Walls of their new-fenced Towns, and had as yet neither Time nor Skill to frame a Domeftick Policy, or Municipal Laws; and far lefs to think of publick Methods of training up their Citizens: *They lived naturally*, and were governed by the *natural Poife* of the Paffions, as it is fettled in every human Breaft. This made them fpeak and act, without other Reftraint than their own native Apprehenfions of *Good* and *Evil*, *Juft* and *Unjuft*, each as he was prompted from *within*. " Thefe Manners af- " ford the moft *natural* Pictures, and proper " Words to paint them."

THEY HAVE a peculiar Effect upon the Language, not only as they are natural, but as they are ingenuous and *good*. While a Nation continues fimple and fincere, whatever they fay receives a *Weight* from *Truth:* Their Sentiments are ftrong and honeft; which al-

Sect. 4. ways produce *fit Words* to exprefs them [i]: Their Paffions are found and genuine, not adulterated or difguifed, and break out in their own artlefs Phrafe and unaffected Stile. They are not accuftomed to the *Prattle*, and little pretty *Forms* that enervate a polifhed Speech: nor are they over-run with *Quibble* and *Sheer-Wit*, which makes its Appearance late in every Country, and in *Greece* came long after the *Trojan* Times. And *this* I take to be the reafon, " Why moft " Nations are fo delighted with their ancient " Poets [k]:" Before they are polifhed into Flattery and refined into Falfehood, we feel the *Force* of their *Words*, and the *Truth* of their *Thoughts*.

In COMMON Life, no doubt, the witty facetious Man is now the preferable Character: But he is only a *middling* Perfon, and no *Hero* [l]; bearing a Perfonage for which there is hardly an Inch of room in an *Epic Poem*. To be witty in a Matter of Confequence, where the Rifque is high, and the Execution requires *Caution* or *Boldnefs*, is *Impertinence* and *Buffoonry*.

VIRGIL

---

[i] Quin ipfe (Tiberius) compofitus aliàs, & velut eluctantium Verborum, *folutius* promptiufque eloquebatur, quotiens fubveniret.
TACITUS.

[k] ————Græcorum funt *antiquiffima* quæque Scripta vel *Optima.*————
Horat. ad Auguftum. Ep. i. Lib. ii.

[l] *Bellus* Homo, & *Magnus* vis idem, Cotta, videri: Sed qui *bellus* Homo eft, Cotta, *pufillus* Homo eft.
Martial. Epigr. Lib. i. 10.

VIRGIL well knew the Importance of this Sect. 4. Imitation of ancient *Manners*; and borrowed from *Ennius* his antiquated Terms, and the ftrong obfolete Turn of his Sentences. Nay, he has adopted as many of the *old Forms* ufed at Sacrifices, Games, Confecrations, and even *Forms of Law,* ·as the Emergencies of his admired *Poem* wou'd permit.

Gravelot inv.   P. Fourdrinier Sculp.

SECT.

Gravelot inv.   P. Fourdrinier Sculp.

S E C T. V.

Sect. 5. **B**Y TRACING the Caufes which have the greateft Influence upon Language, we are led to a Thought that muft give Pleafure to the *truly Good*.   We find that without *Virtue* there can be no *true Poetry* : It depends upon the *Manners* of a Nation, which form their Characters, and animate their Language : If their Manners are found and entire, their Speech will accompany and do them Juftice : And if

we

we rife higher, and fuppofe them not only Sect. 5.
found, but *noble* and *heroic* (as we muft do,
when fpeaking of Manners fit for Poetry) What
is this but *Virtue's Self* in all her Luftre and
Dignity? Your Lordfhip muft have viewed her
at times in this glorious Drefs, and will forgive
me, if I am inquifitive upon fo amiable a Subject.
Is what we call *Heroifm* indeed any thing elfe,
than *A difinterefted Love* of Mankind and our
Country, unawed by *Dangers,* and unwearied
by *Toils?* If it is not, the focial Paffions, and
nobleft Affections muft prevail in an *Epic-Poem.*
They may vary indeed, and fhew themfelves
very differently in different Characters: They
may likewife have their *own Shades,* and muft
be fometimes drawn upon dark Grounds, to
raife and give them a *Relief;* but ftill they muft
be the *principal Figures* in the Piece, if it is
meant to give a real and lafting Pleafure.

　　BUT there is another Conclufion offers itfelf, and appears fo *odd,* that one does not know
what to make of it: For does it not found
fomething like Treafon in *Apollo's* Court, to
fay, *That a polifhed Language* is not fit for a
great Poet? And yet, if the Maxim be true,
" That no Man defcribes well but what he has
" feen, nor talks with Eafe and Maftery, but
" in the Language and Idiom he has been ufed
" to," I apprehend we muft affent to it. Whoever is acquainted with what paffes for Polite-
nefs of Stile, and with the Subjects ufually
treated

Sect. 5. treated of in *that* manner, will eafily forgive me, if I am at no pains to make out the Confequence. I fhall only obferve, that what we call *Polifhing* diminifhes a Language ; it makes many Words *obfolete* ; it coops a Man up in a Corner, allows him but *one Set* of courtly Phrafes, and deprives him of many fignificant Terms, and ftrong beautiful Expreffions, which he muft venture upon, like *Virgil*, at the hazard of appearing antiquated and homely.

A LANGUAGE throughly polifhed in the modern Senfe, will not defcend to the *Simplicity* of Manners abfolutely neceffary in *Epic-Poetry* : And if we feign the Manners, we muft likewife endeavour to imitate the Stile. I have already fhewn how little Succefs we can expect in the Attempt ; and it were eafy to give Proof in *Fact*, that no Learning or Genius is fufficient to fecure us from a Mifcarriage in this Particular. But the Tafk is unpleafant : Let us therefore chufe an Example where we may rather praife than blame.

THE NAME of *Fenelon* calls up the Image of a Man diftinguifhed by every amiable Quality : Like fome powerful Charm, it makes real Virtue, princely Science, and Sweetnefs of Manners, rife to our Imagination. His perfect Knowledge of Antiquity, and flowing Fancy, feemed to qualify him to write the Sequel of the fimple and inftructive *Odyffey*. And yet we know that his enchanting Work has not efcaped Criticifm ;

Criticifm[a]; and that only fuch Parts of it lie Sect. 5. expofed, as attempt a *Mixture* of ancient and modern Manners; that is, when he wou'd reconcile *old Heroifm* with *Politicks*, and make Poetry preach *Reafons of State.*

IT MAY be thought fuperfluous after this to obferve, That an *abfolute* Court muft have a pernicious Influence both on the Variety of Charaters in a Nation, and the Extent of their Dialect : We need but look around us to fee many of the fineft Countries in *Europe*, groaning under baffled Laws and an aibitrary Sway, and giving difmal Proofs of the Truth of this Remark. In fuch Governments not only Matters of Confequence are over-ruled at pleafure, but in the moft indifferent Circumftance of Life, all muft conform to the *Court-Model.* Example hath the Force of Command ; you muft both fpeak and write after *a Copy* ; and no fufpicious Word muft reach the Ears of the miftaken Great. By this means, many things come to lofe their Names, or are foftned into *infignificant* Appellations; and where *thefe* cannot be had, Circumlocutions are called in, to witnefs our Dread of offending by fpeaking plain Truth[b].   BESIDES,

[a] *Critique des Avantures de* Telemaque. A Piece equally cruel and unjuft ; without other Handle in fact, than what arifes from the Glow of an elevated Fancy, and the Incompatibility of Manners.

[b] When the Cardinal *Richelieu* had obliged the *French* Academy to cenfure the *Cid*, a Piece of the celebrated *Corneille*'s, the Author wrote a Letter to the Cardinal's Favourite M. *de Boifrobert*; where he tells him, " J'attens avec beaucoup d'Impatience les " Sentimens de l'Academie, afin d'apprendre ce que dorefenavant " je dois fuivre: Jufques là, je ne puis travailler qu' avec défiance, " & n'ofe employer un Mot en feureté."
                      P. Peliffon. Hift. de l'Acad. Françoife.

Sect. 5. Besides, it is odds, but that in such a Country, there are *formal Reftraints* upon Writing; which muft have yet a worfe Effeƈt. What a lamentable Sight are thofe Countries at this day, which were formerly the *Parents* of *Learning* and *Ingenuity?* How barren now in real Literature! How *diftorted* the little they produce! bearing the Marks of the Violence and *unnatural* State in which it is conceived and brought forth. Inftead of thofe manly Sentiments which do juftice to Virtue and Vice ; inftead of thofe bold Piƈtures of Men and Things of the *prefent* Age, (the Age in which We are moft concerned,) They muft content themfelves with licking up Scraps of *monkiſh* Hiftory, and colleƈting Legends of the Saints : Or if they venture *to reafon*, it muft be upon diftant Faƈts and general Principles, remote from their own Times, without daring to hint a Parallel, or make the fmalleft Application.

Such is *their* State ; while We, with Joy, may view our native Ifle, the happy Inftance of the Connexion between *Liberty* and *Learning*. We find our Language mafculine and noble; of vaft Extent, and capable of greater Variety of *Stile* and *Charaƈter* than any modern Tongue. We fee our Arts improving, our Sciences advancing, Life underftood, and the whole animated with a *Spirit* fo generous and free, as gives the trueft Proof of the Happinefs of our Conftitution.

FORGIVE me, *My Lord,* if a Thought fo Sect. 5.
pleaſant, and which You have ſo great a hand
in making ſuch, has drawn me from a melancholy Subject. One cannot, without Compaſ-
ſion, think of a poor Poet writing under the
Terror of the Inquiſition. He knows not but
ſuch a Verſe may give umbrage to a Right Re-
verend Father *Inquiſitor;* another to a Reve-
rend Father *Prior Inſpector;* this Simile may
ſtartle the Father *Deputy Reviſor,* and that Al-
luſion ſeem dangerous to the *Vicar* himſelf.

No WONDER if the ſlighted Author, haunt-
ed with ſuch *ſable Spectres* inſtead of *Muſes,*
is delivered of a deformed Production. Their
Ghoſtly Appearance muſt damp every liberal
Thought. The Mind dares not exert itſelf,
but *crouches* under the Panick of a *Cenſure,*
backed with the Secular Arm to inforce it.
And can we expect any Grace or Spirit in a
Work that is conceived and faſhioned in ſuch
piteous Circumſtances? No ſurely, nor in a
little time any Works at all: For the *Fathers*
generally obtain their End; and in a Nation
where they are once entruſted with the Power
to effect it, in a little time ſo order Matters,
that ſcarce any one writes but themſelves c. But
theſe

---

c A Book in *Spain* muſt paſs through ſix Courts, before it is
publiſhed. I. It is examined by the *Examinador Synodal* of the
Archbiſhoprick, commiſſioned by the *Vicario.* II. It goes to the
Recorder of the Kingdom, where it is to be publiſhed, *Chroniſta
de Caſtilla, Arragon, Valencia,* &c. III. If approved by them,
it is licenſed by the *Vicario* himſelf, atteſted by a *Notario.* IV. The
Privilege muſt be had from his *Majeſty;* and a *Secretary* counter-
ſigns.

Sect. 5. thefe things have been the Subject of many a
Treatife: I only mention them, to point out
the _Reafon_ of the Antipathy between them and
the fublimer Kinds of Writing. To expatiate
upon the baneful Influences of Tyranny, wou'd
be very unneceffary, when a Man living under
the beft-regulated Government is too much
moulded to its _Manners_, ever to excel in that
original and unlimited Draught of Mankind,
Epic-Poetry.

In oppofition to thefe Opinions, it may be
advanced by fuch as are acquainted with the
Progrefs and Periods of Literature, "That the
"_Interval_ between the high Liberty and En-
"flavement of a State, has been obferved to
"fhew the World fome noble Productions."
The _Fact_ is unqueftionable; and to difcover
the Caufes of it, we need only confider the
Steps by which a Government falls from its
Rights, to be at the mercy of a _fingle Perfon._

In general, this Difafter is laid to the door
of _Corruption_; and very juftly: _Ambition_ and
Luxury feldom fail, when they have attained
their full Growth, to throw a State into Con-
vulfions, and make it ripe for a Mafter. They
difpofe Men to _give_ and _take_, upon certain
Confiderations, which by degrees grow _weighty_
enough

---

figns. V. After it is printed, it goes to the _Corrector General por_
fu Mageftad, who compares it with the licenfed Copy, left any
thing be inferted or altered. And, VI. The Lords of the _Council_
tax it at fo much a Sheet. In _Portugal,_ a Book has feven Reviews
to pafs before Publication. I have fmiled at fome of their Title-
Pages, bearing for the greater Security of the Buyer, _Com todas as_
licenças neceffarias.

enough to affect the Publick: But at the same Sect. 5.
time, there is no Season on Earth when Men
are so throughly known. When the Offers are
tempting, and Bribes run high [d], it is then that
Men discover what they are worth, or for what
they will fairly bargain and sell themselves. The
Man of real Virtue appears with double Lustre
after the Refusal; and he who has withstood
one Temptation, when his *Foible* is found out,
and rightly applied to, gives way upon the second, and fixes his *Price*. Mankind in this
respect are like certain *Indian Feathers*; They
do not shew to advantage in *one* Light only;
but the Disorder and Dangers frequent at such
Junctures, set all their Passions a going, and
turn them into every Shape they are capable
of: And these Attitudes, when well observed,
and justly copied, give us the excellent Pieces
above-mentioned.

BESIDES, the Times of such Struggles have
a kind of *Liberty* peculiar to themselves: They
raise a free and active Spirit, which over-spreads
the Country: Every Man finds himself on such
occasions

d Biduo, per unum servum, & eum ex gladiatorio ludo, con-
fecit totum negotium: Accersivit ad se, promisit, intercessit,
dedit. Jam vero, O Dii boni, Rem perditam! etiam *Noctes cer-
tarum Mulierum*, atque Adolescentulorum nobilium *Introductiones*,
nonnullis Judicibus pro mercedis cumulo fuerunt. *Cicero* writing
to *Atticus* the History of *Clodius's* Acquital by the assistance of
Crassus. 　　　　　　　　　　　　　　Lib. i. Ep. xiii.
　Curio's Bribe to change Sides, and betray his Country, was *Centies* H-S, or 80,729 *l.* 3 *s.* 4 *d.* He wanted this and five times
more to free him of Incumbrances; for he had a Debt of *Sex-
centies* H-S. 484,375 *l.*

F

Sect. 5. occasions his own Master, and that he *may be* whatever he can *make* himself: He knows not how high he may rise, and is unawed by *Laws*, which are then of no Force. He finds his own Weight, tries his own Strength, and if there is any hidden Worth, or curbed Mettle in him, certainly shews and gives it vent. Accordingly we see, that the Genius's produced at these Times, give great Proofs of *Reach* and *Capacity*, especially in politick Managements and civil Affairs, in the largest Sense [e]. The abstract *Sciences* are the Product of *Leisure* and *Quiet* [f]; but those that have respect to *Man*, and take their aim from the human Heart, are best learned in Employment and Agitation.

IT WAS when *Greece* was ill-settled, when Violence prevailed in many Places, amidst the Shock and Confusion of the wandering Tribes, that *Homer* produced his immortal Poem. And it was when *Italy* was torn in pieces, when the little States were leagued against each other; in a word, in the Heat of the Struggle and Bloodshed of the *Guelfe* and *Ghibelline* Parties, that *Dante* withdrew from his Country, and made the strongest Draught of Men and their

Passions,

---

[e] *Thucydides, Aristotle,* and *Demosthenes* among the *Greeks,* and *Cicero, Virgil,* and *Horace* among the *Romans,* were Witnesses to Civil Wars, or Attempts made upon the Publick Liberty. Some of them surviv'd it, and some fell in its Defence.

[f] Καὶ πρῶτον εὑρέθησαν (αἱ Ἐπιστῆμαι) τότοις τοῖς τόποις ὑπὲρ ἐχϐλάσων· διὸ πεεὶ Αἴγυπτον, αἱ μαθηματικαὶ πρῶτον τέχναι συνέστησαν· ἐκᾶ γὸ ἠφεῖθη χολάζειν τὸ τ̄ ἱερέων ἔθνΘ·

ΑΡΙΣΟΤ. μῷ τὰ φυσικ. α· τὸ μεῖζον.

Paffions, that ftands in the Records of modern Sect. 5.
Poetry. The Author of the *Eneïd* lived in a
Time of Diforder and publick Ruin: He faw
the Miftrefs of the World become twice a Prey
to lawlefs Power; her Conftitution deftroyed,
and Prices fet upon the Heads of her braveft
Sons for oppofing a Tyranny.

AND ftill, *My Lord*, it was when unhappy
Britain was plunged in all the Calamities of
Civil Rage, that our high-fpirited Poem took
its birth. It is true, the *Plan* of *Paradife Loft*,
has little to do with our prefent Manners; It
treats of a fublimer Theme, and refufes the
Meafure of Human Actions: Yet it every where
bears fome Analogy to the Affairs of Mankind;
and the Author (who had viewed the Progrefs
of our Mifery) has embellifhed it with all the
proper Images his Travelling, Learning, and
Experience could afford him.

BUT AS few of the Changes which Letters have undergone, efcape your Lordfhip's
notice, it will probably be afked; "Since a po-
"lifhed Language, and the Deference paid to
"an abfolute Court, are incompatible with the
"nobler kinds of Poetry, how came the *new*
"Comedy to excel the *old*, which had all li-
"berty of Language and Manners, while the
"other grew up under the Influence of Luxury,
"and the Awe of the *Macedonian* Power?"

A learned and fententious Writer will not
allow this to be true: "The Old Comedy,
"according

Sect. 5.   " according to him, was employed in the Re-
" formation of *Manners*, in recommending
" *Virtue*, and pointing out the *Abuses* of the
" State ; whereas the New was contented to
" trifle with Punks and Pandars ; the *old Chuff*,
" the *Davus*, or Knave of the Family, and
" his young *Master* : The Scene, he says, is
" always at *Athens*, and all the Pother is some
" little jilting Story, or knavish Prank ; pro-
" posing only some trifling *Mirth* or silly *Pas-*
" *time !*"

BUT ADMITTING the Supposition ;——the
different Nature of the Writing accounts for it.
Nothing can be more opposite than the Stile,
the Language, the Manners of *Comedy* to *Epic* :
The fittest for the one seem the most improper
for the other ; and the most uncomick Character on Earth is that of a Great and Generous
Man.   It is indeed true, that in such a thorough
Democracy as *Athens*, the Limits of *Comedy* and
Tragedy cou'd not be well ascertained, or kept
asunder.   Tragedy being a Representation of
the *high* Characters in Life, and Comedy of the
lower, they were in reality jumbled together in
this State ᴳ, where the vilest and meanest Creature might speak as scurrilously of the Person and
Conduct of the first Citizens, as his Education
and

ᴳ Pinxit & Dêmon (ΔΗΜΟΝ) Athenienfium, Argumento quoque ingeniofo.   Volebat namque varium, iracundum, injuſtum,
inconſtantem ; eundem exorabilem, clementem, mifericordem,
excelfum, gloriofum, humilem, ferocem, fugacemque, & omnia pariter oſtendere.

    Plinius, de Parrhafio, Lib. xxxv. § 10.

and Temper cou'd prompt him. *Here* lay the Sect. 5.
Strength of the *old* Comedy, which cou'd not
fubfift but in fuch a State; and which no doubt
muft have the Preference, if immoderate Laugh-
ter, if Liberty to talk at random, and banter the
higheft Dignities, and beft Men of the Nation,
be advantageous to that kind of Writing. But
if that *Liberty* was often abufed, and if the
Drama is capable of a nobler Turn, and of
giving a more refined Pleafure; if more *Truth*
can be brought into the Manners, and *Men* and
their *Natures* more generally reprefented [h], in
that cafe it muft give way to the *new*.

I MUST however own, that while the high
Democracy prevailed at *Athens*, and the Commonalty were poffeffed of that uncontrouled
Power which *Pericles* put in their hands, and
Cleon exercifed, during that time, *Ariftophanes*
and his Fellows had *Originals* to draw from;
and in that refpect their Wit and Writings, which
appear to us *theatrical* and *falfe*, are *natural* and
true. But that wild licentious Government was
no fooner check'd by Fears from abroad, (which
always produce Regulations at home) than the
ΚΑΛΟΙ ΚΆΓΑΘΟΙ, the Men of Capacity and
Worth, began to diftinguifh themfelves and appear eminent; A *Secretion* was made; Manners
were formed, and Characters obferved and valued.

F 3 HERE

[h] *I Poeti Comici, per farci accorti de gli Andamenti del mondo,
piacevolmente, Nozze, Fefte, Conviti, Roffianefimi Putanefmi,
Ladronezzi, Truffe, Menzogne, Amori & Odii, tali appunto su per
le Scene rapprefentano, quali folete fare & fofferire voi Huomini.*
Speron. Speroni. *della Ufura*.

Sect. 5.   HERE was the Rise of the *new* Comedy;
Ribaldry was banished, and *Menander* wrote.
That is, at a Season when *Liberty* was not lost,
but the Excrescencies of it lopp'd off; when the
Humour of that witty People was not quashed,
but regulated: So true it is, " *That every* kind
" of Writing, but especially the *Poetic*, depends
" upon the Manners of the Age when it is pro-
" duced." The best *Poets* copy from *Nature*,
and give it us such as they find it. When once
they lose sight of this great Original, they write
false, be their natural Talents ever so great. Let
Torquato Taſſo witness the Truth of this, and the
rapid *Arioſto*; each endowed with a fertile Genius, and a happy Expreſſion; but who quitting
Life, betook themselves to aerial Beings and
Utopian Characters, and filled their Works with
Charms and *Viſions*, the modern Supplements
of the *Marvellous* and *Sublime*.

S E C T.

Gravelot inv.   G Van Gucht Sculp.

SECT. VI.

WHEN I reflect upon this way of rea-
Sect. 6.
soning, from the Influence that publick
Manners have upon Writing, I make no doubt
but the Question will recur; Since it is abfo-
lutely the *Conjuncture*, and *Manners* of the
Times, that produce Poets, " How comes it to
" pass that we have but one *Homer?* Cou'd a
" Space of two or three hundred Years, when
F 4 " *Greece,*

Sect. 6.   " *Greece,* and the Coaft of *Afia,* was in a pro-
           " per Temperament for fuch Formations, bring
           " forth but *one* ?"

THE Anfwer is obvious; That tho' it be
abfolutely neceffary, yet it is not the *only Con-*
dition: There are many required befides ; too
many to be here enumerated : there is an univerfal and elevated *Genius* ; a Quality fo rare,
that an excellent Author of our Nation feems
to think, " That of all the Numbers of Man-
" kind, that live within the Compafs of a
" thoufand Years, for one Man that is born
" capable of making a *great Poet,* there may
" be a thoufand born capable of making as
" great Generals, or Minifters of State, as the
" moft renowned in Story [a]." But though this
were exaggerated, there are many fubfequent
Circumftances of Life, many Advantages of
Education, and Opportunities of knowing Mankind in general, and feeing particular Subjects
fit for Poefy, which can hardly meet in one and
the fame Perfon.

TO INSTANCE in one Particular, from
which we may judge of the Import of the
reft : *Much Travelling,* and wide *perfonal Ob-*
fervation, has been the Lot of the greateft
Epic Poets. In this way of Life they had frequent Opportunities to acquaint themfelves with
the *Originals* of their *Draughts* and *Fictions,*
whofe great *Excellency,* whether material or
moral,

---

[a] Sir *William Temple,* Mifcell. Part. ii. Effay 4. POETRY.

moral, is their *Likeneſs* to *Nature* and *Truth*. Sect. 6. But this happens to few Men, eſpecially of a 〰 Poetical Turn: They are commonly none of the healthieſt People, and too delicate to endure the Hardſhips, or face the Dangers that are inevitable in long Voyages. And yet, with all theſe Chances, the Period I have mentioned, when the *Manners*, the *Religion* and *Language* of *Greece* were at their *proper Pitch* for *Poetry*; to that Period, I ſay, the World ſtands indebted for *Linus*, and *Orpheus*, for *Olympus*, *Muſæus*, and *Amphion*; Men who are handed down to us as the Maſters of Verſe, by the greateſt of their Succeſſors [b]. Their Songs, it is true, are long ſince periſhed; but the wiſe and peaceful *Heſiod*, part of whoſe Compoſitions hath reached us, and commands our Admiration, owes his *Birth* to the ſame *Period*.

Nor can there be a greater Proof of the Power that *Manners*, and the *Publick Character* have over Poetry, than the ſurpriſing Reſemblance of the oldeſt Writings. Two things cannot be liker one another, than the *old Oracles*, the *Fragments* of *Orpheus* ſo called, and the *ancient Hymns*, are to *Heſiod's* and *Homer's* Verſes. Not to ſay in general, that they have the ſame *Turn*; but the ſame Epithets of *Gods* and *Men*, the ſame *Sentiments* and *Alluſions*, the ſame *Cadence* and *Structure*; nay, ſometimes the

[b] Muſæum ante omnes —Æneid. vi. Horat. Ode 11. Lib. iii. & de Arte Poetica.

Sect. 6. the very fame *Expreffions* and *Phrafes* are to be met with in them all. Numberlefs are the ΣυνεμπlώμαΤα, or *Coincidencies* obferved by the Criticks; and in fhort, the Collufion of their Metaphor and Imagery is fo palpable, that many have attributed the *Effects* of their being formed upon the fame Models, their Writing from the fame Originals, and in the fame plain Dialect, to downright Copying or Plagiarifm.

Bᴜᴛ there is no need to go fo far: The Caufes affigned are fufficient to produce all this Likenefs; if we remember too, that they commonly make Writers exercife themfelves upon the fame Subjects, which is alfo a part of their Influence. A certain kind of Science is peculiar to every Age, and a particular way of treating it. They are both the Effect of the *Conjuncture* fo often mentioned. And while I am upon this Subject, I cannot pafs over *one* Confequence, which has been long a Problem among the Learned. It is elegantly propofed by a *Roman* ᶜ, who, if his Honefty had been equal to his Underftanding, might have ftood in the firft rank of their *Hiftorians*.

" Tʜo' I have little room for it, fays he,
" yet I cannot help mentioning a thing which
" I have often revolved in my Mind, and can-
" not fatisfy my felf about the Caufe of it:
" For is it not exceeding ftrange, that the
　　　　　　　　　　　　　　　　" *great*

ᶜ C. Vellei Paterc. Hift. Rom. Lib. i. in fine.

" *great Masters* in every Profession and Science, Sect. 6.
" always appear in the fame *Period* of *Time*,
" and are of the fame Caft and Model?——
" One Age, and that at no great diftance of
" Years, produced *Eschylus*, *Sophocles*, and
" *Euripides*, Men of a divine Genius, who
" carried Tragedy to its height. In another,
" the *old Comedy* flourifhed under *Eupolis*, *Cra-*
" *tinus*, and *Ariftophanes*; and the *new* was
" both invented and brought to perfection by
" *Menander* and his Cotemporaries, *Diphilus*
" and *Philemon*, without leaving hopes of Imi-
" tation.

" IN LIKE manner, the *Philofophical* Sages
" of the *Socratic* School, how fhort a while
" did they continue after *Plato* and *Ariftotle's*
" Death? As to *Oratory*, who can be faid to
" have *excelled* in it before *Ifocrates*, or after the
" fecond Defcent of his Scholars? They came
" all fo clofe together, that no one great Man
" can be feen at any diftance of Time from
" another." Then the Hiftorian proceeds to
fhew, that the fame thing had happened among
the *Romans*; and, with great reafon, extends
his Obfervation not only to the fublimer Sciences, but alfo to *Grammarians*, *Painters*, *Statu-*
aries, *Sculptors*, *Founders*, and to all the *fubfer-*
vient Arts. The fame Event might be fhewn
to have fallen out in any Nation, where *Learn-*
ing ever flourifhed, and whofe *Hiftory* is known.

WON-

Sect. 6. WONDERFUL, *My Lord*, have been the Conjectures about this puzzling Appearance ; and many a curious Speculation has been employed to folve it [d] : It has been doubted, "Whether any Influence of *Stars* [e], any "Power of *Planets*, or kindly *Afpect* of the "Heavenly Bodies [f], might not at times reach "our Globe, and impregnate fome favourite "Race with a celeftial Spirit." Supernatural Conceptions, and miraculous [g] Nurfings, have been contrived as a *Salvo* for our Belief, when the *Hero* or *Sage* atchieves things which we fancy above the Reach of *Men*. But our Court-Hiftorian underftands better ; and though he talks a little ftrangely in the End,

---

[d] See *Difcours Phyfique fur les Influences des Aftres* ; where the Planetary Powers are reduced to *Les Cartes'* Principles, and accounted for by the *Materia Subtilis*. 12mo Paris, chez Coignard.

[e] Les Aftres, & principalement les Signes & les Planetes font (aprés Dieu) la feconde Caufe des Mœurs. Le Poete marque la Force qu'elles ont fur la Complexion des Hommes, quand, &c.— Voilà comment Virgile fait l'Horofcope de l'Empire Romain, en fa naiffance. P. Boffu du Poeme Epique Liv. iv.

[f] ———— *Diftat enim, quæ*
Sydera te excipiant, modo primos incipientem
Edere Vagitus, & adhuc a Matre rubentem.
Ventidius quid enim ? Quid Tullius ? Anne aliud quàm
Sydus, & occulti miranda Potentia fati ? Juvenal.

[g] *Hercules, Alexander,* and *Scipio* [*], were faid to be in reality *Jupiter's* Sons, tho' they paffed for *Amphitryon's, Philip's,* and *Pub, Scipio's. Demaratus* belonged to the Hero *Aftrobacus* [†] : and *Orpheus, Homer,* and *Plato,* according to ancient Tradition, had only *Mothers* of the Human Race. *Pindar* was fed with Honey by the Bees themfelves: *Achilles* was nurfed with the Fat of Lions, and Marrow of Deer; and the Founders of *Rome* were fuckled by a Wolf, tho' the Founder of the *Perfian* Empire had only a Bitch to perform that Duty for him [‡].

[*] *Livii Hift. Lib.* xxvi. [†] *Herodot. Erato.* [‡] *Juftin. Lib.* i.

End [h], yet he feems to lay the Strefs of the matter upon a furer Bottom. The way he accounts for it is by *Emulation*, which certainly contributes to the Perfection of every *Art* and *Science*; and was ftrong among the ΑΟΙΔΟΙ, or *Bards*, whofe appearing in a Clufter gave rife to the Queftion [i]: But this Principle is far from giving compleat Satisfaction, which indeed *Velleius* does not affirm.

I w i l l not repeat what has been formerly faid; for I make no doubt of being prevented, and that your Lordfhip has already made the Application. It is the *different Periods* or Steps, naturally fucceeding in the *Progreffion of Manners*, that can only account for the Succeffion of Wit and Literature.

I h a v e marked out thofe of *Greece* in the Hiftory of the Language [k]; they correfpond with admirable Nicenefs to the fucceffive Sets of *Poets, Orators,* and *Philofophers* enumerated by the *Roman* Hiftorian. *For they are fettled and uniform* Caufes, *and never fail to work their Effect, unlefs when external Violence hinders their Operation.*　　I n

---

[h] Naturáque quod fummo ftudio petitum eft, afcendit in fummum, difficilifque in perfecto mora eft, naturaliterque, quod procedere non poteft, recedit.

Velle. P. Hift. R. Lib. i.

[i] In *Hefiod's* Days, who, if not contemporary, lived at no great Diftance of Times from *Homer*, a Poet, or Α Ο Ι Δ Ο Σ, was as common a Calling as a Potter or a Joiner, and as liable to Emulation and Envy.

Καὶ Κεραμεὺς Κεραμεῖ κοτέει, κ᾽ Τέκτονι Τέκτων ἱ
Καὶ Πτωχὸς Πτωχῷ φθονέει, καὶ Α Ο Ι Δ Ο Σ Α Ο Ι Δ Ω ͺ
'Ησιοδ᾽. 'Εργ. καὶ 'Ημερ.

[k] See Page 44, 45, and 46.

Sect. 6. IN THE early Ages of the *Grecian* State, the wild and barbarous Inhabitants wanted the Affistance of the Mufes to foften and tame them. They ftood in need of being impreffed with an Awe of fuperior and irrefiftible Powers, and a liking to *focial* Life. They wanted a *Mythology* to lead them by *Fear* and *Dread* (the only Holds to be taken of a rude Multitude) into a Feeling of *natural Caufes*, and their *Influence* upon our Lives and Actions. The *Wife* and *Good* among the Ancients faw this Neceffity, and fupplied it: The oldeft of the infpired Train were the

> *Pii Vates, & Phœbo digna locuti* [1] :

They had *Religion* for their Theme, and the *Service* of Mankind for the End of their Song. How unlike in this to fome late *Authors* of our own Growth!, who, I hardly know for *what* End, have written againft the *Religion* of their Country; and without pretending to fubftitute any thing better, or more practicable, in its place, wou'd deprive us of our happy Eftablifhment, meerly, as it wou'd feem, for the Pleafure of pulling down, and doing Mifchief.

BUT THE firft Men of Science in *Greece*, better inftructed in Human Nature, and knowing the Advantages of national Rites, wrote in

a

[1] Virgil Æneid. vi. It was for this reafon that *Ariftotle* calls them, and the early Philofophers, πρῶτος θεολογήσαντας, the firft who fpoke of the Nature of God.

'ΑΡΙΣΟΤΕΛ. Μέλα τὰ Φυσικὰ. See Pag. 85, 86,

a different Strain: The Formation of *Things*, Sect.6.
the Birth of the *Gods*, their Properties and Exploits, first informed their Numbers: Next
were celebrated the Heroes, who had extirpated
Tyrants, destroyed *Monsters*, and subdued *Rob-*
bers.   They sung the Flood of *Deucalion*, and
Reparation of *Mankind*; the Wars of the *Cen-*
taurs, and the Fate of the *Giants*.

> *Et sævos Lapithas, & nimium Mero*
> *Hylæum, domitosque Herculeâ manu*
> *Telluris Juvenes; unde Periculum*
>   *Fulgens contremuit Domus*
>   *Saturni veteris.——* m

THESE, *My Lord*, ╲ were their Subjects:
They are some of the ΒΡΟΤΩΝ ΘΕΛΚΤΗΡΙΑ,
as *Penelope* calls them n; some of the

ΕΡΓ' ΑΝΔΡΩΝ ΤΕ ΘΕΩΝ ΤΕ, ΤΑΤΕ ΚΛΕΙΟΥΣΙ ΑΟΙΔΟΙ·

Doings of Gods and Men, which Poets use
To celebrate.—— o

They are as old as our Knowledge reaches in
the *Grecian* Antiquity, and the ΑΟΙΔΟΙ or *Bards*
who made and sung them, are among the ear-
liest Characters.
    THIS APPEARS from the Accounts given
of them by *Homer* himself: particularly when
                                                    he

---

m Horat. Carm. Lib. ii. Od. 12.
. n *Songs to sooth Mankind.*   Οδυσ. α.
  o Ibid.

Sect. 6. he relates, how the greateſt Prince of the confederate *Greeks* put his beautiful Wife under the
Tuition of a *Bard*; and takes care to let us
know, that the *Lady* was inacceſſible, until that
faithful Guardian was removed. *Many* of them
lived contemporary with *Homer :* No Prince's
Court ſeems to have been without one or more
of them; and they reſorted to the great Feaſts
and high Solemnities all over *Greece*, to aſſiſt
at the Sacrifices, and entertain the People.
We know ſome of their Names, who tuned
their Lyres to the foregoing Subjects; but their
Songs are loſt, and with them many a *Strain*
of true *Poetry* and *Imitation.*

Gravelot inv.   P.d Gucht Scul.

S E C T.

Gravelot inv.   *G. V.^{dr} Gucht Sculp*

S E C T. VII.

HITHERTO we have viewed *Homer's*
publick Advantages, and have found that
they afforded him the fitteſt *Manners* for Poetical Compoſitions, and the nobleſt *Language* to
expreſs them. We have viewed theſe firſt in
their *own Beauties*, and then tried them both
by the *Foils* of their Contraries, and *Strength*
of their Conſequences; and have found them to
be genuine and true. His *Perſonal Good-fortune*

G   is

Sect. 7. is now before us; I mean, " What effect, his
" private *Education*, his Way of *Life*, and *Suc-*
" *cess* in it, muſt have upon him as a *Poet*."

THE TRADITION concerning his Educa-
tion is very lame. *Plutarch* having related his
Mother's Adventures about the time of his Birth,
paſſes over the firſt part of his Life in ſilence.
But if the Relation of it aſcribed to *Herodotus*
be true, he was educated in the only way that
Learning was to be had at that time. *Letters*
were then but little known, and it ſeems ſtrange,
that in ſuch a Place as *Smyrna*, where, according
to the cruel Practice of theſe Ages, the *Lydians*
had been juſt expelled by another Tribe, there
ſhould be any Perſon who underſtood or taught
them.

BUT THE low Circumſtances of *Homer's*
Family carried him and his Mother to *Phe-*
mius's Houſe, and left him his Succeſſor in the
School. I take *Phemius* to have been one of the
ΑΟΙΔΟΙ, or *Bards*, who might, when at home,
inſtruct Youth in Letters: For I ſuppoſe Learning was not then common enough to make a
Profeſſion by itſelf. If there was any Knowledge in the Country, it muſt be in ſuch a
Man's hands [a]. And *this* is indeed the important

---

a Τὸν δὲ ΦΗΜΙΟΝ, ἡ παλαιὰ ἱςοεία, διδάσκαλον γενεᾶς λέ-
γει τῦ Ποιητῦ, ἄνδρα σοφὸν, ἢ μέσαις κάτοχον —— φιλόσοφΘ
γὸ ὁ ΦήμιΘ, καὶ ἢ πᾶς ΑΟΙΔΟΣ.
        Ἐυςαθ. εἰς τὴν α Ραψῳδ. Ὀδυσ.

He is ſaid to have written a Poem, ΝΟΣΤΟΝ τ᾽ ἀπὸ Τροίας
μετ᾽ ἈγαμέμνονΘ ἀνακομισθέντων.
        Ἡρακλ. παρὰ Πλυταρχ. περὶ Μυσικῆς.

portant part of the Queſtion, *What Learning* Sect. 7.
was then in Being, and what kind of Knowledge
it was poſſible, in that Age, to acquire?

ONE OF the moſt learned and laborious
of the *Roman* Writers, after great Searches into
Antiquity, has left it doubtful *when* or *where*
Poetry was firſt produced : But adds, " It is
" certain there were Poems before the *Trojan*
" War b." As this was the *form* in which
Learning firſt appeared in *Greece*, it wou'd have
been highly entertaining to have known the
Opinion of that great Scholar concerning theſe
early Productions ; not only *what* they were ;
but whether the Poems ſtill extant in his Days,
were the genuine Works of the Authors whoſe
Names they bore? For it was the Practice of
the ancient Poets, and particularly the *Epic* or
Rhapſodiſts, to conceal their *Names,* which indeed the Nature of their Work did not invite
them to mention. We have a convincing Proof
of this in the ΚΥΠΡΙΑ ΕΠΗ, a Poem of the
Wars of *Cyprus,* believed by People in After-
Times, to be the Work of no leſs a Man than
Homer himſelf. It appears that this Opinion
was ſtill entertained in the Days of *Herodotus,*
who confutes it by comparing a Paſſage in that
Poem, with another in the *Iliad* c. For want
of ſuch a Guide to point out the *Species* of

G 2   Learning

---

b De *Poëmatum* Origine magna quæſtio eſt : *ante Trojanum*
Bellum probantur fuiſſe.   *Plinii* Hiſt. Nat. Lib. vii. Cap. lvi.
   c Herodot. Euterpe, Lib ii.

Sect. 7. Learning that prevailed in *Homer's* Time, we must try to find out the *Rise* of the National Opinions of his Countrymen ; because in order to judge *what kind* of Knowledge they, or any People were addicted to, the first Step must be, *To search for it at the Fountain.*

WHILE the *Policies* of *Greece* were yet but forming, *Assyria*, *Phœnicia*, and *Egypt* were mighty Kingdoms, flourishing under regular Governments, and happy in the Richness of their Soil, and their Methods of improving it. In a course of Years, the long Peace they enjoyed, and the *Arts* which such Times produce, having brought a great part of the Administration into the hands of the *Sacred Order*, they took all possible Methods to keep up their *Authority*, and aimed at nothing more than the raising their Reputation for Wisdom and Knowledge. *This* render'd them first envious of their *Discoveries*, and then at pains to find out Methods, " How to transmit them to " their *Descendants*, without imparting them " to the *Vulgar*." Here was the Origin of *Allegory* and *Parable* ; and the Foundation of the received Saying among the Ancients, 'Αλληγορεῖν ὅρημα τ̄ 'Αιγυπλιῶν. *To allegorize is an* Egyptian *Invention.*

THE Sense I would put upon this Maxim is, Since it is natural to all Nations to employ Allusions, and speak in Similitudes, the *Egyptian* Priests have built upon it, settled the

Tropes

Tropes and Metaphors, and improved it into Sect.7.
an *Art.* Nor did they ftop here; but, as
a fecond *Wrapper,* and a Remedy againft the
growing Knowledge of the *Country,* they invented, or borrow'd a *new Charaƈter* for writing
thefe Allegories. They called it ιερα γραμματα, or *Holy Letters,* becaufe they muft be
known by none but the Priefts, nor ufed by
them but in *divine* Matters.

YOUR LORDSHIP will remember that *Da-*
naus [d] the *Egyptian, Cadmus* the *Phœnician,* of
Egyptian Extraƈt, and the *Phrygian Pelops,*
were the firft Planters, or Improvers of *Greece.*
But befides the deep Impreffion of *Afiatic* and
Egyptian Manners, which thefe Founders of
Cities and Kingdoms muft give their new Sub-
jeƈts [e], it is agreed on all hands, that the firft
Sages among the *Greeks* drew their Science
from thefe Countries, and their *Theology* in particular from *Egypt* [f].

IT IS TRUE, there was as yet no *Separa-*
tion of *Wifdom:* The Philofopher and the Divine, the Legiflator and the Poet, were all united in the fame Perfon [g]. Such was *Orpheus,*

G 3 and

---

[d] Ἁι ΔΑΝΑΟΥ θυγατέρες ἦσαν, ἁι τὴν τελετὴν ταύτην (τὴν
Θεσμοφορείαν Δήμητρ⊙) ἐξ Ἀιγύπτε ἐξαγαγῦσαι, ϗ διδάξασαι
τὰς Πελασγιώτιδας γυναῖκας. Ἡρόδοτ. Ἐυτέρπῃ.

[e] Ἄλλαι μὲν (Μυθοποιίαι) ἐπὶ Μάγοις γεγόνασιν (to wit in
Affyria or *Babylon*) ἄλλαι ἢ παρὰ Φρύξι, ϗ ἤδη παρ᾽ Ἀιγυπτίοις,
&c. Φορνύτ. Περὶ τ παραδεδομένων Μύθων. Cap. 17.

[f] Σχεδὸν ἢ ϗ πάντα τὰ ὀνόματα τ θεῶν ἐξ Ἀιγύπτε ἐλήλυθε
ἐις τὴν Ἑλλάδα. Ἡρόδ]. Ἐυτέρπῃ.

[g] See Page 99.

Sect.7. and his Scholar *Musæus*; *Onomacritus* too, and *Thales* [h]; and in general, all the ancient *Law-givers* employed the Muses to difpenfe their divine Inftructions, and recommend their Morals [i].

THE great Men who came after them, and were bred in this ancient School of *Religion* and *Politicks*, finding the Governments of *Greece* already fettled, kept to Philofophy; as *Democritus*, *Pythagoras*, and the *Milefian Thales*: Thefe, befides their Travels into *Egypt*, wander'd over the greatest part of the *Eaſt*. *Democritus* [k] and *Thales* falling in Times of lefs difguife, plainly publifhed their Opinions: But *Orpheus*, *Musæus*, *Onomacritus*, and even *Pythagoras* himfelf, drank deep of the *clofe referved Manner* of their *Masters*. They taught in Allegory, and affected a *Mysticifm* in their commoneft Actions.

PYTHAGORAS, tho' he lived lateft, feems to have principally aimed at eftablifhing a Sect, or rather a Semblance of a *Common-wealth*; which made him take particular ways to form his Difciples, and raife the Admiration of Men: And indeed with them all, *Silence* and *Super-ftition* made a neceffary Part of their Inftitutions. But

[h] ΘΑΛΗΣ, Μελοποιός ἀνὴρ, ᾗ νομοϑετηκός. Strabo, Lib. x. *Lycurgus*, they fay, in his Travels found *Thales* in *Crete*, and fent him to *Lacedemon*.

[i] Πρότερον μὲν ἐν ποιήμασι ἐξέφερον ὁι φιλόσοφοι τὰ δόγματα, ᾗ τὰς λόγας, ὥσπερ ΟΡΦΕΥΣ ᾗ Ησιόδ⊙. ΠΛ8ταρχ. περὶ Πυϑ. ᾗ ΕΙ.

[k] *Pythagoras & Democritus—-ambo, peragratis Perfidis, Æthiopiæ, Arabiæ, Ægyptique Magis.* Plin. Lib. xxv. cap. ii.

But happily for *Greece*, though they cou'd wrap Sect. 7.
up their Doctrines in *Fable*, they had not an
unknown Character to write in ; fo that their
Precepts and Opinions came to appear, when
their Verfes were publifhed, and their Manner
known.

LINUS is faid to have written, in the *old
Pelafgic* Letters, the *Expedition* of the firft *Bacchus*; and to have left Relations of other Tranfactions of the fabulous Ages [1]. He wrote of
the *Generation of the World* and *Rife of Things*,
the common Foundation of the *Egyptian*, and
thence of the *Grecian Theology*. As he is
reckoned the Parent of their Poetry, fo in the
Egyptian Records, kept by their Priefts, he
ftands at the Head of the Worthies who came
to that Country in queft of Knowledge [m]. *Lа-
ertius* [n] has preferved the firft Line of his Poem
of the Creation,

Ἦν ποτὲ χρόνος ὅτῳ, ἐν ᾧ ἅμα πάντ᾽ ἐπιφύκει.

It contains an Idea of the ancient *Chaos*, or
that primigenial State of Nature, when the
Elements lay blended together, and Confufion
and Darknefs exercifed an uncontrouled Dominion. The fame Author adds, That *Anaxagoras* was thought to have taken occafion
from thence to advance his celebrated *Pofition*,

G 4 " That

[1] Diodorus Sicul. Biblioth. Lib. iii.
[m] Ibid.
[n] In Procemiâ.

Sect. 7. "That originally, all things lay jumbled to-
"gether in one jarring and diforderly Mafs,
"but that a *Mind* came and put them in
"order [o]."

COEVAL with *Linus* was *ANTHES* of
Anthedon [p], a Town in *Bæotia*. He wrote
Hymns [q], celebrating the Gods; that is, the
Powers and Productions of *Nature*; whofe
ftronger Afpects, and ftriking Senfations, feem
to have been the Origin of *Rapture* and *Verfe*.
Feafts and Sacrifices would help forward the
Tranfport, and are finely fitted to this Situation
of the human Mind. *Horace* makes the Beginning of the *Roman Satire* to have been at
the Harveft-home of the old *Italians*, when
they facrificed to the *Earth*, and poured out
Milk to the Genius of the Woods [r]; and the
very Invention of *Heroic Meafure* is afcribed to
a *Female, PHEMONOE*, the firft Prieftefs
of *Apollo* [s].

PAMPHO, a Native of *Attica*, and Difciple of *Linus*, firft fung of the *Graces*, without

[o] Copied by *Virgil*,
    Principio, Cœlum ac Terras, Campofque liquenteis
    Lucentemque Globum Lunæ, Titaniaque Aftra
    SPIRITUS intùs alit: totamque infufa per Artus
    MENS agitat Molem.——   Æneid, Lib. vi.
[p] *Paufanias*, Bœot. Lib. ix.
[q] *Plutarch*. De Muficâ.
[r] TELLUREM Porco, SILVANUM Lacte piabant;
    Floribus & Vino GENIUM, memorem brevis Ævi.
                        HORAT. Ep. I. Lib. ii. ad AUGUSTUM.
[s] Ἐξαμετρων ϰαταρξαι λέγεται τῆς ΦΗΜΟΝΟΗ γυνὴ Περ-
φητης Ἀπόλλωνος.   Ευσαϑ Περοίμ. πρὸς Ὅμηρον.
And *Strabo*, Πρώτλω δὲ ΦΗΜΟΝΟΗΝ φασι γενεϖϑ Πυϑιαν.
                                           Lib. ix.
[t] *Paufanias* Bœot.

out defining their Number, or giving their Sect. 7.
Names. He bewailed his Master's Death in a 〰
Dirge called οιτολινοσ : He sung the *Rape
of Proserpine* by the Infernal God, and wrote
Hymns to *Jupiter, Diana,* and *Ceres. Phi-
loſtratus* says, that *Homer* copied the *Hymn to
Jupiter,* and changed it much for the better [u].

But *ORPHEUS,* that Great Name in
Poetry, has eclipſed the Fame of all the reſt :
He likewiſe is ſaid to have been one of *Linus'*
Scholars ; tho' *Plutarch* expreſly affirms, that
he imitated no Man in his Poetry or Muſick,
but was himſelf an *Original* [w]. It is however
certain, that he made the ſame Voyage as his
ſuppoſed *Maſter* had done, into *Egypt ;* where
he ſtaid long, and was let into the Secrets of
their Philoſophy and Religion.

At his *Return* he did greater Services to
his Country ; or rather to the People among
whom he choſe to live, for he is thought to
have been originally from *Thrace.* His Actions
are themſelves involved in *Allegory,* and related
in the ſame kind of Fable as he was wont to
employ about his *Gods* and *Heroes.* Whether
he left any thing of his own *in Writing,* is to
me a great Doubt. I find no reaſon to conclude

---

[u] *Pampho* had ſaid, Ζεῦ κύδιςε, μέγιςε θεῶν, εἰλημμὠψε κότρῳ.
   Μηλωη τε, ϗ ἱππίη, ϗ ἡμιονέῃ.
Inſtead of which, with more dignity *Homer* has turned it,
      Ζεῦ κύδιςε, μέγιςε, κελαινεφὲς, αἰθέι ναίων.
         Φιλοςεφ]. Ἡρωικῶν.

[w] Ὁ δὲ Ὀρφεὺς οὐδένα φαίνεται μεμιμμѱθ. Πλε. Μυς:κῆς.

Sect. 7. clude he did not.   But the Fame of his Knowledge was fo high, that we have from *Suidas* x,
the *Titles* of fixteen or feventeen Poems written under his Name, chiefly by the *Pythagoreans*, who embraced his Doctrine ; and from
others, we may reckon up twice the number.
They are *philofophical, prophetical,* and *religious* ; and were believed to contain his real
Opinions and the native Strain of his Verfe.

H E B E G U N his Song with ancient *Chaos*,
its Transformations and Changes, and continued it through the various Steps of *Creation* :
The Offspring of *Saturn*, or *Time*, the *Æ-
ther, Love,* and *Night* ; the Birth and Progeny of the *Giants* ; and ended in the Formation of *Man* y.   He directed thefe his my-
ftical Leffons to raife an Awe of the *Gods* in
the Breafts of his Hearers, that he might re-
ftrain them from Barbarity and Bloodfhed, and
charm them into Humanity and Social Manners z.   *Ariftophanes*, when he wou'd give the
Sum of his Services, fays,

'ΟΡΦΕΥΣ

x In *Orpheo.*

y He fung, 'Αρχαίν μθὺ πρῶτα ΧΑΟΣ ἀμέχαρτον ἀνάγκlω,
   Καὶ ΚΡΟΝΟΝ, ὅς τ' ἐλόχευσιν ἀπειρεσίοισι ὑφ' ἕλκεις
   ΑΙΘΕΡΑ, ἰ διφυῆ σέιοπία κυδρὸν ΕΡΩΤΑ,
   ΝΥΚΤΟΣ ἀειγεννήτης Πατέρα κλυτὸν ; ὅν ῥα ΦΑΝΗΤΑ
   'Οπλότεροι καλέυσι βερτοὶ, πρῶτΘ ὲ ἐφάνθη.
   ΒΡΙΜΟΥΣ τ' ἐυδνάτοιο γονὰς ; ἠδ' ἔργ ἀΐδηλα
   ΓΙΓΑΝΤΩΝ, δι λυγρὸν ἀτ' Ουρανῦ ἐςάξαντο
   Σπέρμα γονῆς τὸ πρότθεν, ὅθεν γένΘ ἐξεγίνοντο
   ΘΝΗΤΩΝ, δι κατὰ γαίαν ἀπείειτον αἰὲν ἔασι.

'ΟΡΦΕΥΣ 'Αργοναυτ-

z Horat. ad Pifon.

ΌΡΦΕΥΣ μϐ γὰρ πλετὰς δ' ἡμῖν κατέδιξε, Sect. 7.
φόνων τ' ἀπέχεϑαι.

Orpheus *our Prayers prefcrib'd, and holy Rites,
And Abftinence from Murder* ᵃ.——

As his *Name* for many Ages was the firſt
in *Greece* for Sanctity and Wiſdom, his Doctrines, if they were not by himſelf committed
to Writing, muſt be current by *Tradition.* The
Prince of the Philoſophers quotes two Lines
from his *Theogony* without inſinuating any Su-
ſpicion of their not being genuine ᵇ; as *Ariſtotle,* the grand Critic, does both from him ᶜ, and
from his Succeſſor ᵈ.   Nay, ſo late as the Reign
of *Auguſtus Cæſar, Diodorus* the *Sicilian* mentions the *Poem of Orpheus* as a Piece then held
in great Admiration, both for the Matter it
contained, and the particular Harmony of its
Compoſition ᵉ.   And truly I cannot doubt, but
that the Writings which paſſed under his Name,
whether written by *Muſæus* or *Onomacritus,*
contained his genuine Dogma's ᶠ.
   MUSÆUS was *Orpheus'* famed Scholar,
or perhaps his Son.   *Virgil* ſpeaks of him as
the

ᵃ ΒΑΤΡΑΧ·
ᵇ ΌΚΕΑΝΟΣ πρῶτ۞ καλλιρρόου ἦρξε γάμοιο,
 ῍Ος ῥα κασιγ:ήτην ὁμομήτορα Τηϑυν ὄπυιεν.   Κράτυλ۞.
ᶜ Ἀριςοϑ· Ὀικονομικῶν α.
ᵈ Φησὶ γδν ἡ Μουσαἰ۞ εἶναι,——ΒΡΟΤΟῖΣ ῝ΗΔΙΣΤΟΝ
ΆΕΙΔΕΙΝ.   Ἀριςοϑ· Πολιτ· ϑ.
ᵉ Καὶ γδ Ποίημα συνέταξε τὸ ϑαυμαζόμϑψον ἡ κατὰ τὴν ὡδὴν
ἐμμελείᾳ διαφέρον.   Διοδ· Σικελ· βιϐλιοϑ· δ.
ᶠ They were called the ΟΡΦΙΚΑ ΕΠΗˑ ἐν τοῖς Ὀρφικοῖς
καλυμϑίοις ἔπεσι, ſays *Ariſtotle,* περὶ ψυχῆς α.

Sect. 7. the greateſt of *Poets*.   He ſeems to have med-
dled leſs in the governing or reforming Manners than his Maſter; deterred perhaps by the
unhappy End of the *Theological Hero*.   Yet
he compoſed *Prophecies* and *Hymns*, and wrote
ſacred Inſtructions which he addreſſed to his
Son.   He preſcribed *Purifications* and *Atone-
ments*, ſung the Wars of the *Titans*, and left
ſomething upon *Aſtronomy*.   But his great Work,
and what brought moſt Honour in thoſe days,
was a *Theogony* or Hiſtory of the *Creation* ᵍ.
Pauſanias is of opinion, that an *Hymn to Ceres*
is the only genuine Remain of this philoſophi-
cal Poet ʰ.   He had a Son and a Daughter,
Eumolpus and *Helene*, both touched from *Helicon*.   The Son wrote of the *Myſteries of Ceres*
and Rites of *Bacchus*, and the Lady is reported
to have ſung the *Trojan* War ⁱ.

CONTEMPORARY with theſe was *SYA-
GRUS*, whoſe Character is ſtill more confined
to the Province of a Poet.   ᵏ *Elian* ſays, that
he too ſung of the War at *Troy*, and was " the
" *firſt* who gave a Looſe to his Muſe upon
" that noble Subject."   *D. Laertius* calls him
SAGARIS, and brings him down to *Homer's*
own

ᵍ *Diog. Laertius* in Procem: Where he gives a Principle of
Muſæus' Philoſophy.
    Ἐξ ἑνὸς τὰ πάντα γίνεσθαι, ϰỳ εἰς τ'αὐτὸν ἀναλύεσθ.
  ʰ *Atticis & Meſſeniacis.*
  ⁱ *Hephæſtio* apud *Photium* CODICE CXC. *Suidas* in *Eumolpo.*
  ᵏ "Ότι ΣΤΑΓΡΟΣ τις ἐγένετο Ποιητὴς μετ' Ὀρφέα ϰ Μυ-
σαῖον, ὃς λέγεται τὸν ΤΡΩΙΚΟΝ ΠΟΛΕΜΟΝ πρῶτ⊙ ἆσαι
μεγίςης ἀτ⊙ ὑποθέσεως λαβόμψ⊙, καὶ ἐπιτολμήσας ταύτη.
    Αἰλιαν. Ποιϰιλ. Ἱςορ. βιβ. ιδ. ϰεφ. α.

own Days; whofe Rival and Enemy he fays Sect. 7.
he was while alive, as *Xenophanes* proved after
he was dead [l].

WE CAN tell with more certainty, that
Amythaon's Son, the prophetick *MELAM-*
PUS, brought the Myfteries of *Proferpine* from
Egypt into *Greece.* He taught them the Story
of the *Titans*, and according to *Diodorus*, τὸ
σύνολον, τἰω πεὶ τὰ ΠΑΘΗ ΤΩΝ ΘΕΩΝ ἱϛορίαν,
" The whole Hiftory of the Tranfactions and
" Difafters of the Gods [m]." He is celebrated
by *Homer* himfelf, who without all doubt was
acquainted with his *Mythology* [n].

ABOUT the Age of *Linus* came *OLEN*
from *Lycia* [o], and compofed the firft Hymns
that were fung in *Delos* at their Solemnities,
which were among the oldeft in *Greece* [p]. *Ho-*
mer himfelf frequented thefe Feafts, to celebrate the fair Offspring of *Latona*, and fing to
the *Ionians* that repaired to *Delos* in vaft Numbers

[l] In Prœmio, And in *Xenophanes*' Life, γέγραφε δὲ καὶ ἐν
Ἐλεγείαις, καὶ Ἰάμβοις ϰαϑ᾽ ΗΣΙΟΔΟΥ καὶ ΟΜΗΡΟΥ,
ἐπισκόπτων αὐτῶν τὰ πεὶ θεῶν εἰρημένα.

[m] Diodor. Biblioth. Lib. i.

[n] Ὀδυσ. Ῥαψωδ. λ. and again, Ῥαψωδ. θ.

[o] ΟὗτΘ δὲ ὁ ΟΛΗΝ καὶ τὲς ἄλλυς τὲς παλαίυς ὕμνες ἐ-
ποίησε ἐκ Λυκίης ἐλθὼν τὲς ἀειδομένυς ἐν Δήλῳ.——
Ἡρόδοτ. Μελπομώνη βιβ. δ.

[p] Λύκιθ δὲ ΩΛΗΝ ὃς καὶ τὲς ὕμνυς τὲς ἀρχαιοτάτυς ἐ-
ποίησεν Ἕλλησι. Παυσαν. Βοιωτ.
   Plutarch upon the Authority of *Anticles* and *Iftrus*, two ancient Authors, fays, that the Statue of *Apollo* in *Delos* had a Bow in
one Hand, and with the other fupported the three *Graces*, who held
each an Inftrument of Mufick; one a Lyre, another a Flute, and
the third a *Syrinx*, or 'Pipe. As to the Antiquity of it, they
faid, ὅυτω δὲ πάλαιον ἐsὶ τὸ ἀφίδρυμα τῦτο, ὥsε τὲς ἐργασαμθνους
ἀυτὸ, ᾗ ϰαϑ᾽ Ἡρακλέα μεεσπων φασὶ γραι. Περὶ Μυσικῆς.

bers upon thefe Occafions.   He glories in being ΗΔΙΣΤΟΣ ΛΟΙΔΩΝ, the fweeteft of the
Singers that came there ᑫ.

 THYMOETES, Laomedon's Grandfon,
and *Orpheus's* Cotemporary, is recorded as the
greateft of the early *Travellers*. Befides the
Countries then known, to wit *Afia* and *Egypt*,
which he vifited, he is faid to have paffed thro'
Africk to the *Weftern* Region : There he faw
the Ifland in which the ancient Inhabitants affirm that *Bacchus* was nurfed ; and having learned from the *Nyfæans*, the Exploits of the *God*,
at his Return he compofed in the old Dialect,
and wrote in the old Letters, the Piece called
the Phrygian Poems ʳ.

 Iᴛ ᴡᴀs indeed from the leffer *Afia* that the
Greeks had their Regular *Mufick*.   The Forti-
fier of *Thebes*, the famous *Amphion*, is called
the *Inventer of Mufick*, I fuppofe in *Greece :* He
is allowed the Honour of firft framing a *Lyre* ˢ,
and certainly employed both his Melody and
perfuafive Strains, to induce the wild Inhabitants to wall their Town, and live orderly :
But with what Propriety he is called the Inventer of the *Lydian* Meafure, I hardly underftand ᵗ.

            Tʜᴇ

ᑫ See below, Page 109.
ʳ Diodor. Biblioth. Lib. iii.
ᵗ *Plato,* fpeaking of the Invention of *Arts,* fays, Τὰ μὲν
ΔΑΙΔΑΛΩ καταφανῆ γέγονε τάδε ΟΡΦΕΙ, τάδε ΠΑΛΑΜΗ-
ΔΕΙ; τὰ δὲ περι Μσικὴν, ΜΑΡΣΥΑ καὶ ΟΛΥΜΠΩ, περι
λύραν δὲ ΑΜΦΙΟΝΙ.   Νομων. γ.
ᵗ Muficam invenit *Amphion*; Fiftulam & Monaulum (MO-
NAΥΛΟN) *Pan* Mercurii; obliquam Tibiam *Midas* in Phry-
                 giâ;

THE *Phrygian MARSYAS* ᵘ claims the Sect. 7.
Invention of the *Double Flute*, and of the *Mea-*
sure that bears the Name of his Country. He
was in high esteem with the Ancients, and
seems to have been but too sensible of his Vein
and Accomplishments, as appears from the Story
of his Contest with *Apollo*. Some believe the
Foundation of that Fable to have been the fatal
End of the Musician, who went mad, and threw
himself into the *River* that bears his Name ʷ.

HIS SCHOLAR, *OLYMPUS*, shares with
him the Glory of the Invention of the *Phry-*
gian Measure ˣ, and pretends to be the first himself, who sung a *Nænia* or funeral Song. He
is said on the Death of *Python*, αὐλῆσαι ΕΠΙ-
ΚΗΔΕΙΟΝ Λυδίςι, " To have play'd a funeral
" Tune upon the Flute in the *Lydian* Strain ʸ."
His Compositions are selected by *Aristotle* as the
most rapturous, and the aptest to inspire Passion and Enthusiasm ᶻ into the Minds of the
Hearers.

giâ; geminas Tibias *Marsyas* in eâdem gente; Lydios Modu-
los, *Amphion*; Dorios, *Thamyras* Thrax; Phrygios, *Marsyas*
Phryx: Citharam, *Amphion*; ut alii *Orpheus*; ut alii *Linus*;
septem Chordis additis *Terpander*; octavam *Simonides* addidit;
nonam *Timotheus*. Citharâ sine voce, cecinit *Thamyras* primus,
cum Cantu, *Amphion*; ut alii *Linus*. Citharœdica Carmina com-
posuit *Terpander*; cum Tibiis canere voce, Trœzenius *Darda-*
nus instituit. Plinii Histor. Nat. Lib. vii. § 56.

ᵘ *Suidas* in Μαρσύας.

ʷ Xenophon. Ἀνάβασ. βιβλ. α.

ˣ Νόμοι δ' ΟΛΥΜΠΟΥ καὶ ΜΑΡΣΥΟΥ Φρύγιοι καὶ Λύ-
διοι; καὶ Ὀλύμπυ Ἐπικήδειοι. Πολυδεύκ. Ὀνομαστικόν.

ʸ Πλύταρχ. περὶ Μυσικῆς. He says there were two of that Name.

ᶻ Ὀλύμπυ μελῆ, ὁμολογυμβῷως ποιεῖ τὰς ψυχὰς ἐνθυσιαςικάς.
Πολιτικ. δ'. And a little afterwards, speaking of the different
Harmonies and their Effects, he says, Ἐνθυσιαςικὸς δ' ἡμᾶς ποιεῖ
ἡ Φρυγιςὶ (ἁρμονία); So that *Olympus* has been the Author.

Sect.7. Hearers. And he hath the Testimony of the knowing *Plutarch*, of having greatly advanced his Art, by introducing some kinds of Musick 'till then unknown to the World, and of being the Prince and Inventer of the beautiful *Grecian* Manner [a].

THE MUSES Lover in more Senses than one [b], the *Thracian THAMYRAS* first played upon a Lyre without singing. This he did to show the Variety of his Genius, for at the same time he composed *Hymns* [c], the pious Exercise of the ancient Poets. He likewise sung the Wars of the *Titans* [d], and wrote a Poem of three thousand Verses upon the great Foundation of their Religion and Morals, the ΚΟΣΜΟΓΟΝΙΑ, or *Generation of the World*, or the ΘΕΟΓΟΝΙΑ, which is an equivalent Expression [e].

THE *Trœzenians* [f] boast an Epic Poet, *OROEBANTIUS* by Name, who wrote before *Homer*, I cannot tell upon what Subject: But *MELESANDER* the *Milesian*, sung the Battle of the *Lapithæ* and the *Centaurs* [g],

which

---

[a] Φαίνεται δ᾿ Ὄλυμπ☉ αὐξήσας Μυσικὴν, τῷ ἀγγένητον τι καὶ ἀ᾿νούμϕον ὑπὶ τ᾿ ἐμπερϑεν εἰσπασαγῖν, καὶ ἀρχηγὸς γενέας τ᾿ Ἑλληνικῆς καὶ καλῆς Μυσικῆς.   Πλυταρχ· ibid.

[b] See the Catalogue Ιλιαδ΄. β and the Article of the *Pylians* under *Nestor*, where *Homer* mentions *Thamyris*; as also *Eustathius*' Notes.

[c] Πλατων· Νόμων η.

[d] Πλυταρχ· περὶ Μυσικῆς·

[e] Suidas in *Thamyre.*

[f] ᾽Ότι ἦν OPOIBANTIOY τῦ Τρεζηνίε ᾽Επη πρὸ ῾Ομήρε, ὡς ϕασι οἱ Τρεζήνιοι λόγοι. Καὶ ὁ Φρύγα δὲ ΔΑΡΗΤΑ, ὁ Φρυγίαν ᾽Ιλιάδα ἔπι καὶ νῦν ἀποσωζομένην οἴδα, πρὸ ῾Ομήρε καὶ τυτον γενέσαι λέγυσι.——— ᾽Αιλιαν· Ποικιλ· ἱσορ· βιβ· ια· κεϕ· C.

[g] Μελίσανδρ☉ ὁ Μιλήσι☉, ΛΑΠΙΘΩΝ καὶ ΚΕΝΤΑΥΡΩΝ Μάχην ἔγεαϕεν.   Ibid.

which feems to have been an Action of great Sect. 7.
Fame in the early Ages, and to have affor-〰
ded much Exercife to the young Mufes of
Greece.

THE WISE *PALÆPHATUS* [h] is faid
to be a Son of *Hermes,* and not long after
the celebrated *Phemonoë.* There have been fome
great Men fince of the Name; but this admired Ancient fung the Generation of *Apollo* and
Diana, and the Conteft of *Minerva* and *Neptune.* He wrote a Poem upon *Latona's Locks,*
(ΛΗΤΟΥΣ ΠΛΟΚΑΜΩΝ) and another of an uncommon nature, " The Voice and Speech of
" *Venus* and *Love* [i]." He likewife compofed
a ΚΟΣΜΟΠΟΙῚΑ, or Hiftory of the Creation of
the World, in five thoufand Verfes.

THESE are fome of the Men in whofe
hands the ancient *Mythology* and *Poetry* grew
together. When I review them, I think it
happy that *Hefiod's* noble Work has reached
our Times. We fhould fcarcely know elfe
what to make of fo many ΘΕΟΓΟΝΙΑ's, ΚΟΣ-
ΜΟΠΟΙῚΑ's and ΚΟΣΜΟΓΟΝΙΑ's as we have
enumerated: But from it we know, that the
Birth of the Gods, the *Rife of Things,* and the
Creation of the World are but reciprocal Terms,
and in the ancient Stile ftand for juft the fame
thing. They were the common Theme of
the firft *Poets* and *Lawgivers,* (the earlieft Philofophers)

[h] Suidas in Παλαίφατ☉.
[i] Φόνας ἢ λόγυς Ἀφροδίτης ἢ Ἔρωτ☉. Id. ibid.

H

Sect. 7. lofophers) who by their feveral Improvements and Additions enabled *Hefiod* and *Homer*, their Succeffors, to give their Theology a *Body*, and reduce it to a Standard, that flourifhed while *Greece* was a free Country, and lafted fome time after their Liberty was gone.

A N D N O W I would willingly fpare your Lordfhip the trouble of hearing any more concerning the Books that might be in *Phemius*'s or his Scholar's Library, was there not a Prefumption, " That thefe Writings I have na-
" med, are *later* than our Poet:" And of this Opinion is that great Hiftorian, and Antiquary of *Greece*, *H E R O D O T U S the Halicarnaf-
fean.* As for the *Gods*, fays he, " Whence each
" of them was defcended, or whether they
" were always in being, or under what Shape
" or Form they were, the *Greeks* knew no-
" thing 'till very lately. *Hefiod* and *Homer*
" were, I believe, about four hundred Years
" older than myfelf, and no more : And thefe
" are the Men who *made* a *Theogony* for the
" *Greeks*; who gave the Gods their Appella-
" tions, defined their Qualities, appointed their
" Honours, and defcribed their Forms. As
" for the Poets who are faid to have lived be-
" fore thefe Men, *I am of Opinion they came*
" *after them* k."   So far the Hiftorian ; who no doubt means *Linus, Orpheus*, and their Scholars, by the Poets he does not name.

W H A T

---

k 'Ευτέρπη. βιC. C.

WHAT HE fays of *Hefiod* and *Homer*, muft Sect.7. be true in one or other of thefe refpects; That either they brought their *entire Syftem* immediately from *Egypt*, and publifhed it in *Greece*, 'till then ignorant of Religion and Rites: Or that, without other affiftance than their own Wits, they *contrived* it wholly themfelves. But they are both equally incredible.

WHOEVER knows any thing of the *Nature* of that kind of Writing, needs make but one Reflection, to be convinced that a *THEO-GONY* is a Piece of *deep Learning*, and vaft *Labour*. " It is *a Syftem of the Univerfe, di-* " *gefted and wrought into an Allegory:* It is a " Compofition, made up of infinite Parts, each " of which has been a *Difcovery* by itfelf, " and delivered as a *Myftery* to the initiated[1]:" The contriving and putting them together has been a Work of fome Ages, and is a conjunct Effort of *Politicks* and *Philofophy*.

NEITHER, on the other hand, were *Hefiod* and *Homer* the *firft* who learned Religion in *Egypt*, and brought it over Sea to *Greece*. A fmall Acquaintance with their Writings will convince any Man of Tafte that they wrote from *Life*; and defcribe the Exercife of a Worfhip long fince eftablifhed in their Country. An hundred Paffages in both Authors make it abundantly plain, that the *Greeks* knew the

H 2 Names

[1] Γνώσεαι ἀθανάτων τε θεῶν θνητῶν τ' ἀνθρώπων,
ΣΥΣΤΑΣΙΝ, ἦ τε ἕκαστα διέρχεται, ἦτε κρατέωσι.
ΠΥΘΑΓΟΡΟΥ Χρυσ. ἔπη.

Sect. 7. Names and Natures of their Gods, had Sacrifices and Ceremonies; Temples, Priests, Prayers, and Songs, long before either *Hesiod* or *Homer* were born.

But it is to no purpose to use other Arguments than this noble Historian's own Words.
In the beginning of the same Book, speaking
of the Origin of the Word Ocean [m], he says,
ὌΜΗΡΟΝ δὲ, ἢ τίνα τ̅ ΠΡΟΤΕΡΟΝ ΓΕΝΟΜΕΝΩΝ
Ποιητῶν, δοκέω τὸ ὄνομα εὑρόντα, ἐς τὴν Ποίησιν
ἐσενείκασθαι. " *Homer*, I believe, or some of
" the Poets *who lived before him*, having in-
" vented the Word, inserted it into their Po-
" etry." Or if we should be so indulgent as
to allow, that he spoke *negligently* in this place,
and according to the vulgar Opinion; how
shall we reconcile it, when he tells us expresly
that *Melampus*, a Man placed by *Homer* [n] himself three Generations before the *Trojan* War,
" first taught the *Greeks* the Name and Sacri-
" fices of *Bacchus* [o]? That the Rites about
" Funerals called *Orphic* and *Bacchic*, were
" really and originally *Egyptian?* And in ge-
" neral, that the *Egyptians* were the first of
" Mankind who used Solemnities, made Pro-
" cessions, and appointed Initiations; and that,
" παρὰ ΤΟΥΤΩΝ Ἕλληνες μεμαθήκασι [p], *from*
" *them* the Grecians *learned to do the same?"*

FOR

---

[m] It seems to be a *Punick* or *Phœnician* Word (Og,) which signifies a *Boundary*; because the Sea is the *Limit* of the Land. This
perhaps is the Reason why *Homer* calls the River *Nile*, the
Ocean, Ὠκεανοῦ τε Ῥοὰς.———See Pag. 137. n.

[n] Ὀδυσσ. Ραψωδ. Ο.　　[o] Εὐτέρπη. βιϐ. C.　　[p] Ibid.

FOR is it not an eafy Conclufion, that if Sect.7. Funeral Rites, Sacrifices, and the Name of ~~~ *Bacchus* be found in *Homer*; and the Hifto-rian tells us, that *Melampus* and *Orpheus firft* brought them from *Egypt*, and taught them the *Greeks*; Is it not eafy, I fay, to conclude,

" That this great Author, having his Fancy
" full of the Antiquity of the *Egyptian* Rites,
" in oppofition to the upftart Religion of
" *Greece*, has fallen unawares into an Incon-
" fiftency, when he fays, that *Homer* and *He-*
" *fiod* were the Men who *made* a Theogony
" for the *Greeks*, and *firft* informed them of
" the Names and Natures of their Divinities ?"

It remains then, that thefe Fathers of our Poetry, had themfelves, if not Patterns to work by, as feems to have been *Hefiod*'s cafe [q], at leaft plenty of Materials to work upon; which cou'd be no other than the Doctrines, whether traditional or in Writing, of the Men I have juft now mentioned [r].

AND THUS we find an Anfwer to the Que-ftion, What *Learning* was then in Being; and

H 3 *what*

---

[q] Ἀλλὰ τῶ μᾶρ᾽ Ἡσιόδε τελειότερον τότ᾽ ἂν ἡ ἐξήγησις γίνοιτο, (fpeaking of the Nature of *Saturn*) τὰ μᾶν τινα, ὡς οἶμαι, παρὰ τ᾽ ΑΡΧΑΙΟΤΑΤΩΝ αὐτῶ παρειληφότ⦿, τὰ δὲ μυθικώτερα αὐτῶ περιθέντ⦿· ᾧ τρόπῳ κὶ πλεῖςα θεολογίας διεφθάρη.

ΦΟΡΝΟΥΤ. Περὶ τ᾽ παραδεδομᾶρων Μύθων. κεφ. ιζ.

[r] —— Fuit hæc fapientia quondam,
Publica privatis fecernere, facra profanis;
Concubitu prohibere vago, dare jura maritis,
Oppida moliri, leges incidere ligno:
Sic honor & nomen *divinis* Vatibus, atque
Carminibus venit. POST *bos* infignis Homerus, &c.

Horat. ad Pifones.

Sect. 7. *what kind* of Knowledge it was poffible in *Ho-mer's* days to acquire? It was wholly *fabulous* and *allegorical.* " The Powers of Nature, and " Human Paffions were the Subject; and they " defcribed their various Effects with fome " Analogy and Refemblance to *Human Actions.* " They began with the *Rife* of Things, their " Viciffitudes and Transformations, defined " their Nature and Influence; and, in their " metaphorical Stile, gave to each a *Perfon,* a " *Speech,* and *Method* of *Operation,* conforma- " ble to their fancied *Qualities.*" This they called *a Hiftory of the Birth of the Gods* ; of the *Heaven,* to wit, the *Earth, Air,* and *Sea;* of the *Sun, Moon,* and Divifions of the *Stars* ; of the *Rivers, Woods, Rocks, Fountains,* and the other conftituent Parts of the Univerfe[f]. They related their Loves and Hatreds; their Marri-ages, Difafters, Seditions, and Wars; or in other Terms, the *Struggles* of their oppofite Natures, and the *Concord* arifing from their *Equilibrium :*

Quid velit, aut poffit, Rerum Concordia difcors.

SUCH was the Science of the early Ancients; Nor is there any other kind of Learning to be
met

---

[f] Sic deinde effatus, frondenti Tempora ramo
Implicat, & *Geniumque* loci, *primamque* Deorum
TELLUREM, NYMPHASque, & adhuc ignota precatur
Flumina ; tum NOCTEM, Noctifque orientia SIGNA,
Idæumque JOVEM, Phrygiamque ex ordine MATREM
Invocat, & duplicis *Cæloque Ereboque* Parentis.
                             VIRGIL. Æneid. VII

met with in *Homer*: I mean such Learning as Sect. 7.
we acquire by Books and Masters; for what 〰️
Knowledge he picked up as a *Traveller*, is of
another kind, and falls in more properly to
be considered in another place.

Gravelot inv.   P.ª Gucht Scul.

Gravelot inv.   V.Gucht del.

S E C T. VIII.

Sect. 8. **B**UT HERE, begging your *Lordſhip*'s par-
don, I muſt be permitted to think of my
own good Fortune in addreſſing this Enquiry
as I have done: Whoever has a Diffidence of
his own Opinions, naturally ſeeks for a wiſer
Man than himſelf, with whom to communicate
them: And if he is conſcious of any ſingular
Humour, or Inclination to judge with a *few*
againſt the Multitude; to laugh perhaps at what
they

they highly efteem, and efteem what they Sect. 8.
think contemptible, he muft then find either
one of the fame Sentiments with himfelf, or,
if he fhould be miftaken, one of that Can-
dour and Knowledge of Mankind, as will
make Allowances, and bear with the Infirmi-
ties of his weaker Friend. In this cafe, *My
Lord,* I find myfelf bound to give fair Warn-
ing of the Forbearance I fhall want ; fince I
am upon the matter about to affert, " *That*
" *Homer's being born poor, and living a*
" *wandering indigent Bard, was, in relation*
" *to his Poetry, the greateft Happinefs that*
" *cou'd befall him.*"

WE HAVE already feen fome of his Obligations to his Poverty. It put him in the *only
Road of Life* in which Learning was then to
be acquired ; with the peculiar advantage of
living in the Houfe with his Mafter, in the double Relation of a Scholar and a Son. Had he
been the Child of a rich Father, or of one
who cou'd have barely fupported him, or even
taught him his own Trade, he had never gone
to *Phemius,* to be doubly inftructed in Philofophy and Poetry, which at that time, as has
been already obferved, were not *feparate Studies.* The fame. Neceffity made him glad to
be his *Succeffor,* and teach his School after his
death ; an Exercife, if not too long continued,
of the higheft Tendency to ftrengthen the Mind
and correct the Fancy. But the grand *Good-
fortune*

Sect. 8. *fortune* that *Homer*'s Poverty procured him
was this, " That it forced him to take up, and
" continue in the Profeſſion of an ΑΟΙΔΟΣ,
" or *Stroling Bard.*"

To comprehend the full Extent of this
Happineſs, We muſt remember, that this is a
Grecian Character, which took its riſe in that
Country, and was formed upon no borrowed
Model. The Poetry and Allegory of the
Egyptians, was, like every thing elſe that cou'd
influence their Manners, bounded and preſcribed by Law ². *Diodorus* tells us, that *Men* were
forbidden the Practice of Muſick, as tending
to effeminate their Minds : And indeed the Attention both of this, and of the *Perſian* and
Babyloniſh Governments ſeems to have been
more turned to their *Hiſtory* and *Records*, or to
Aſtronomy and *Numbers*, than the Encourage-
ment of the *Muſes*.

But in *Greece*, where Nature was ob-
ſtructed in none of her Operations ; and no
Rule or Preſcription gave a check to Rapture
and Enthuſiaſm, there ſoon aroſe a Set of Men,
who diſtinguiſhed themſelves by *Harmony* and
Verſe. The wonderful Tales which they told,
and the Melody with which they accompanied
them, made them the Delight of theſe ſimple
Ages ; and their Knowledge of Things both *natural* and *divine*, gave them a great Aſcendant
over the Spirit and Belief of their Cotemporaries.   Tho'

---

² See Page 146. in the Notes.

THO' WE had no remaining Teftimonies
of the Honours paid to this Profeffion by the 〰
Ancients, we might fafely conclude from its
Nature and *Functions*, that it would meet
with univerfal Approbation. A Man who has
it in his power to charm our Ears, entertain
our Fancies, and inftruct us in the Hiftory of
our Anceftors; who informs his wond'ring
Audience of the fecret Compofition, and hidden Harmony of the *Univerfe*, of the Order of
the *Seafons*, and Obfervation of *Days*, fuch
a Man cannot mifs of Efteem and Attention [b]:
But if he adds a *Sanction* to his Doctrine and
Art; if he pretends " That he is under the
" Direction of the *Gods*; that he defcribes
" their *Natures*, announces their *Names*, and
" *Decrees*; that he does this by their imme-
" diate Orders, and then leads the way him-
" felf in the new Devotion;" he muft needs
become the Object of their Admiration and
Reverence.

THAT

[b] On the old Altar of PAN, fays Sannazaro, *Pendeano due
grandi Tavole di Faggio, fcritte di rufticane lettere, lequali conte-
nevano le antiche Leggi, e gli Ammaeftramenti della Vita paftorale.
Nell' una eran notati tutti i Dì dell' Anno, i Mutamenti delle fta-
gioni e la inequalità della notte e del giorno; infieme i Pronoftici
delle Tempeftati, e quali giorni fon della Luna fortunati, e quali
infelici alle Opere de' Mortali; e che ciafcuno in ciafcuna hora doveffe fuggire ò feguitare per non offendere le offervabili volontà de
gli Dij. Nell' altra fe leggeva qual Governo fi convenga alle Pecore;
quale doveffe effere la bella forma della Vacca e del Toro, e le età
idonee al generare, &c.* And the ancient Prieft of the God had
perfect Knowledge of *e la Terra, e'l Cielo, e'l Mare; lo infati-
gabile Sole, la crefcente Luna, e tutte le Stelle di che il Cielo fi ador-
na; e cofi per confequente, i tempi del arare, del metere, di pian-
tare le Viti e gli Olivi; di ineftare gli Alberi, veftendoli di adottive
frondi.*   Sannazaro Arçadia.

Sect. 8.   THAT THIS was their Conduct, appears from no weaker Authority than the ingenuous *Pindar's*, the Prince of the *Lyricks:* He lets us know, that the *Homeridæ* (a Family in *Chios*, thought to be defcended from our Poet) followed the Occupation of their Founder, and were for the moft part, what he calls, *Singers of flowing Verfe:* It was, he fays, their conftant Practice to ufher in their Song with a *Prayer* to *Jupiter* [c]: A Cuftom of a very devout Appearance, and which they obferved fo ftrictly, as to hand it down in a religious kind of *Tradition*, to the Poets of after-times. *Piety* was indeed the chief part of a *Bard's* Profeffion; and fome of their Worthies, fuch as *Eumolpus*, *Melampus*, and *Epimenides*, are reported to have done as great *Feats* in this Capacity, as the *Law-givers* did in theirs.

IN OTHER refpects, we find the Teftimony of the oldeft Poets ufed by the later Writers as the *Great Mafters* of Science: They are quoted as the Fountains of Hiftory, the Judges of Politicks, and Parents of Philofophy. We have a noble Inftance of this in *Hecatæus* the *Milefian*, whofe Knowledge and Capacity fairly diftinguifhed him in the grand Affembly of the *Ionians* [d]. The Queftion in agitation was of no lefs Importance, than " Whether
" they

c Ὄσσεν περ κỳ Ὀμνείдαι,
   Ῥαπτῶν ἐπέων τὰ πόλλ' Ἀοιδοὶ,
   Ἄρχονται ΔΙΟ῀Σ ἐκ σεροιμίν. ▬ Πινδάρε Νεμ. Ἐιδὸς β.
d Herodotus, Τερψιχωρῇ.

" they ſhould continue in their Obedience, or Sect. 8,
" rebel againſt the *Great King?*" So they called the *Perſian* Monarch.   *Hecatæus* diſſuaded
the War; and produced a thing 'till then rarely
ſeen, *A. Map of the* Perſian *Dominions*, and
from it nade a Computation of their Power:
But like a Maſter of the Argument, if, on the
other hand, they were reſolved to try the Fortune of War, he gave them good Advice, and
pointed out the *only Method* of carrying it on.
They neglected both Parts of his Counſel, and
were ruined in the Iſſue.

    IT IS TRUE *Hecatæus* lived ſome time after
Homer: But we find the Character the ſame in
his Writings both for Sanctity and Science. An
ΑΟΙΔΟΣ or *Bard*, according to him, muſt know
ΠΟΛΛΑ ΘΕΛΚΤΗΡΙΑ, *many ſoothing Tales*; their
Subject muſt be ΕΡΓΑ ΑΝΔΡΩΝ ΤΕ ΘΕΩΝ ΤΕ,
The Deeds of Gods and of Men; and their Oc-
cupation is

    ΘΕΟΙΣΙ ΤΕ, ΚΑΙ ΑΝΘΡΩΠΟΙΣΙ ΑΕΙΔΕΙΝ.

    To Mortals and Immortals both to ſing.

    THAT *Homer* himſelf was one of the Num-
ber, is what I can find no reaſon to doubt.   It
was the concurring Opinion, and conſtant Tradition of all Antiquity *that He was ſo :* And
the Place where he makes the moſt immediate mention of himſelf in his own Writings,
declares him to be an ΑΟΙΔΟΣ, and the *fore-
moſt* of the Profeſſion.   I touched upon the
                                        Paſſage

Sect. 8. Paſſage before, which is wonderfully wrought, and of vaſt Simplicity. It is addreſſed to *La-tona*, and her prophetick Offspring *Apollo* and *Diana*, whoſe Feaſt was held at *Delos*, and was frequented by vaſt Multitudes of People from *Ionia*, and the adjacent *Iſlands*, " Hail, *Hea-* " *venly Powers*, ſays the Bard, whoſe Praiſes " I ſing; let me alſo hope to be remembred " in the Ages to come : And when any one " born of the Tribes of Men, comes hither " a weary Traveller, and enquires ᵉ, *Who* is " the ſweeteſt of the *Singing Men* that re- " ſort to your Feaſts, and whom *you* moſt " delight to hear ? Then do you make an- " ſwer for me; ᶠ *It is the blind Man that* " *dwells in* Chios;——*His Songs excel all that* " *can e'er be ſung.*"

BUT I muſt deal fairly upon this point, and own, that this ſame *Hymn* is ſaid by ſome to be none of *Homer*'s; but the Compoſition of one *Cynæthus*; a *Chian* too, and a great Rhapſodiſt, who has the honour to be the firſt Man that ſung *Homer*'s Works in *Sicily*; and is ſaid to have been the Author of a good many Verſes, that paſs under the Poet's Name in the *Iliad* and *Odyſſey*. Theſe Poems, they tell you, *Homer* did not commit to Writing himſelf;

---

* ——Τίς δ' ὔμμιν ἀνὴρ ἥδισ֦Θ ΑΟΙΔΩΝ
  Ἐνθάδ σωλεῖται; καὶ τέῳ τέρπισθε μάλιστα!
ᶠ Τυφλὸς ἀνήρ· οἰκεῖ δὲ Χίῳ ἐνὶ σαιπαλοίσσῃ·
  Τῦ πᾶσαι μετόπισθεν ἀεισσύεσιν Ἀοιδαί.
              Ὅμηρ. Ὕμνος εἰς Ἀπόλλωνα·

himfelf; but his Pofterity in *Chios*, and the Sect. 8.
Rhapfodifts who were for ever reciting them,
came at laft to have them by heart; and this
Cynæthus, their Chief, while he preferved *Homer's* Verfes, and put them together, did inter-
mix a good many of his own Invention. The
Hymn to *Apollo*, in particular, is pointed out
as one of his Compofitions; fo that we could
not draw much from it relating to *Homer*, if
there was fufficient Authority to fupport the
Affertion.

BUT THERE is not: All we have for it,
is the *Word* of a namelefs *Scholiaft* of *Pindar's*, who fpeaks faintly of it himfelf; and
the Men of that Clafs, tho' very ufeful in their
way, we all know, have but fmall Pretenfions
to great Credit in Facts; Or if their Teftimony was of any weight, the fame Scholiaft has
preferved three Lines of *Hefiod's*, which feem
to determine the Queftion ᵍ. They affert, that
this, or fome fuch Hymn was of *Homer's* Compofure, and that he was wont to make Voyages to *Delos* on the fame Errand. There is,
however, ftill better ground to believe it his; I
mean the Authority of the learned and accurate *Thucydides*, who quotes this very Hymn as
an original Compofition of our Poet's ʰ, and
whofe Judgment is of more weight than a hundred Annotators.

It

ᵍ 'Εν Δήλῳ, τότε πρῶτος ἐγὼ καὶ Ὅμηρος Ἀοιδὶ
Μέλπομεν, ἐν νεαρῖς ὕμνοις ῥάψαντες ἀοιδὴν,
Φοῖβον Ἀπόλλωνα χρυσάορον, ὃν τέκε Λητώ·
ʰ Lib. i.

Sect. 8. IT WAS neceſſary to clear ſo important a
Point, becauſe this is the only Piece of *Homer's*,
which fixes the Place, if not of his *Birth*, at
leaſt of his *Abode* [i] : It ſhews in what he placed his *Merit*, and how he wiſhed to be talked of among Poſterity : It likewiſe favours the
received Opinion of his loſing his Sight in the
Decline of Life, and leaves no doubt of his Occupation.

THE *Iſland* CHIOS was no ill-choſen Retreat:
It enjoyed the diffuſive Benignity of the Climate, in common with the reſt of that delicious Coaſt ; but peculiar to itſelf, it produced
the *richeſt Wine* that *Greece* could boaſt [k] ;
and abounded in the other Ingredient of the
Pleaſures of the Ancients, *the fineſt Oil*. What
made this ſo neceſſary, was the uſe of the *Hot
Bath*; an Article in their living they rated ſo
high, as to ſet it upon a footing with the Joys
of *Wine*, and the Charms of the *Fair :* And
the *three* together were thought ſo ſweet by
the *ancient* Men of Pleaſure, that *Life* in
their Opinion was not worth keeping without
them [l].

THE

---

[i] *Ariſtotle* was of opinion, that *Homer* was a Chian.

[k] Athenæus Deipnoſophiſt. Lib. xii.

' Quo *Chium* pretio cadum ?——   Horat. Lib. iii. Ode xix.

OINON ΑΡΙΣΤΟΝ φέρεται Τ' Ελληνικῶν, (Χίος). Στραβ. βιℂ. ιδ'.

[l] BALNEA, VINA, VENVS, CORRVMPVNT CORPORA NOSTRA.

SED VITAM FACIVNT, BALNEA, VINA, VENVS.

Homer himſelf, when he deſcribes a Man newly come out of the
Bath, and anointed with Oil, generally adds, that he appeared *taller*
and *larger* than before, and was grown Εοίκελος Αθανατοισιν
Something like the Immortals.

THE Inhabitants of *Chios*, *Homer*'s Com- Sect. 8.
panions, bore an excellent Character among the
other Iflanders, and particularly proved fuch
excellent Seamen, that while the Power of
Greece was but yet in its Infancy, they were
able to fit out a powerful Fleet, and even formed Defigns upon the *Sovereignty* of the Seas:
and fome time afterwards, when a fuperior
Force attacked them, they fhewed great Spirit in the Defence of their Liberties [m]. Our
Poet therefore in this Situation was fettled as
it were in the *middle*, between *Ionia* and *Greece*.
He had the advantage of going to either when
he pleafed; and cou'd be eafily tranfported to
Delos, which was juft in his Neighbourhood,
to attend the Feaft of his *favourite Divinity*.

IT IS, I think, generally allowed that *Homer*
took his Characters from *Nature* or *real Life*;
and if fo, the Picture of the ΑΟΙΔΟΣ is his
own. He does indeed omit no opportunity to
do honour to the Profeffion, nor even to mention it. He has painted every Circumftance of
it, draws Similies from it, tells its effects upon
the Hearers, and of all the Wooers who had
been devouring *Ulyffes'* Eftate in his abfence, he
fpares not one, fave *Phemius* the *Bard*, and a
ΚΗΡΥΞ, or *Publick Servant* [n].

FEW PEOPLE have conceived a juft Opinion of this Profeffion, or entered into its
Dignity. The Reafon of which I take to be,

I　　　　　That

---

[m] Strabo Lib. xiv.　　[n] 'Οδυσ. 'Ραψωδ. χ.

Sect. 8. That we have no modern Character like it:
For I fhould be unwilling to admit the *Irifh* or
Highland Rüners to a fhare of the Honour;
tho' their Bufinefs, which is to entertain a Company with the Recital of fome Adventure, re-
fembles a part of the other. The *Trovadores* or
Troubadours of *Provence*, the earlieft of the
Moderns who difcovered any Vein for Poetry,
have a better Claim °. They fung their Verfes to
the Harp, or other Inftrument they cou'd ufe,
and attained to a juft *Cadence* and *Return* of
Verfe in their *Stanza's*; but had neither Manners nor Language for great Attempts.

THIS IGNORANCE of an ancient Character has made fome ingenious Men, and Admirers of *Homer*, take pains to vindicate him from
it, as a mean and contemptible Calling; or at
leaft to diffemble and flur it over. It was indeed no Life of Wealth or Power, but of great
Eafe and much *Honour*. The ΑΟΙΔΟΙ were
welcome to Kings and Courts; were neceffary
at Feafts and Sacrifices; and were highly reverenced by the People. The *Pheacian Poet*
is defcribed

——— ΕΡΙΗΡΟΝ ΑΟΙΔΟΝ
ΔΗΜΟΔΟΚΟΝ, ΛΑΟΙΣΙ ΤΕΤΙΜΗΜΕΝΟΝ.

———*valde amabilem Vatem,*
Demodocum, Populis honoratum.

IT

* See *Sperone Speroni*. The Name remains ftill in *Spain*, as
Todos o los mas Cavalleros andantes de la Edad paffada, eran grandes *Trobadores* y grandes *Muficos*. Parte I. Lib. iii, de *Don Quixote*.

IT WILL eafily be granted, that Men pinch- Sect. 8.
ed in their *Living*, and forced to have their
Thoughts ever upon the ſtretch for Subſiſtence,
cannot have room for rapturous Views, and poetick Strains [p]. The ſame Reaſon excludes all
Men of *Buſineſs*, who are thoroughly ſo, from
the Society of the *Muſes* [q]; not only becauſe
our Capacities are narrow, but becauſe our
Minds as well as Bodies, when once inured
to a Habit, ſeldom or never quit their wonted
Track: Or if at any time, by main force, we
are beaten out of it, yet " a certain Manner
" of thinking and reaſoning always recurs,
" bearing a *Reſemblance* to the Education and
" Courſe of Buſineſs we have run through."

I REMEMBER a Saying of *Plato's* upon
an Occaſion of this nature. There was one
Anniceris a Gentleman of *Cyrene* in *Africk,*
who had acquired a wonderful Dexterity at
driving a Chariot. He was willing to give the
Philoſopher a proof of his Art; and, in pre-
ſence of abundance of People, drove ſeveral
times round the Academy with ſo ſteady a Rein,
as to leave but *one Print* of his Chariot-Wheels.

I 2

Plato

[p] *Sed Vatem egregium,* ———
  Hunc, qualem nequeo monſtrare & ſentio tantùm,
  Anxietate carens Animus facit ; omnis acerbi
  Impatiens, cupidus Silvarum, aptuſque bibendis
  Fontibus Aonidum. Neque enim cantare ſub Antro
  Pierio, Thyrſumve poteſt contingere mœſta
  Paupertas, atque Æris inops ; quo noɛe diæque
  Corpus eget ———
  Pectora noſtra duas non admittentia Curas.   Juv. Sat. vii.

[q] Or the ſmall Genius which my Youth cou'd boaſt,
  In *Proſe* and *Buſineſs* lies extinct and loſt.   PRIOR.

Sect. 8. *Plato* said, " It was impoffile that a Man who
" had beftowed fuch infinite Pains upon a
" Trifle, fhou'd ever be good for any great
" Matter." In fhort, whoever confines his
Thinking to any *one* Subject, who beftows all
his Care and Study upon *one* Employment or
Calling, may excel in that ; But cannot be
qualified for a Province that requires the *freeft*
and *wideft*, as well as the moft fimple and difinterefted Views of Nature.

N o w if we were to fit down and contrive,
what kind of Life is the leaft obnoxious to thefe
Inconveniences, we fhall find none fo free from
Care, Bufinefs, or *Want,* as that of a BARD.
It is exactly the eafy, independent State, that
is unawed by *Laws,* and the *Regards* that mo-
left us in Communities ; that knows no Duties
or Obligations but thofe of Hofpitality and Humanity : that fubjects the Mind to no Tincture
of Difcipline ʳ, but lays it open to all the *natural Senfations,* with which the various Parts
of the Univerfe affect a *fagacious, perceptive,
mimicking Creature.*

As THIS Condition is in itfelf of the ut-
moft Importance to a *Poet,* the Confequences
of it are almoft equally happy : The ΑΟΙΔΟΙ,
or *Bards,* were under a neceffity of frequent
Travelling, and every now and then exercifing
their *Vein* upon the greateft Subjects. In this
Situation did *Homer* begin to wander over
Greece,

ʳ *Plato* calls a *Mind* fit for Poetry, ψυχὴν ἄζεπυ. Φαῖδρϴ.

Greece, carrying with him thofe *Qualities* that Sect. 8.
procured him a *Welcome* wherever he came ᶠ. I
have already fhewn what a noble Scene for Travelling the *Grecian Cities* and young Common-
wealths then afforded. *Homer* ftaid fo long in
each of them, as was neceffary *to fee*, but not
to be *moulded* into their Manners. The *Order*
of a Town, and the *Forms* brought into the
common City-life, elude the Paffions ᵗ, and
abate their Force by turning them upon little
Objects. But he neither led a Town nor
Country-Life; and in this refpect was truly a
Citizen of the Univerfe.

THE GREAT Philofopher I lately mentioned, has dropt an Expreffion in the third Book
of his Laws, which characterizes very nicely
both the *Life* which *Homer* led, and the *Manners* that are defcribed in his Poems. He introduces a *Lacedemonian* faying, That his Countrymen, the *Spartans*, ufed to read this Poet's
Verfes, Καίπερ ΙΩΝΙΚΟΝ ᵘ ΛΑΚΩΝΙΚΟΝ ἐ-
χᾶς·οῖε δὲλ.θων βιὸν, tho' he every where painted
the *Ionic*, and not the *Lacedemonian* Way of
Living. The Oppofition is, between the

I 3   Strict-

ᶠ The Poet himfelf, when fpeaking of the People we gladly admit into our Houfes, enumerates Μάντιν *(a Diviner)* ἢ Ἰητῆρα κακῶν *(or a Phyfician)* ἢ Τέκ]ονα δὲρων *(a Houfe-Carpenter.)*

Ἡ καὶ θέσπιν ΑΟΙΔΟΝ, ὅς κεν τέρπῃσι ἀείδων. Ὀδυσ. Ῥαψωδ.ρ.
A divine Bard, to charm us with his Song.

ᵗ A great Man, who had reafon to know it, fays that he never
faw the Populace in fuch a Fury, but the Hour of Dinner or Supper
wou'd cool them. They don't like what they call *Se défheurer*.
                              Memoir. de *Retz*.

Sect. 8. Strictness of the *Spartan* Rules, in their Diet, Hours, Exercises, and Diversions ; and the *Ionian* Liberty in all these Points. The severe Discipline of *Thebes* and *Lacedemon* was indeed no Friend to Poetry: It made many a noble Patriot and gallant Soldier ; But there was never a Poet a Native of *Sparta* [u] ; and *Pindar* the only one produced in *Thebes*, kept but little at home, and seems not much to have affected the Character of his Countrymen [w].

THE NEXT Advantage of *Homer*'s Profession, was the *Access* it gave him into the Houses and Company of the *Greatest Men*. The Effects of it appear in every Line of his Works; not only in his Characters of them, and Accounts of their Actions ; but the more *familiar* Part of Life ; their manner of Conversing and method of Entertaining, are accurately and minutely painted. He knows their Rarities and *Plate*, and can hold forth the Neatness and Elegance of their *Bijouterie*. He has nicely inspected the Trinkets their Ladies wore ; their *Bracelets*, *Buckles*, and *Necklaces*, whose Prettinesses he sometimes talks of with great Taste and Exactness. He has a delicious Pair of *three-stoned Ear-rings*.

——'Ἐρ-

[u] Quæ Urbes (Thebæ & Lacedæmon) talium Studiorum steriles fuêre ; nisi Thebas unum Os Pindari inluminaret: Nam Alcmana Lacones falsò sibi vindicant.
Velleii Paterc. Hist. Lib. ii. § ult.
[w] See his Life and Writings ; Διπαρᾶν ἀπὸ ΘΗΒΑΝ.
Φέρων μελὸς ἔρχομαι, Πυθ. β.

——————'Ερματα δύω,　Sect. 8.
Τερ̃λϰ̀ ἱμερόεντα· χάρις δ' ἀπελάμπετο πολλή.

And a curious *Gold Necklace* set in Amber in
the form of a *Sun*.

—————— πολυδαίδαλ☉ ΟΡΜΟΣ
Χρύσε☉, ἠλέκἸρoισι ἐερἸμ̀ϓ☉, ἠέλι☉ ώς.

He has them too of several Sizes; for *Lucina*
was to receive at *Latona*'s Lying-in, from the
Goddesses that were Gossips,

——————— ΜΕΓΑΝ ΟΡΜΟΝ
Χρυσέοισι λίνοισι ἐερἸμένον, ἐννεάπηχυν.

—————— *A Necklace huge,*
Strung upon golden Threads, three Yards in
length.

In a word, there is scarce a Circumstance in
Oeconomy but what he has somewhere described,
or made it evident that he knew.

Nor cou'd it be otherwise, if we consider
the daily Life of the ΑΟΙΔΟΙ. The Manner
was, when a *Bard* came to a House, he was
first welcomed by the Master, and after he had
been entertained according to the ancient Mode;
that is, after he had bathed, eaten, and drunk
some ΜΕΛΙΗΔΕΑ ΟΙΝΟΝ, *heart-chearing Wine*,
he was called upon to entertain the Family in
his turn: He then tuned his *Lyre*, and raised

I 4　　　　　　his

Sect. 8. his *Voice*, and sung to the liftening Crowd fome Adventure of the *Gods*, or fome Performance of *Men*.

MANY Advantages accrue from hence to the *Poet*: He is under a happy Neceffity of making no *fanciful Conceits*, or profound Verfes in an uncommon Language: But if he would fucceed, he muft entertain his wondering Audience in a fimple, intelligible Stile. He might indeed tell wonderful Stories of ftrange Performances, and Places ftrange: but they muft be *plainly* told, and with a conftant eye to *natural Manners* and *human Paffions*: He needed not keep ftrictly to them; *that* wou'd raife no Admiration; but with an Analogy or Likenefs, fuch as the Tenour and Circumftance of the *tender* or *woeful* Tale wou'd bear.

HERE TOO was abundance of Opportunities not only of *judging* what was amifs, what was true or falfe in his *Song*; but of *helping it*. While he was perfonating a *Hero*; while his Fancy was warming, and his Words flowing; when he had fully entered into the *Meafure*, was ftruck with the *Rhythmus*, and feized with the *Sound*; like a Torrent, he wou'd fill up the Hollows of the Work; the boldeft Metaphors and glowing Figures wou'd come rufhing upon him, and caft a *Fire* and *Grace* into the Compofition, which no Criticifm can ever fupply [x].

As

[x] Πλάτων· ΙΩΝ ἢ ΡΑΨΩΔΟΣ.

As TO the *Audience*, I might shew the Good- Sect. 8.
fortune of our Poet in that particular, by re-
minding your Lordship of the Monitor of the
younger *Gracchus* [y], or the *Slave* who directed
and check'd the most fluent Orator of *Augustus'*
Court [z]; but *Moliere's* old *Woman* comes nearest
our Purpose. It was by her Ear and Taste that
that celebrated Comedian tried the success of
his Comic Scenes, and as they affected her more
or less, so he judged of their Force and Failures[a].
Thus the most approved Writer among the
Moderns makes choice of a Circumstance for
his Rule that *Homer* was obliged to regard in
every Performance.

THE MORE we consider its Influence upon
Poetry, the stronger and wider it appears: To
this Necessity of pleasing his Audience, I wou'd
ascribe that *just Measure* of *Probability and
Wonder* which runs thro' the greatest part of
his Works. The People must be entertained:
that is, they must be kept at *a gaze*, and at
the same time must comprehend the Dangers,
and feel the Passions of the Description.   The
Adventure must be such as they can understand;
and the Method in which it is brought about,
must surprize their Imagination, draw forth
their Attention, and win their Heart [b]. This
at

[y] See *Plutarch* in his Life.
[z] Excerpta è Lib. iv. Controverf. Senecæ: in Procem.
[a] Her Name was *la Forêt*.
[b] Καὶ τὸ μῷ' ὅλον παρ' αὐτῷ διήγησις τ̃ πρᾳγμάτων, ΠΑΡΑ-
ΔΟΞΟΣ, ὠ ΜΥΘΩΔΗΣ καθεσκεύασαι. ὑπὲρ τὸ πληρουῶ ἀργίας
ὠ ναυμαῖϑ τὲς ἐπιζάνονἰας, ὠ ΕΚΠΛΗΚΤΙΚΗΝ τὼ
ἀκρόασιν καθιστάναι.   ΠΛΒταρχ. βίος Ὁμήρε.

Sect. 8. at once accounts for the Stories which *Homer* tells, improbable indeed in themselves, and yet bearing such a *Resemblance* to Nature and Truth.

HIS CARE to please his Audience appears from a Maxim he has advanced concerning the Subjects that are listened to with most Pleasure.

Τὼ γὸ ᾿ΑΟΙΔΗΝ μᾶλλον ἐπικλείουσι ᾿Ανθρωποι
῾Ητις; ἀκρουόντεσσι ΝΕΩΤΑΤΗ ἀμφιπέληται [c].

For his Poems were made to be *recited*, or sung to a *Company*; and not read in private, or perused in a Book, which few were then capable of doing: and I will venture to affirm, that whoever reads not *Homer* in *this View* loses a great Part of the Delight he might receive from the Poet.

HIS STILE, properly so called, cannot be understood in any other light; nor can the *Strain*, and *Manner* of his Work be felt and relished unless we put ourselves in the place of his Audience, and imagine it coming from the Mouth of a *Rhapsodist*: Neither, to say the truth, is there any thing but *this* situation, that will fully account for all his Heroes telling miraculous Tales as well as himself, and sometimes in the *Heat of a Battle*. But when we remember his *Profession*, and his common *Audience*, we see the

Necessity

[c] ᾿Οδυσ. ῾Ραψωδ. A.

Neceffity of *Stories*, and of fuch as he ufually Sect. 8.
tells.   It was not the Inhabitants of a *great*
luxurious City he had to entertain with unnatural
Flights, and lewd Fancies; but the martial Race
of a wide and free Country, who willingly liften
to the Prowefs of their Anceftors, and Atchievements of their Kings.

IT wou'd be tedious to infift upon every particular in the Life of a *Rhapfodift*; but there are
two Advantages more which deferve our notice.
The firft is. the *Habit* which the Poet muft
acquire by finging. *extemporary Strains.* We
have daily proofs of the power of *Practice*
in every Art and Employment.. An Inclination indulged turns to a *Habit*, and that, when
cultivated, rifes to an *Eafe* and *Maftery* in the
Profeffion.   It immediately affects our Speech
and Converfation; as we daily fee in *Lawyers* [d],
Seamen, and moft Sets of Men who converfe
with eafe and fluency in their *own* Stile, tho'
they are often puzzled when forced to affect another. To what height fuch a *Genius* as *Homer's*
might rife by conftant Culture, is hard to tell;
Euftathius fays, " That he breathed nothing
" but *Verfe*; and was fo poffefs'd with the
" *Heroic Mufe*, as to fpeak in *Numbers* with
" more eafe than others in *Profe* [e]."

THE SECOND Peculiarity which attends a
Stroling Life is, *great Returns of Mirth and*
Humour.

[d] See Peliffon. Hiftoire de l'Acad. Françoife.

[e] Ὅτι ἔπνει ΕΠΗ ΟΜΗΡΟΣ· ἠ ἔπως ἔιχε τ̃ πειέργε ἠ
ΕΜΜΕΛΟΥΣ ΜΟΥΣΗΣ, ὡς ἰδὲ τᾶ ἐν ἀπλότητι πεζολογεῖν
ἔπεςι.   Ευςαθ. Πεοοίμ.

Sect. 8. *Humour.* After suffering Cold and Fatigue, a flood of Joy comes impetuous upon a Man when he is refreshed, and begins to grow warm f. His Heart dilates, his Spirits flow, and if there is any *Vein of Humour* or Thought within him, it will certainly break loose, and be set a running g. The *poetick*, and most kinds of Strolers, are commonly Men of great Health; of the quickest and truest Feelings: They are obliged to no exhausting Labour, to stiffen their Bodies and depress their Minds. Their Life is the likest to the plentiful State of the *Golden Age*; without Care or Ambition, full of Variety and Change, and constantly giving or receiving the most natural and elegant Pleasures.

It is an ingenious but cruel Story which the Poets have contrived, to express the Train of Cares brought into Life by *Prometheus* or Foresight: The Chains which fasten him to the Rock, and the insatiable Vultur that rends his Vitals every Morning. The wandering Songsters were almost the only People who escaped the Doom: With a free unanxious Mind they passed their Days; .

> ———*Versus amat, hoc studet unum :*
> *Detrimenta, Fugas Servorum, Incendia ridet.*

Their very *stroling* from one little State to another wou'd enrich their Fancies. *Solitude*
is

---

f The Poet has describ'd it himself, we may suppose from Experience, ———Μετὰ γάρ τε ϰ, ἀλγεσι Τέρπεται ἀνὴρ, Ὅσις δὴ μάλα πολλὰ πάϑη, ϰ, πολλ᾽ ἐπαληϑῆ. Οδυσ. ο.

g Satur est cum clamat *Horatius*, EVOE ! Juvenal. Sat. vii.

is a Friend to Thought; as a perpetual Circle Sect. 8.
of Pleasure and Diversions, is its greatest Ene- ᗅᑎ
my. When alone, we are obliged to furnish out
our own Entertainment; We must recollect ourselves, and *look within*, if there be any thing *there*
that merits our Attention. When in Company
the regard we owe to every Person in it, *dissipates*
the Mind, and hinders Reflection. The way to
think little, is to hurry from one Amusement to
another, that we may fly from *ourselves*. But
the Man who lives plain, and at times steps
aside from the *Din of Life*, enjoys a more genuine Pleasure: He obtains ravishing Views of
silent Nature, and undisturbed contemplates her
solitary Scenes. He often turns his Attention
upon *himself*, canvasses his own Passions, and
ascertains his Sentiments of *Humanity*.

IT IS true, there are many Hermits who
are not much given to Meditation, and some Persons whose business it is *to travel* are remarkable for Stupidity. But it is not the Life of a
Recluse that is here meant; nor the busy Jour-
neys of such as traverse Countries for a Livelihood. It is the short Retreat of a chearful
Mind, whose Business it is *to please*; who must
entertain the first Company he meets in the
most lively and affecting manner. This is quite
a different Situation: a Situation that must ob-
lige the Poet, not only to study the *Passions* of
his Hearers while he recited; to observe their
Features, watch every Motion of their *Eye* and
Turn

Sect. 8. *Turn* of Thought; but to look around him when *alone*, and lay up store of such Images, as Experience told him wou'd have the strongest Effect.

Before I leave the subject, I woud observe once for all; that the Ancients believed both *Homer*'s *Poverty*, and his subsisting by his *Muse*. A Man of great Learning and Eloquence, says [h], " That many thought his *Life* more wonder- " ful than his *Poetry :* that to live *poor* and *wan-* " *dering*, and earn just so much by his Poems " as barely to support him, is a noble Proof " of his Fortitude and Magnanimity [i]." This, *My Lord*, is spoken a little in the Spirit of an ancient *Cynick* or modern *Capuchin ;* where Poverty is a Merit, and a contempt of Wealth, a title to deserve it. But *Dion* is not singular as to the Matter of fact. *Plato* is of the same Opinion : He seems to have dealt a little hardly with *Homer*, because his *Theology* and the ΙΩΝΙΚΟΣ ΒΙΟΣ, the *free Ionian Life* which he described, were not compatible with the Manners of his high-modelled *perfect City ;* but it is plain he has studied him with all the Attachment and Pleasure of a professed Admirer.

In the tenth Book of his *Republick* he gives several strokes of his Life. He there makes it a Question, " Whether *Homer*, who had imitated " or

---

[h] Dion. Chrysostome.

[i] Τὸ γ̀ ἐν πενίᾳ διαγενέϲϑϑ, κ̀ ἀλώμενον, κ̀ τοσ̃ν ἀπὸ ᷅ Ποιημάτων πος̌ον]α, ὁπόσον ἀποζῆν, ϑαῦμα ᷅ ἀνδρείας κ̀ μεϳα- λοφϱοσύνης. Διώγ Χρυσοϛ. λογ. νγ.

" or reprefented Actions of all forts, had ever Sect. 8.
" done any great thing *himfelf?*" He feems to
think *that he had not*; and draws his Conjecture
from the Poet's Friends: He mentions one *Creophilus a Samian*, as the chief of them; " Whofe
" *Name*, fays he, however ridiculous [k], will be
" lefs fo than the Figure he himfelf makes in
" Learning [l]: and if what is told of the Poet's
" Life be true, his Friends feem to have been very
" carelefs about him. In this refpect *Homer* has
" not been able, like *Prodicus* the *Cean*, or
" *Protagoras* of *Abdera*, to gain Admirers, or
" inftruct his Followers from a *real Skill* or
" Knowledge of the things he defcribes; but
" has only been good at *mimicking* and de-
" fcribing others. For do you imagine *Glauco!*
" (this is *Socrates'* Companion in the Dia-
" logue) that *Homer's* Cotemporaries wou'd
" ever have permitted *him* and *Hefiod to wan-
" der up and down the Country, finging* and
" playing the *Rhapfodifts*, had they been able
" to improve their Manners, or promote their
" Affairs military or civil? Wou'd they not
" have thought they had fallen upon a *Treafure*
" when fuch Men came to their Town, done
" them all poffible Honours, and *penfioned*
" them to ftay? Or if they cou'd not fix them,
    " wou'd

[k] We wou'd tranflate it *Lovemeat*, or Mr. *Flefhly*.
[l] He is faid to have entertained *Homer* in his Houfe upon condition he wou'd give him fome Work, to be publifhed under his
(*Creophilus'*) Name; and accordingly got a Poem upon the taking
and facking of O *Echalia*. Καὶ ὑποδεξάμϑνον Ὁμήρον, λαϐεῖν παρ'
αὐτῶ τὸ Ποίημα τὴν δ' Ὀιχαλίας ἅλωσιν. Σκιδ'. ἐν Κρεωφίλω.

Sect. 8. " wou'd they not have *followed* thefe Poets
" wherever they went, until they had fully
" learned the Science of fo great Mafters? *Pro-*
" *tagoras* and *Prodicus* can demonftrate, that
" no Family nor City ever thrives without their
" Inftructions, and are fo reverenced by their
" Difciples, that they wou'd almoft bear them
" upon their Heads!"

T H I S' P A R T then of *Homer's* Life, I mean
his exercifing the Profeffion of an ΑΟΙΔΟΣ, may
be confidered at the fame time as the chief Part of
his Education. To it he owed many of the *Spe-*
ciofa Miracula ᵐ, which are admired by *Horace*.
For as he travelled over the feveral Provinces of
Greece, he might pick up the *Country Miracles :*
They commonly take their Rife either from the
natural Hiftory of the Place, or they are *Tra-*
ditional Stories of their mighty Progenitors.
They are always happy in fome *Air of Probabi-*
lity, and have fome foundation in *Nature* ;
fomething in the Mountain, Cavern, or River
which at firft ftruck the gazing Mortals that approached it, and made them conceive ftrange
notions concerning the *Caufes* of the apparent
Wonder. Thefe, paffing from hand to hand, are
enlarged, their Circumftances varied and refined,
until they grow by degrees into an *Allegory* or
myftick Tale ⁿ.

I M A K E little doubt but this was one great
Fund of *Homer's* Learning; as the Neceffity he
　　　　　　　　　　　　　　　　　　　lay

ᵐ Beautiful ftriking Miracles.
ⁿ It is an Obfervation of *Strabo's* concerning our Poet, ὅτι μηδενὸς
δ' ἀληθῶς· κρίνην ἀπάτῃην πεϱπολογίαν, ὐχ Ὁμηϱικὸν. Βιβ. α·

lay under of a daily *Practice* was his beſt In- Sect. 8.
ſtructor in the *Art of Poetry:* If your Lordſhip
will be pleaſed to make the Reflection, it will be
found, that in all that wide *Plan* of Mankind,
contained in his two Poems, there is not any ſingle Character marked out ôr diſtinguiſhed by
acquired Knowledge, as we underſtand the word.
The Knowledge and Virtues of his Perſons are all
natural; ſuch as ſpring up without other culture
than the native *Bent* of their Genius, and their
Converſe among Mankind.　Thus *Ulyſſes* grew
up a ſagacious, ſubtle, bold, perſuaſive Man,
without the aid of Maſters of *Rhetorick* or Lec-
tures of *Politicks: Agamemnon* was lofty, royal
and ambitious; a vigilant and brave General,
dreading Diſgrace, and careful of his People;
and all this without ſtudying *King-craft* or the
Art of *War*.　It continued ſo until *Homer*'s own
days; there was but little *Erudition* in the World:
and what they had was *allegorical*; and deſcend-
ed, as appears from the former Account, to the
Bards from the firſt LAWGIVERS, who profeſ-
ſed both Characters.

　IN THIS reſpect, the TALENT of their Poets
was truly *natural,* and had a much better title
to Inſpiration than their learned Succeſſors; I
mean learned by Books; tho' I do not ſay that
Homer or *Heſiod* had no Learning of this ſort:
But perhaps *(ut vineta egomet cædam mea)* the
leſs of it the better.　Certainly, *My Lord,* the
Scholaſtick Turn, *Technical* Terms, imaginary

Re-

Sect. 8. Relations, and wire-drawn Sciences, spoil the
natural Faculties, and marr the Expression. But
the Ancients of early Times, as *Nature* gave
Powers and a Genius, so they fought, or plow-
ed, or merchandized, or sung ; Wars, or Loves,
or Morals, ὡς ἡ Μῦσα ἐδίδυ, *just as their Muse
or Genius gave Permission.*

HOMER's blind Bard[o] sings by meer Inspi-
ration, and celebrates things he had no access to
know but in *that way:* which, as it is the greatest
Recommendation to the *Bard's Trade*, if, at the
same time, it *has a foundation*, and is *such* a Lye
as he uses to make, (that is, *like to Truth)* it must
shew " How much these ancient *Songsters* trust-
" ed to their *Vein* ; and were accordingly be-
" lieved to know something more than *Men.*"

IT IS WORTH while to observe another Picture of them given by the Poet in the Character of *Phemius.*   He had been forced by *Penelope's* Wooers to sing at their Feasts ; and was
shut up with them in the great Hall, where
Ulysses had begun to take a dreadful Revenge.
When the Slaughter was well over, he came
out from the Hollow of a Door where he had
lurked, threw down his Lute, and springing
to the Hero besmear'd with Blood, fell down
before him with these Words :

ΓΟΥΝΟΥΜΑΙ Σ' ΟΔΥΣΣΕΥ. —[p]

Ulysses! at thy Knees I beg for Pity!
'Twill gaul thy Soul hereafter, if thou killest

A

[o] DEMODOCUS the Pheacian.   [p] 'Οδυσ. X.

A Bard, *who sings both to the Gods and Men :*
Untaught *by others, in my Mind I bear,*
By GOD *himself implanted, all the Strains*
Of Melody *and* Verse.——

INDEED, the Epithets he bestows, and the
Insinuations he makes concerning the Characteristick of his Brethren, wou'd make one suspect
that they were frequently under the power of
an *Impulse*. A Bard with him, is ΘΕΙΟΣ, *Di-*
vine, ΘΕΣΠΙΣ, *Prophetick*, ΕΡΙΗΡΟΣ, *most ve-*
nerable : He is the *Darling* of the *Muses* [q]; he
sings from *the Gods* [r]; and if he touches upon an
improper Subject, 'tis not the ΑΟΙΔΟΣ, or BARD,
that is to be blamed, but *Jupiter*; who manages Mortals just as he pleases [s]. In a word,
he never begins to sing, until he feel the *Stir-*
rings [t] of his Mind, and hath the Permission of
his Muse [u].

THE OTHER Parent of our Poetry, the
peaceful *Hesiod*, tells us, " That it is by Inspi-
" ration of the *Muses*, and of the *far-shooting*
" *Apollo*, that there are singing Men upon

K 2   " the

---

[q] Τὸν περὶ Μῦσ' ἐφίλησε.   'Οδυσ. θ.

[r] 'Ως δ' ὅτ' ΑΟΙΔΟΝ ἀνὴρ ποτιδέρκεται, ὅς τε ΘΕΩΝ ΕΞ
Ἀείδει, δεδαὼς ἔπε' ἱμερόεντα βροτοῖσιν,
Τοῦ δ' ἄωτον μεμάασιν ἀκουέμεν ὁπότ' ἀείδῃ.   'Οδυσ. ρ.

[s] He sings, 'Οππῃ οἱ ΝΟΟΣ ὄρνυται; 'Ου νυ τ' ΑΟΙΔΟΙ
Ἄιτιοι ἀλλά ποθι ΖΕΥΣ αἴτιος, ὅς τε δίδωσιν
Ἀνδράσιν ἀλφηστῇσιν, ὅπως ἐθελῃσιν ἑκάστῳ·   'Οδυσ. α.

[t] —— Καλέσασθε ΘΕΙΟΝ ΑΟΙΔΟΝ
Δημόδοκον· τῷ γὰρ ῥα ΘΕΟΣ περὶ δῶκεν ἀοιδὴν
Τέρπειν· ὅπῃ ΘΥΜΟΣ ΕΠΟΤΡΥΝΗΣΙΝ ἀείδειν.   'Οδυσ. θ.

[u] ΜΟΥΣ' ἄρ' Ἀοιδὸν ΑΝΗΚΕΝ ἀειδέμεναι κλέα ἀνδρῶν.'Οδυσ.θ.

Sect. 8. " the Earth, and Players upon the Harp [w]."
Nor is it only the *Poetick Tribe* who make thefe
Pretenfions, or the credulous Multitude that be-
lieve them; but we find the Men of greateft
Knowledge and fevereft Thought, both admit-
ting and fupporting their Claim.

It is a ftrange Saying to come from the
Mouth of a wife Philofopher, " That God, de-
" priving the Poets of their Underftanding,
" ufes them as his *Minifters*, *Sooth-fayers*, and
" *holy Prophets*, to make us, the Hearers
" know, that it is not of themfelves they fay
" fuch wonderful and high things, not being
" in their Wits: but that it is *God* himfelf who
" fpeaks to us, and pronounces by them [x]."
" For inftance, he names *Tynnichus* the *Chal-*
" *cidean*, who never in his Life made a Poem
" worth mentioning, except the celebrated
" *Pæan*, or Hymn to *Apollo*, which was in
" every body's mouth, and was perhaps the
" fineft Poem that ever appeared. This he
" fays he compofed, ΕΥΡΗΜΑΤΙ ΜΟΥΣΑΝ,
" *by the Invention of the Mufes.*"

THESE

[w] Ἐκ γὸ ΜΟΥΣΑΩΝ, καὶ ἑκηϹόλε ΑΠΟΛΛΩΝΟΣ
Ἄνδρες ΑΟΙΔΟΙ ἔασιν ἐπὶ χθόνα, καὶ ΚΙΘΑΡΙΣΤΑΙ. Θεογ.
[x] Διὰ ταῦτα ᾗ ὁ ΘΕΟΣ ἐξαιρύμϕϘ τέτων νῦν, τέτοις χρῆ-
ται ΥΠΗΡΕΤΑΙΣ, καὶ τοῖς ΧΡΗΣΜΩΔΟΙΣ, καὶ τῇ
ΜΑΝΤΕΣΙ τῆς ΘΕΙΟΙΣ, ἵνα ἡμεῖς οἱ Ἀκέοντες ἐιδῶμϟ
ὅτι ΟΥΚ ΟΤΤΟΙ εἰσὶ οἱ ταῦτα λέγοντες, ἔτω πολλῆ ἄξιας
οἷς νῦς μὴ πάρεσιν, ἀλλ᾽ ὁ ΘΕΟΣ ΑΥΤΟΣ ΕΣΤΙΝ ὁ λέ-
γων, διὰ τέτων δὲ φθέγγεται πρὸς ἡμᾶς.
                    ΠλάτωνϘ ΙΩΝ, ἢ σελ Ιλιάδ

To the fame Purpofe *Guarini*,
     Quefta Parte di Noi, che intende e vede,
     Non è noftra virtu; mà vien dal Cielo:
     Effo la dà, come a lui piace, e toglie.

THESE ARE high Pretenfions, and fhou'd Sect. 8.
be ftrongly fupported before they are admitted:
But if one uninfected with the Poetical Spirit
was to fearch for their meaning *in Profe*, it
fhou'd feem to fay, "That as there is no Poetry
" without Genius, fo that Genius itfelf has its
" Fits and Seafons, which are provoked and in-
" dulged no where fo happily as in the ftroling
" unanxious Life of an ΑΟΙΔΟΣ, or BARD."

K 3　　　　*S E C T.*

ynrielet inv.   G. Tarelt gucht sculp

S E C T. IX.

Sect. 9. **H**OW noble and natural soever the A-
spects of Mankind might be, which
Homer had from the young *Common-Wealths*
that were beginning to form themselves all
over *Greece*, yet his Views were not confined
to them. The Manners of his Poems are generally of the *Grecian Stamp* ; but he quits
them at times, and by some artful Touches
inserted here and there, he lets us know, *that*
he

he is not ignorant of other Nations, nor un-Sect. 9.
acquainted with the State of Foreign Countries. He appears, upon occasion, a great *Ge-*
nealogift, a knowing *Hiftorian,* and, which is
moft to our purpofe, an admirable *Geographer.*
This, no Infpiration will account for: We
muft therefore accompany him in the fecond
Part of his Travels, his vifiting *Egypt* and the
Eaft.

AMONG the many Stories contrived by his
Admirers, there is one told by *Hephæftion* [a],
which conceals a Meaning very different from
its firft Appearance. He fays, " That a Lady
" of *Memphis,* the Daughter of *Nicarchus,* by
" Name PHANCY, *excelling in Wifdom,* com-
" pofed two Poems; the *War of Troy,* and the
" *Wanderings of Ulyffes*; and laid them up in
" the *holy* Place of the Temple of *Vulcan* at
" *Memphis*; that *Homer* coming there, found
" means to get Copies of them from the *Sa-*
" *cred Scribe* PHANITES, out of which he
" compofed his *Ilias* and *Odyffey.*" The Senfe
put upon this by the Learned, is, That *Homer*
was either an *Egyptian* born, (for fo many
have fufpected;) or, that his great Genius having been cultivated by an *Egyptian Education,*
he was thereby enabled to compofe his admired Poems.

BESIDES the conftant Belief among the Ancients, of his having been in that Country;

K 4   and

---

[a] *Apud* Photium, in Biblioth. § 190.

Sect. 9. and befides the *Authority* of the *Egyptian* Priefts themfelves, who affirmed it upon the *faith* of their *Records* [b], there are other Prefumptions in his Works, which will probably have confiderable Weight with fuch as can take them from the *Original.*

I am obliged to fay fo; becaufe, tho' it be very pleafant to trace the Likenefs between the Cuftoms of one Country, and thofe of another derived from them; to fearch into the Origin of the borrowed Rites, and the *natural* Foundation of the new *Mythology*; yet their Connexion is delicate, and the Perception of it generally *too fine*, to be turned into a direct Proof: It cannot be felt at all, without a nice Knowledge of the Mother-Country and of its. Manners, as well as of their *moral Progeny.* But fuch a Draught of the parallel Cuftoms of two Countries, would, I am afraid, prove tedious. It has afforded Materials for fome ingenious Books, and is of late the Subject of the moft entertaining Converfations. I will not therefore undertake to defcribe the Proceffion at the Funerals of *Apis,* or its Progrefs through *Heliopolis,* up the *Nile;* upon which *Orpheus* and *Homer* founded their Defcription of the *Paffage* of Souls to *Hell* [c] :

Nor

---

b Diodorus Sicul. Lib. i. Biblioth. in fine.

c Παρ᾽ δ᾽ ἴσαν Ὠκεανῦ τε ῥοάς, καὶ Λευκάδα Πέτρην,
Ἠδὲ παρ᾽ Ἠελίοιο πύλας, καὶ Δῆμον Ὀνείρων
Ἤισαν· Αἶψα δ᾽ ἵκοντο κατ᾽ Ἀσφοδελὸν Λειμῶνα·
Ἔνθα τε ναίυσι ψυχαὶ, ΕΙΔΩΛΑ ΚΑΜΟΝΤΩΝ.
Ὀδυσ: Ω.

Nor will I meddle with the Lake near *Mem-* Sect. 9.
phis, which was the Pattern of *Acheron*; nor
the Manner of burying in the delightful *Mea-*
dows around it, that gave rife to the peopling
the *Elyfian* Fields.

LET me only obferve, That thefe Places
were extant, and thefe Cuftoms ftill kept up,
fo late as the Time of *Diodorus* the *Sicilian*;
and that the *Egyptian* Priefts affirmed to him,
That from thefe Places and Cuftoms *Homer*
had taken his religious Doctrines. They gave
further Inftances, in the Temple of *Darknefs*
or *Gloom*; the Brazen Gates of *Cocytus* and
Lethe; the Archetype of *Charon*'s Boat, and
the Etymology of his *Name* d; with many
other Parts of the *Grecian Creed*, (too many
to mention here) which were *Realities* in
Egypt : There was a real Temple, real Gates,
a wooden Boat, and an honeft Ferry-man,
all fairly exifting in *this* World; though
transferred by *Orpheus* and *Homer*, and applied, perhaps typically, to *that which is to*
come e.

BUT there is *one* Proof given by the Sacred Order, of *Homer*'s having been in their
Country, by much too curious to be omitted.
It is taken from that Part of his Writings,
where he relates, how the beauteous *Helen*,
when fhe entertained *Telemachus* in her Houfe,
had

d CHARONI in the old *Egyptian*, fignified fimply a *Ferry-*
man.   e Diodorus Siculus, Lib. i.

Sect. 9. had put into the Wine a *Drug* of such Virtue, as to inspire Mirth and Joy, occasion a perfect Oblivion of past Ills, and an Insensibility of present Misery. *This,* says the Poet, she received as a Present from *Polydamna* the Wife of *Thon* the *Egyptian* [f] : And *this,* say the Priests, with all its Circumstances, (the surprising Qualities of the Drug, and Names of the Persons) he could learn no where so exactly as in *Egypt.*

To give this Argument fair play, we must remember, that in those rude Ages of the World, *whoever* discovered any Knowledge of the Customs or Inhabitants of a *distant* Country, was of course supposed *to have been* in that Country. There was no Correspondence of Letters, little Trade, and the Writing of History was a thing unknown. Knowledge therefore implied Travelling; and if that Knowledge extended *to Persons,* and the Peculiarities of their Manners, it fixed the Travelling to the Country where those Persons lived : The Character of the Man who understood the *Tempers,* and knew the *Mind* of many People, was He, Ὅς μάλα πολλὰ ——— πλάγχθη [g], *who far had stray'd* —— *o'er many Lands.*

I MUST own, *My Lord,* this looks plausible: But there are some other Considerations which give it still a greater Air of Veracity. From the most authentick Accounts we have of *He-*
len's

[f] Ὀδυσ. Δ.   [g] Ὀδυσ. Α.

len's Adventures [h], it appears, that she was for
some time in the power of this *Thon*, (whether
a Prince of the Country, or the Governour of
a Province) when she and *Paris* were driven
upon the *Egyptian* Coast, in their Voyage from
Greece to *Troy*; and consequently that she must
have been in company with his Lady: For we
can never suppose, that so beautiful a Creature,
so discreet, and of such high Birth, should be
treated as an ordinary Prisoner [i].

IT appears also, that the *Egyptian Ladies*
were much addicted to the use of this Medicine; and if we believe a later Historian, *They*
were the first People in the World who found
out an Antidote against *Grief* and *Sorrow* [k].
The *Egyptian* Complexion, which was thoughtful and melancholy, made them fonder of an
enlivening Potion, than an airy People would
have been; and the same excellent Writer, *Diodorus*, when he was himself in the Country,
found the *Recipe* still known, and as much in
vogue as ever.

THO' I could take this upon the *Sicilian's*
Word; yet, I confess, what makes it, and
the whole Story, appear the more probable
to me, is, That I find the same Medicine *still*
in use in the same Country, and the Effects of
it

[h] 'ΗΡΟΔΟΤΟΥ 'Ιστόρια. Βιβλ. β.

[i] *Har che non può di bella Donna il pianto?*
Et in lingua amorosa i dolci Detti?
Esser da vaghe Labbra amata Catena,
Che l' alme, à suo voler, prende et affrena.
                                             Tasso.

[k] Diodorus Siculus. Biblioth. Lib. i.

Sect. 9. it *now*, exactly such as *Homer* ascribes to his Heroine's *Anodyne* :

Νηπενθὲς, ἀχολόν τε, Κακῶν τ' ἐπιληθὲς ἁπάντων.

Pow'rful to banish Grief, to calm our Ire,
And sweet Oblivion bring of every Ill.

It is not much above a Century and a half, since a young Physician, who proved afterwards very eminent in his Profession, went down to *Egypt* with the *Venetian* Consul, whose usual Residence was then at *Gran-Cairo*. He staid there some Years, and after his Return to *Italy*, published the Observations he had made, in a Treatise *De Medicinâ Ægyptiorum*. He has a Chapter in it, of the Medicines which that People swallow *for pleasure* ; to elevate their Fancies, and make them imagine themselves in Groves and Gardens, and other Places of Delight. The first mentioned is the *Affion*, (our common *Opium*) *Quo devorato*, says the Physician, *referunt, Homines hilares admodum evadere, multæque ac varia loqui, fortioresquè ad quæcunque obeunda munera sibi videri: Præterea, subdormientes hortos etiam & viridaria multa, arboribus, herbis, ac floribus variis perbellè ornata spectare.*

The *first* of these are the very Virtues of *Homer*'s Opiate: And to shew that he knew the *Place* where it grew, as well as the Persons

who

who uſed it, *Diodorus*, after he has told that Sect.9.·
Thon and *Polydamna* were *Thebans*, immediately ſubjoins, that the Ladies of *Dioſpolis* (the
ancient *Thebes*) had the Honour of the Invention : And the Phyſician, as if he had travelled with him, adds to his former Account,
" *Hunc ſuccum, quo omnes utuntur, ex locis*
" Saieth, *ubi olim* THEBARUM *erat Urbs*
" *præclariſſima deferunt.*" It is true, they uſe
Opiates for pleaſure all over the *Levant* ; but
by the beſt Accounts of them, they had them
originally from *Egypt* [1]; and *this* one appears
plainly to be a Production of that Country ;
and a Cuſtom, which your Lordſhip ſees can
be traced from *Homer* to *Auguſtus*'s Reign, (under whom *Diodorus* lived) and from thence to
the Age preceding our own.

IT IS indeed natural to ſuppoſe even *now*,
when we hear any one talking of another
Country, deſcribing the Places and Perſons,
and telling an exact Story of any Occurrence
in it, with a number of minute Circumſtances ;
it is natural, I ſay, to ſuppoſe, that the Man
who talks in this manner *muſt have been* in that
Country. The Account of *Polydamna*'s Preſent is very particular ; and yet ſhe is not the
only *Egyptian* Acquaintance of the *Grecian*
Beauty

---

[1] All over the Eaſt, they call the fineſt ſort of their Opium,
Miſti, and *Meſeri,* which is to ſay, *Egyptian :* For *Egypt* is
called *Miſti,* as far as the *Indies.* It is a Corruption of *Meſeri,*
which is plainly from *Mizraim,* the old Name of *Egypt.* See
Jac. Bontius de Medicinâ Indorum, Lib. iii, *Cap.* 4.

Sect. 9. Beauty recorded by *Homer*. She had another,
" ALCANDRA, the Wife of *Polybus*, who
" dwelt likewife in the *Egyptian Thebes*, the
" richeft City then in the World. Her Huf-
" band, *Polybus*, made a Prefent to *Menelaus*
" of two Silver-Baths, two Tripods, and ten
" Talents of Gold : and the Lady made a
" feparate Prefent to *Helen* of a golden Spindle,
" and a Work-Bafket of Silver, of an oval
" Form, gilt round the Edges ᵐ."

THE happy Concurrence of Circumftances
in this Obfervation has tempted me to put
them together : But any Perfon who reads *Homer* with a tolerable Tafte of ancient Manners,
will find other Marks of his having been in
Egypt no lefs convincing.

No *Traveller* who does not defcribe a Country of defign, has given more Hints of his
knowing its Nature and Situation ⁿ. He feldom mentions *Sailing*, but he names *Egypt* as
the Place of the greateft *Refort*. When *Ulyffes*
appears to the Wooers in the figure of a poor
old Man, the moft probable Lye he can tell
of the way he was reduced to Poverty, is,
That,

ᵐ ——— ἀργύρεον Τάλαρον ——— τὸν δὲ ἔδωκε
ΑΛΚΑΝΔΡΗ Πολύβοιο δάμαρ, ὃς ἐναί ἐν ΘΗΒΗΣ
ΑΙΓΥΠΤΙΗΣ, ὅθι πλεῖστα δόμοις ἐνὶ κλήματα κεῖται·
Ὃς Μενελάῳ δῶκε δύ' ἀργυρέας Ἀσαμίνθας,
Δοιοὺς δὲ Τρίποδας, δέκα δὲ χρυσοῖο Τάλαντα.
Χωρὶς δ' αὖ ἘΛΕΝΗ Ἄλοχῷ πόρε κάλλιμα δῶρα·
Χρυσέην τ' Ἠλακάτην, Τάλαρόν θ' ὑπόκυκλον ὄπασσεν
Ἀργύρεον· χρυσῷ δ' ἐπὶ χείλεα κεκράαντο.   Ὀδυσ. δ.

ⁿ See *Strabo*, Book I.

That, as was the Cuſtom of the ancient *Greeks*, Sect. 9. he had gone a *privateering* into *Egypt*; where he was taken, and ſold for a *Slave* [o]. He had told the *ſame* Tale more particularly to his Servant *Eumeus* before, and even ſpecified the *preciſe Time* it takes to ſail, with a favourable Gale, from *Crete* to the only *Egyptian* Port; (πεμπ7αῖοι ἱκόμεϑα) *in five Days.*

WHEN *Antinoüs*, one of the Wooers, is diſpleaſed with *Ulyſſes*'s Behaviour, the firſt Threat that offers to him, is, *to ſend him as a Slave to* Egypt *or* Cyprus [p]. And in his Hymn to *Bacchus*, the Poet repeats the *ſame two Places* as the Common Market for *Slaves*. He takes occaſion to give a nice Deſcription of the Pirates Method of ſcouring the Coaſt, from the Story of their having once ſeized upon *Bacchus*, as ſome noble Youth, for whom they expected an immenſe Ranſom: After they had dragged the God aboard, he makes the Captain of the Crew ſay to the Steerſman, (who was beginning to ſuſpect that their Captive would prove troubleſome, and was adviſing to let him go)

Mind you the Wind, and hoiſt aloft the Sail;
Haul in your Tackle: We'll *ſee to the Priſ'ner;*
He'll

[o] Ὅς (Ζεύς) μ᾽ ἅμα ληῑσ7ῆρσι πολυπλάγκ7οισιν ἀνῆκεν
ΑΙΓΥΠΤΟΝ δ᾽ ἰέναι, δολιχὴν ὁδὸν.——' Oδυσ. ρ.

[p] Be gone, ſays he,
Μὴ τάχα πικρὴν ΑΙΓΥΠΤΟΝ ᾗ ΚΥΠΡΟΝ ἵκηαι.
'Oδυσ. ρ.

Sect. 9. *He'll visit, as I judge,* Egypt *or* Cyprus,
Or sail the Northern Seas : ——*Unless he tell*
His Name and Quality, and Friend's Estate [q].

As to the Country itself, the Poet has made
his *Hero, Achilles,* (instructed perhaps by his
Father, or by the wise *Chiron* [r]) give a noble
Description of the *Metropolis,* Thebes; and
in the compass of a few Lines, has shewn
its *Form,* its *Wealth,* and *Policy* [s]. Nor is he
less acquainted with the Nature of the *Egyptian Soil,* and the various Productions of that
Land of Wonders [t]. He could scarcely hear
of the *Ethiopians* in any other place but *Egypt ;*
much less could he learn their *Situation,* and
the *Division* of their Tribes [u]; and less still,
that they were among the ancientest of Nations, and the oldest and purest *Votaries of the
Gods* [w].

These

[q] Copied by *Ovid,* in his *Metamorph.* Lib. iii.

[r] Pellusium, oppidum nobile, qued Peleus, Achillis Pater
dicitur condidisse.   Ammian. Marcellin. Lib. xxii.

[s] Iliad. i.   [t] Odyss. Δ.

Ἀιγυπτίη, τῇ πλεῖςα φέρει ζείδωρος ἄρερα

Φάρμακα, πολλὰ μὲν ἐσθλὰ μεμιγμένα, πολλὰ δὲ λυγρά.

Some of those I take to have been, the Μύερν λεύκον Ἀιγύπιον
εὐῶδες, so often mentioned by *Hippocrates ;* the Σέσινον μύερν, in
the same Author: It was an Extract of Lilies used by the Ladies, and retains the *Egyptian* or *Asiatic* Name, from *Susan,* a
Lily. *Hippocrates* likewise mentions the Ἀκάνθα Ἀιγυπία, the
Βόλζιον Ἀιγυπίον, the ΒάλανΘ' Ἀιγυπίος, the Ἀιγυπίη ςυπηνεία,
and even the ΑΙΓΥΠΤΙΟΣ ΟΠΟΣ itself. This last is
thrown out by a *various Reading,* or rather a Conjecture ; the
more improbable, that in another Place, he prescribes the
ΟΠΟΣ ΜΗΚΩΝΟΣ, and the ΜΗΚΩΝΙΟΝ ΥΠΝΩ-
ΤΙΚΟΝ.

[v] Iliad. i.   [w] Ibid.

THESE, *My Lord*, are some of the Presump- Sect. 9.
tions of *Homer's* having been in *Egypt*, which
are to be met with in his Works. They a-
mount not perhaps to a strict Proof; but if sur-
vey'd, as they stand in the *Author*, they carry
a high Probability, and will possibly leave but
little room for doubting, when we consider,
that he sailed with MENTES, a *Merchant* and
Ship-master; and that no considerable Trade
was carried on in *those days*, but with *Egypt*,
Phenicia, or *Cyprus* : They furnished the *chief*
Commodities then known ; *Greece* at that time
labouring under a great Ἀχρηματία [x], as *Thucydides* calls it, and having no Superfluities to
barter ; but fetching the little Wealth they had,
and the Beginnings of their Arts, from these
Fountains of Science and Government [y].

Now

[x] Want of Goods or Merchandize.

[y] The *Greek* Historians have been all condemned by *Bochart*,
a Man of very great Learning, for asserting, that the lower
Egypt was a Plain made out by the continual Congestion of the
Slime, which their wonderful River swept along, in its Course
thro' *Ethiopia* and the high Country. He has likewise chastised
Homer, who favours that Opinion in his Account of the Distance of the *Pharos* from the Land. He founds his own Opinion upon the small Alteration which the River has made upon
the *Egyptian* Coast, for Two thousand Years and upwards :
For it is so long since *Alexandria* was built, which still continues a Sea-port Town : And he sees no Reason, why it
should not be making constant Additions to the Land, if it had
ever made any. But there is a Reason why that Effect of the
River should cease. Where-ever the wide Communication of
the Sea, and the Agitation that is frequent on the Main Ocean,
is broken by the Intervention of *Promontories*, there Slime and
Mud, and all the Dregs of a mighty River, fall to the ground,
and settle; being neither driven by the Stream, now dissipated,
nor tossed by the Waves : and the Slime thus settled, will receive

Additions,

Seƈt. 9.　　Now if to ſo many Marks of *Homer's* being a Travᵉller, we join the Charaƈter given of him in *two* Words by a Man of the ſame Caſt, in what he calls το ΦΙΛΕΙΔΗΜΟΝ, ΚΑΙ ΤΟ ΦΙΛΕΚΔΗΜΟΝ ΤΟΥ ΠΟΙΗΤΟΥ ᶻ, *his Love of Knowledge and of Travelling*, we both increaſe the Probability of his having been in *Egypt*, and find a *Speƈtator* worthy of ſo auguſt a Scene: Here he might ſee, " What the " utmoſt Stretch of *Human Policy* is able to " perform:" He might ſee *Riches*, *Pleaſures*, and *Magnificence*, reconciled (as far as the Nature of things will allow) with *Safety* and *good Order*. Here was the nobleſt *Contraſt*, and moſt inſtruƈtive Oppoſition, that *any* Conjuncture can offer to our View: He came from a Country where *Nature* governed; and went to another, where from the higheſt Atchievement to the ſmalleſt Aƈtion in Life, every thing was direƈted by *ſettled Rules*, and a *digeſted Policy* ª.

HERE

Additions, as long aɔ it is proteƈted by ſuch powerful Bulwarks, *and no longer.* The ſame River, if it find any Rocks at a ſmall diſtance from its Mouth, will heap Earth upon them, form an Iſland, and continue to increaſe it, until it leave only Space ſufficient for a free Egreſs to itſelf, and the natural Play of the Waves on either hand, as they are direƈted by the adjacent Shore. The Mouths of the *Ganges*, the *Euphrates*, the *Danube*; and nearer home, the *Mæander* and the *Po*, are all Proofs of what is aſſerted above.

ª Strabo, Geograph. Lib. i.

ª 'Ου ϒδ μόνον τᾶ χρηματίζειν ἢ κείνειν ἦν καιρὸς ἀειομίνΘ, ἀλλὰ ϗ τᾶ ΠΕΡΙΠΑΤΗΣΑΙ, ϗ τᾶ ΛΟΥΣΑΣΘΑΙ, ϗ ΚΟΙΜΗΘΗΝΑΙ ΜΕΤΑ ΤΗΣ ΓΥΝΑΙΚΟΣ, ϗ καθόλυ 7 κⁿ 4 βίου πραϑομίνων ἁπάντων.

Διοδ᠂ Σικιλ᠂ Βιβλιοθ᠂ ӕ᠂
Their

HERE was a *People* so throughly moulded Sect. 9.
to their Government, that *Education* seemed
to have taken place of *Nature*; and by a Depth
of Thought in the Legislature, was laid so *true*,
and made to take such *hold* of the Passions,
that it seem'd rather to *create* than *direct* them.
This appeared long after *Homer*'s days, in their
Tenaciousness of their own Customs, under a
frequent Change of Masters [b], and their in-
fecting all the Nations that learned their Religion or Politicks from them, with the same
Stubbornness and *Bigotry*.

BUT when our Poet went down to *Egypt*,
they had received no Shocks from the *Persian* or *Macedonian* Power: They were living
in Peace and Splendour; flourishing in all the
Arts they chose to encourage; reverenced for
their Wisdom, and renowned in Arms. *Here*
he might fill a capacious Mind, and satiate
that Thirst of Knowledge, which is the Characteristick of the greatest Souls. In *Greece* he
must have learned many *Allegories*, while he
exercised his Profession; but here he would see
their Source and Design: He would be instructed in the *Rise* and *Use* of the Doctrines he had
imbibed: He would gain an Ease and Exact-
L 2 ness

Their very *Musick* and *Sculpture* was circumscribed by Law,
and continued invariable, says *Plato*, for many Thousands of
Years. Legum, Lib. ii.
  [b] Ægyptii plerique subfusculi sunt et atrati, magisque mœsti-
ores.——Controversi, et reposcones acerrimi.——Nulla tor-
mentorum vis inveniri adhuc potuit, quæ——invitum elicere
potuit, ut nomen proprium dicat. Ammian. Marcellin. Lib. xxii.

Sect. 9. ness in applying them, and be able to raise his
Moral to that stupendous Height we so justly
admire. For what might we not expect from
the Affluence and Fire of his Imagery, when
ranged and governed by a *Mind* now *Master* of
the Subject?

I AM very sensible, that *Homer's Mythology* is but little understood; or, to express it
better, is *little felt*: and for this reason, the
Effects of his *Egyptian* Education are lost upon
the greater part of his Readers. There are but
few who consider his *Divine Persons* in any
other Light, than as so many *groundless Fictions*,
which he made at pleasure, and might employ indifferently; giving to *Neptune*, for instance, the Work done by *Apollo*, and introducing *Venus* to perform what he now ascribes
to *Minerva*. But it is mere want of Perception.
His GODS are all *natural Feelings of the several Powers of the Universe*: or, as the Bishop
of *Thessalonica* calls them, " ΕΝΝΟΙΩΝ ΕΥΓΕ-
" ΝΩΝ ΣΚΙΑΙ ΕΙΣΙΝ Η ΠΑΡΑΠΕΤΑΣΜΑΤΑ,
" *Shadowings, or Wrappers of noble Sentiments.*"
They are not a Bundle of extravagant Stories;
but the most delicate, and, at the same time,
the most *majestick Method* of expressing the
Effects of those natural Powers, which have the
greatest Influence upon *our Bodies* and *Minds* ᶜ.

THERE

ᶜ Πᾶς δ᾽ ὁ, περὶ τ̄ θεῶν λόγος ἀρχαίας ἐξετάζει δόξας κὴ μύ-
θυς, ἀπιθομένων τ̄ παλαίων ἃς εἶχον ΕΝΝΟΙΑΣ ΦΥΣΙ-
ΚΑΣ

THERE is scarcely a Page in *Homer's* Poems, Sect. 9. where we meet not with Proofs of this Asser- ᔕᔕ tion; and if we confider the Stroke it muft have in Poetry, we fhall find, that *here* is an Advantage for Defcription loft beyond retriev- ing: When to thefe *natural Senfations*, the Be- lief of *Sanctity* was joined, and the Apprehen- fions of a *Divine Prefence* was filling the Mind, the Image would be *irrefiftible*, and raife fuch *Affections*, as beft account for this Poet's being *deïfy'd* by the Ancients [d], and *doated* on by the Moderns.

IT MAY look odd to fay, that even the *Ignorance* of thefe Ages contributed not a little to the Excellency of his Porms: But it was certainly fo. The Gods were not called in doubt in thofe days; *Philofophers*, and fpecu- lative incredulous People had not fprung up, and decry'd Miracles and fupernatural Stories; they rather made it their bufinefs to invent and propagate them, for the Good of Society, and the keeping Mankind in order:

L 3

Ex-

ΚΑΣ *πος̃* τ̃ *πρᾳγμάτων*, ϰ̀ *πρς·ιθέντων* ἀ↵ τοῖς λόγοις τ̃ Μ Υ Θ Ο Ν. Στραβ. Βιβ. Ι.

And the excellent *Vincenzo Gravina : Perloche gli antichi Poeti con uno medefimo Colore, efprimevano fentimenti* teologici, fifici e morali *: Colle quali fcienze, comprefe in un folo corpo, veftito di maniere popolari, allargavano il campo ad alti e profondi Mifteri.*
Della Ragion Poetica, Lib. i. § 8.

[d] ΕΙ ΘΕΟΣ ΕΣΤΙΝ ΟΜΗΡΟΣ, ΕΝ ΑΘΑΝΑΤΟΙΣΙ ΣΕΒΕΣΘΩ, ΕΙ Δ᾽ ΑΥ ΜΗ ΘΕΟΣ ΕΣΤΙ, ΝΟΜΙΖΕΣΘΩ ΘΕΟΣ ΕΙΝΑΙ.
Ἐπίγραμμ. Βιβ. δ.

Expedit esse Deos, &, ut expedit, esse putemus :
Dentur in antiquos Thura Merumque focos e.

By *this* means, here too, the Poet described
from *Realities* ; I mean, such things as had
a double Weight, by being firmly believed,
and generally received for *sacred Truths :* And
he must have had a good *Faith*, or at least a
strong Feeling of them himself, to be able to
tell them with such Spirit and Complacency.

ONE of the wildest Stories in the whole
Iliad, if taken literally, is in the very beginning
of the fifteenth Book ; where *Jupiter* reminds
his Spouse, how, upon occasion of a former
Quarrel, "He had fastened two Anvils to her
" Feet, and twisted a golden permanent Chain
" about her Arms ; and so mounting her aloft,
" had hung her up between the Clouds and
" the Sky." And yet this Legend was so
well believed, "That in the Neighbourhood
" of *Troy* they *shewed* the two *Lumps of Iron*
" which had been hung about the Goddess,
" and which *Jupiter* informs us he let fall
" there, in order to give future Ages a certain
" Proof of that memorable Transaction f."

WOULD not *this* tempt one to conclude,
that the *Commonalty* in all Ages is the *same ?*
always

---

e Ovid. de Arte Amandi, Lib. i.
f ——————————Μύδϱις δ' ἐνὶ Τϱοίη
Κάϐϐαλον, ὄφϱα πέλοιτο ϗ ἐσσομένοισι πυθέϛαι.
Καὶ δείκνυται, φασὶν ὑπὸ τ πεϱιηγητῶν, ὅτι ταῦτοι Μύδϱι,
ὡς ἀνωτέϱω ΑΚΜΟΝΑΣ ἵππν.
'Ευϛαθ. εἰς την Ο 'Ραψωδ. 'Ιλιαδ.

always ready to swallow a wondrous Tale, be Sect. 9. it ever so gross or senseless, and to believe a Metaphor in its literal Meaning. Our modern *Sages* are indeed widely different from the ancient : *They*, as I observed, employed their Wit in *composing* sacred Allegories, and their Authority ᵹ among the People in supporting them. They look'd upon them as the great *Bridle* of the Multitude, to whose Passions they knew it was necessary to speak, without pretending to govern them by *Reason* and *Philosophy*. But many of the *Moderns*, who would fain be thought wise, employ their Talents and Learning, such as they are, to very different Purposes.

But what Use soever may be made of it, it is certain that *Fiction* and *Lying* are inseparable from Poetry. This was the first Profession of the *Muses*; as they told *Hesiod* one day they appeared to him, while he fed his Lambs in a Vale of *Helicon* : " *Shepherd,* said " they,

L 4

Ἴδμεν

ᵹ *Plato* having first mentioned what he calls his ΤΟ ΟΝ ἀεὶ, γένεσιν δ' ὐκ ἔχον· and Ο ΓΕΡΟΝ ΩΣ τι, ἠ̓ ΩΝ, ἠ̓ ΕΣΟΜΕΝΟΣ μόνℨ·, with great Modesty adds, Περὶ δὲ τ͞ ἄλλων διαιρόταν ἐιπεῖν, ἠ̓ γνῶναι ἢ γένεσιν ΜΕΙΖΟΝ ἢ κῶθ' ἡμᾶς. Πειστέον δὲ τοῖς ἐιρηκόσιν ἔμπροσθεν ΕΚΓΟΝΟΙΣ μὲν ΘΕΩΝ ἔσιν, ὡς ἔφασαν· σαφῶς δὲ τε τές τε αὐτῶν προγόνυς ἐιδόσι. Ἀδύνατον ἒν τοῖς Θεῶν παισὶν ἀπισεῖν, καί-περ ΑΝΕΥ τι ἐικότων ἠ̓ ἀναγκαίων ἀποδείξεων λέγυσι, ἀλλ' ὡς ὀικεῖα φάσκυσιν ἀπαγγέλλειν, ΕΠΟΜΕΝΟΥΣ ΤΩ ΝΟΜΩ, πιστευτέον.   *Timaeᵹ.*

Sect. 9.

Ἴδμεν ψεύδεα πολλὰ λέγειν ἐτύμοισιν ὁμοῖα :
Ἴδμεν, δ'υτ' ἐθέλομεν, ἀληθέα μυθήσαθαι.

'Tis ours false Tales to frame, resembling true ;
And ours, t' unfold the Truth itself to Men.

" Then they gave him a fair Rod, a Shoot
" of verdant Laurel, breathed into him a di-
" vine Song, and taught him to celebrate
" things *past*, and things *to come*."

ANOTHER Ancient, of a lofty Strain and
unbounded Flight, has made a sort of *Apology* for this part of his Profession: He has
founded it upon the Nature of Mankind, of
which he seems to have had the strongest and
most forcible Perceptions of any Poet. It is
in the Story of *Pelops*; ——— ' the Love
' that *Neptune* bore him after he was taken
' out of the Kettle, where he had been boil-
' ed, and all the Pieces of his Body put to-
' gether, without losing a bit, save the Top
' of one Shoulder, which they made up with
' another of Ivory.' Then most *naturally* he
adds [h], " *Wonders are every where : and still,*
" ——*some way,* —— *an artful Tale,* —— *dress'd*
" *up with various Lyes, beguiles the Thoughts*
" *of mortal Men, and pleases more than Truth.*"

THE

[h] Ἦ θαῦμα τὰ πολλά
Καί που τὰ κὴ βερτῶν φρένα,
Ὑπὲρ ⳨ ἀληθῆ λόγον,
Δεδα δαλμένοι ψεύδεσι ποικίλοις
Ἐξαπτῶσι ΜΥΘΟΙ.
Πινδίρ ᾽Ολυμπ. Α.

THE *eloquent Attic* Moralift is of the fame Sect. 9. Opinion: " *Thofe*, fays the Orator [i], who would ∿
" write or paint any thing agreeable to the
" *Vulgar*, fhould not chufe the moft profit-
" able, but the moft fabulous Subjects. For
" this reafon, *Homer*, in his *Epic*, and the
" Inventers of *Tragedy*, deferve our Admi-
" ration. They obferved this original Biafs
" in Mankind, and have adapted their *Poe-*
" *try* to it. *Homer* has wrapt up the Wars
" and Conflicts of the *Heroes* in Fable; and
" the Tragedians, in the publick Games,
" entertain us with the fame Fables, by Ge-
" fture and Action."

IT was indeed a very extraordinary Project of our ingenious Countryman, *To write
an Epic Poem*, without mixing Allegory, or
allowing the fmalleft Fiction throughout the
Compofure. It was like lopping off a Man's
Limb, and then putting him upon running
Races; tho' it muft be owned, that the Performance [k] fhews with what Ability he could
have acquitted himfelf, had he been found and
entire.

BUT WE have at prefent fo little Fiction,
and fo much Poetry, that it will not be amifs
to hear, among the reft, *Socrates*'s Senfe of the
matter. He had been often commanded in
his Sleep, to apply himfelf to *Mufick* : At firft,
he

[i] 'ΙΣΟΚΡΑΤ· πρὸς Νικοκλέα·
[k] Sir *W. Davenant*'s GONDIBERT.

Sect. 9. he underftood the Admonition as if it related to *Philofophy*; *That* being, in his Opinion,
the trueft Harmony, which confifted *in the
Numbers and Meafures of Life.* But at laft,
being in Prifon, he bethought himfelf, that it
was fafeft for him to apply to the common
Poetry. Wherefore he firft fet about compo-
fing an Hymn to *Apollo*, whofe Feaft was then
celebrating : But upon a little farther Reflection, " That a Poet, if he would be. *really*
" *fuch*, muft *make*, and *feign*, and not juft
" write *Difcourfes in Metre* [1] ;" and having no
Talent at *Allegory* himfelf, he took the firft
Fable he remembred of *Efop's*, and put it in
Verfe.

THERE is not a Circumftance of this little Story, which affords not a Maxim to a Poet,
But it feems ftrange, that a Man fo capable
and quick-fighted in Characters, and fo great
a Mafter of Irony. as *Socrates*, fhould have no
Genius for Mufick [m], and be barren in *Mythology.* I believe he *reafoned* too much; was
apt to canvafs his Fancies, and not be indulgent enough to his *Imagination*, which is the
prime Faculty of a Mythologift. It is this,
that diftinguifhes the *real Poet*; and one Stroke
of its *plaftick Power* difcovers him more, than
the greateft Magnificence of Words, and Pomp
of Defcription.

WE

[1] Ἐννοήσας ὅτι τ̀ Ποιητὴν δέοι, ἔιπερ μέλλοι ΠΟΙΗΤΗΣ
ἔιναι, ποιεῖν ΜΥΘΟΥΣ, ἀλλ᾽ οὐ ΛΟΓΟΥΣ.
Πλάτων᾽ Φαίδων.

[m] *Plato,* Πολιτίας Γ.

. WE are told by the Author of the beauti- Sect. 9.
ful Essay upon the Pleasures of the Imagination ⁿ, "That Mankind receive more Delight
" from the *Fancy* than from the *Understand-*
" *ing.*" Few are capable of Pleasures purely
intellectual; and every Creature is capable of
being pleased or disquieted in some degree by
the *Fancy.* Hence, plain naked Truth is either not perceived, or soon disrelished. But
the Man who can give his Ideas *Life* and *Co-*
louring, and render the subtil Relations and
mutual Influences of natural Causes sensible
and striking; who can bestow upon them a
human Appearance, and then weave them into
a strange and passionate Story; to *him* we listen
with Wonder, and greedily learn his soothing
Tale. We find a pleasure in comparing it
with the *Truth* which it covers, and in consi-
dering the Resemblance it bears to the several
Parts of the *Allegory.*

ORPHEUS had never been said to have
charmed the wildest Beasts of the Woods, and
to have made the rigid Oaks keep time to
his Numbers, had he simply told the Import
of his Song: Had he acquainted his savage
Audience, " that *Time* and *Space* were the
" ancientest of things; that they had brought
" forth many wild and strange Productions,
" arising from the jarring Natures and un-
" couth Combinations of the various *Seeds* of
                                  " *Being*;

ⁿ *Spectator*, Numb. 411.

" *Being*; but at length, *in Time*, the Hea-
" vens appeared, with the Air, the Earth,
" and Seas; which were the laſt of Things,
" Time having neither been able to deſtroy
" them (as it had done its former Productions)
" nor to make additions to them, and bring
" forth the like." Such Doctrine as this had
found no admiſſion into the Minds, nor welcome from the Fancy of the uncultivated Crowd:
They could receive little Pleaſure from the Narration, and be impreſſed with no Reverence
for the Subject.

But when, after ſtriking his *Lyre*, and
ſoftening every ruder Thought, he took up another Strain, and began to unfold the ancient
Reign of *boary Saturn*, the Marvels of the *Golden
Age*, and the ſtrange Relation of his *Progeny*;
" How the old Monarch was married to *Ops*
" or *Rhea*, and had by her many Children;
" *Theſe* the cruel Father himſelf devoured ſoon
" after they were born; until at length ſhe
" brought forth *Jupiter* and *Juno*, *Ceres* and
" *Neptune*, who rebelled againſt their voracious
" Parent, made the beneficent *Jupiter* King,
" and deprived *Saturn* for ever, both of the
" Power to deſtroy his new Offspring, or yet
" to beget any more :" *It was then* that the
ſtubborn Multitude opened their Hearts to the
wondrous Tale; and with a pleaſing Amazement received his Sayings: They conceived a
high Reverence for their Teacher, and were
                                    ſtruck

ftruck with an Awe and Dread of the Deities Sect. 9. which he fung.

I AM under a neceffity of having recourfe to Examples, becaufe the Subject is of a nature fo ticklifh and delicate, as not to admit of a direct Definition: For if ever the *Je ne fçais quoi* was rightly applied, it is to the *Powers* of Mythology, and the *Faculty* that produces it. To go about to defcribe it, would be like attempting to define *Infpiration*, or that *Glow of Fancy* and *Effufion of Soul*, which a Poet feels while in his *Fit* ; A Senfation fo ftrong, that they exprefs it only by Exclamations, Adjurings, and Rapture!

> *Auditis? An me ludit amabilis*
> *Infania? Audire & videor pios*
> *Errare per Lucos, amœnæ*
> *Quas & Aquæ fubeunt & Auræ!*

WHEN a Favourite of the Mufes is in this condition, *Nature* appears in her gayeft Drefs; The nobleft Objects come in view; They turn out their beauteous Sides; He fees their various Pofitions, and ftays for nothing but *Refemblance* to join them together. The Torrent of the Poetick Paffion is too rapid to fuffer *Confideration*, and drawing of Confequences: If the Images are but ftrong, and have a happy Collufion, the Mind joins them together with inconceivable Avidity, and feels the Joy of the Difcharge,

Sect. 9. charge, like throwing off a Burthen, or Delive-
rance from a Pressure [o].

BUT at the same time, this *Force* and *Collu-
sion* of Imagery is susceptible of very different
Meanings, and may be viewed in various,
and even *opposite* Lights : It often takes its
rise from a Likeness which hardly occurs to a
cool Imagination; and which we are apt to
take for downright Nonsense, when we are
able to find no Connexion between the strange
Comparison and its intended Object. It is, in
reality, the next thing to *Madness*; obscure
and ambiguous, with intermixed Flashes of
Truth, and Intervals of Sense and Design [p].
There is *Lycophron's* CASSANDRA, for instance; an admirable Imitation of a *Prophetick Fury*, which is not so obscure for being a
Prediction (having, like other Heathen Prophecies [q], foretold things that had fallen
out before it was wrote) : But it is clouded
by the dark Manner of hinting at *Men* and
Things, in such Resemblances and Allusions, as
render

---

[o] At Phœbi nondum patiens, immanis in Antro
Bacchatur Vates; magnum si pectore possit
Excussisse Deum   Tanto magis ille fatigat
Os rabidum, fera Corda domans, fingitque *premendo*.
          Virgil. Æneid. Lib. vi.

[p] Ἐςὶ δὲ φύσει ἡ Ποιητικὴ ἡ σύμπασα αἰνιγματώδης, κ̀ ὐ τῦ
προσηχόντος ἀνδρὸς ξυνεῖναι. Ἔτι δὲ πρὸς τὸ φύσει τοιαυτὴ
εἶναι, ὅταν λαβεῖται ἀνδρὸς φθονερῦ τε, κ̀ μὴ βελομένε ἡμῖν
ἐνδείκνυσθαι, ἀλλ᾽ ἀποκρύπτεσθαι ὅτι μάλισα τὴν ἑαυτῦ σοφίαν,
ὑπερφυῶς δὲ τὸ χρῆμα ὡς δύσγνοσον φαίνεται, ὅ τι ποτὲ νοῦς τε
ἔχεσθ᾽ αὐτᾶ.   ΠΛΑΤΩΝ. Ἀλκιβιάδ. β.

[q] See *Aristotle's Rhetor.* Lib. iii. § 17. of *Epimenides.*

render it one continued Train of *wild* and *da-*Sect. 9.
ring Metaphor.

But it is time, *My Lord*, to look back, and
remember that we are treading upon *enchant-*
ed Ground; for fo is every Inch that belongs
to the Poets: And as we have lately been informed of certain Countries where every thing
in Nature is *reverfed*, it is exactly the Cafe
here, where a little Folly is preferable to the
deepeft Wifdom, and Perfons of cool Senfe
are incapable of the higheft Honours: Nor
have the *Poffeffed* any caufe to complain,
while they may comfort themfelves that they
are not without Company ; and thofe of the
moft eminent of Mankind. " *That* there is
" a Grain of Folly incident to *Great Minds*,"
is an Obfervation not entirely confined to
Poetry; but extending itfelf to Perfons that
excel in every Art and Character of Life: The
fame Flow of Spirits, and Energy of Thought,
which enable them to excel in Science, and
reach the *Heights* of their Profeffion, hurry-
ing them often beyond the *common Meafures*
of ordinary Life ; by which alone the Vulgar
judge of Wifdom and Folly. In *natural*
Knowledge it makes a *Democritus* or an *Ar-*
chimedes, who were fometimes thought a little crazy by their Countrymen. But when
it was applied to what *They* thought *divine*
Matters, it affumed a more venerable Habit and
feverer Mien: It then required *Submiffion* and
Obe-

Sect. 9. *Obedience* [r]: Yet still, it preserved something of the Air and Look of the original Passion ; something of the *ecstatick Manner* of an agitated Mind. This is so true, that those who were inclined to falsify the Character, and wanted to pass themselves upon Mankind for the truly inspired, were obliged to adopt likewise the *Appearance*, and affect a maddish Behaviour, to give a Sanction to the *Cheat* [s].

WHAT may be the *Appearances*, or Aspects of Things natural or divine, which have the virtue thus to shake our Frame, and raise such a Commotion in the Soul, I will not so much as enquire: The Search, I should suspect, would be fruitless, if not *irreverent* [t]: It would be like prying into the Author of *Fairy-Favours*, which deprives the curious Enquirer of his present Enjoyment, while the *courted Phantom* mocks his eager Grasp, or presents him with a Turf,

[r] Sic fieri jubet ipse *Deus* ; sic magna Sacerdos
   Est mihi *divino* vaticinata *Sono* :
   Hæc ubi Bellonæ motu est agitata, nec acrem
   Flammam, non *amens* verbera torta timet.
   Ipsa bipenne suos cædit violenta lacertos,
   Sanguineque effuso spargit inulta Deam :
   Statque latus præfixa verû, stat saucia pectus,
   Et canit eventus quos Dea magna monet.
                      Alb. Tibul. Eleg. 1, 6.

[s] ———Bona pars non Ungues ponere curat,
   Non Barbam ; secreta petit loca, Balnea vitat ;
   Nanciscetur enim pretium nomenque *Poetæ*, &c.
                   Horat. de Arte Poët.

[t] Καθόλε μὲν γὰ ἐν ταῖς ἱσορυμέναις ΜΥΘΟΛΟΓΙΑΙΣ ἐκ ἐκ παντὸς τέρτε πικρῶς τὴν ἀλήθειαν ἐξετάσεον.
                  Διοδ. Σικελ. Βιβλ. δ.

Turf, or Stone, inftead of a Goddefs. The Sect. 9.
Objects, they fay, of this Paffion, difcover ～～.
themfelves, like a *coy Beauty* [u], but by halves;
it is well if you obtain a Side-Glance, or a
paffing Smile: They cannot bear to be ftared
at, and far lefs to be criticized, and taken to
pieces: It is unlawful to doubt of their Charms,
and the ready way to elude their Force, and
rob ourfelves of the delightful Aftonifhment.
But thus far perhaps we may prefume to carry
our Enquiry without offence, and venture to
fay, *That* the original Caufe of this Paffion
muft be fome *wondrous fublime thing*, fince it
produces fuch admired Effects; Its Dictates, in
many places, are received with profound Submiffion, and the Perfons touched with it are
held in high veneration.

MODERN *Hiftory* informs us of certain
Countries, where they pay a devout Regard
to *mad People*. They look upon them as favoured with fome *nearer Afpects* of heavenly
things than are allowed to other Men, and
as having fomewhat about them *facred* and
divine. As I do not pretend to account for
this ftrange Opinion, I can only as it were
guefs, by parallel Cafes, what may be the Reafon of it: And without looking fo far back as
the *prophetic Sibyls*, or the truth-telling, but
difregarded *Caffandra*, we find abundance of
Examples

---

[u] *Non copri fue Bellezze, e non l' efpofe.* Taffo.

M

Sect. 9. Examples in later Antiquity, of the Deference
paid to the Ecſtatick Race. The ancient
Greeks have expreſſed the Senſe they had of
their Condition, by the very Name they gave
them w : From its Origin we know how inſeparable they thought the Symptoms of *Mythology* and *Madneſs.* They ſaw the Perſons
under either Paſſion, neither looking nor ſpeak-
ing like *other Mortals* : They were amazed at
their Change of *Voice* and *Feature*; and could
not perſuade themſelves, but that they muſt
be actuated by ſome higher *Genius* than was
competent to Mankind.

B u t it was not only the *Appearance* that
ſtruck them ; They were led into the ſame
way of thinking, by the imagined *Effects*
of this Paſſion. Some of the Proficients in
it, they thought capable to inform them of
the *Will of Heaven*, and deſcribe the Deeds
of Heaven-born Heroes; Others of them, to
foretell what would happen *on Earth*; and
eaſily inferred the Sacredneſs of the Cauſe
from its wonderful and beneficent Influence.
They were not able to imagine that mere
Humanity could penetrate into the Depths
of Futurity, or unravel that Combination of
Cauſes, which they called *Chance :* Their
acuteſt Obſervers could diſcover no Path to
guide them thro' the *Abyſs of Ages*, to the
Fates of Families and Nations latent in the
Womb

w MANTIΣ.

Womb of Time [x]: Of course therefore, they Sect. 9.
admired the darkest Hint given by an *Oracle*,
and received the most distant Notice of an approaching Event, as a Message from *Heaven*.
" We reap, says the Philosopher, notable Ad-
" vantages from *Madness*, which comes to us
" as a Gift of the Gods. There is, for in-
" stance, the Prophetess of *Delphi*, and the
" Priestesses of *Dodona*, who in their Mad-
" ness have done great and signal Services to
" *Greece*, both of a publick and private na-
" ture, but little or nothing *when in their*
" *Wits*. It would be tedious to enter upon
" the Story of the *Sibyls*, or tell of many
" others, who, under the Power of a furious
" divining Spirit, have forewarned numbers
" of People of things that were to come. At
" times there fall upon certain Families some
" cruel Distempers, or other severe Affliction,
" to punish them for the Crimes of their
" Progenitors; but if any one of them is
" seized with this *ecstatick Spirit*, and begin
" to *prophesy*, a *Cure* is found : They fly to
" Prayers and Holy Ceremonies, and light
" upon certain expiatory and mystick Rites
" which free the Person thus inspired, and
" is a standing Remedy in all such Cases to
" Posterity.

M 2 " BUT

[x] Πρήγματ@ ἀπρήκτε χαλεπώτατόν ἐσι τελευτὰν
Γνῶναι, ὅπως μέλλει τέ]ο Θεὸς τελέσαι.
Ὀργὴ γὸ τέ]αται· πεὸ δὲ τῷ μέλλον]Θ. ἐσοχ
Ὀυ ξυνετὰ ϑνητῆς πιερΐ ἀμηχανίης.

ΘΕΟΓΝ. ΓΝΩΜΑΙ.

Sect 9.   " B u t the moſt *beautiful Madneſs,* and
" amiable Poſſeſſion, is, when the *Love* of the
" *Muſes* ſeizes upon a ſoft and ſuſceptible
" Mind: It is then that it exalts the Soul,
" and throwing it into Ecſtaſies, makes it
" break forth in *Hymns* and *Songs,* or other
" Strains of Poeſy, and at once celebrate the
" high Atchievements of ancient Times, and
" inſtruct the Generations to come. This is
" ſo certain, that whoever he be that pretends
" to the *Favours* of the *Muſe,* without parta-
" king of this Madneſs, from an Opinion per-
" haps, *That Art alone is ſufficient to make a*
" *Poet,* he may aſſure himſelf that he will *fail*
" in his *Character*; his Work will be lame;
" and while the Productions of the *inſpired*
" *ecſtatick Train* are read and admired, his
" *ſober* Performance will ſink in Oblivion y."

LET us acquieſce in this Sentence, *My Lord,*
in ſo far as it regards Poetry; and after a fruit-
leſs Attempt or two, get looſe at laſt from an
infectious Subject.

y *Plato* in *Phædro.*

S E C T.

SECT. X.

I HAVE somewhere read of a famous Painter, Sect. 10. who, to give proof of his Art, had painted 〰 a *sleeping Satyr*; that after the first Design was finished, he began to think it might be proper to diversify and enliven it, with the addition of a Country Boy standing aside and gazing at the Creature, as if afraid to awake him. He tried it; and expressed so happily the Curiosity and Wonder in the innocent Face

Sect.10. of the young Peasant, that when the Picture was exposed to view, and the People came flocking to see it, their whole Attention turn'd upon the Adjunct of the Piece : They admired the wondering Boy, were delighted with the native Simplicity and Surprize in his Look ; and all the Master's Art, in expressing the Character and uncouth Proportions of the *principal Figure*, was over-look'd and thrown away.

I MAKE little doubt but this may be frequently the Case of those who attempt to design after *moral Originals*, as well as *natural ones*. They enter so deeply into *one* Passion or Bias of *Humanity*, that, to use the Painters Phrase, they quite *over-charge it*. Thus I have seen a whole System of Morals founded upon a single Pillar of the inward Frame; and the entire Conduct of Life, and all Characters in it, accounted for, sometimes from *Superstition*, sometimes from *Pride*, and most commonly from *Interest*. They forget how *various* a Creature it is they are painting; how many Springs and Weights, nicely adjusted and balanced, enter into the Movement, and require a *just* Allowance to be made to their several *Clogs* and *Impulses*, e'er you can define its Operation and Effects. But few of them are willing to acknowledge so much; and, like the honest Painter, go and dash out the *superfluous* Boy, how beautiful soever in him-

himſelf, becauſe he eclipſes the principal Re-Sect. 10.
preſentation.

WHETHER any ſuch Enormity has happened in ſome Step or other of this Enquiry,
or whether it would be worth while to lop
off the Excreſcence, if it prove troubleſome,
I ſubmit to your Lordſhip's Determination.
All I wiſh for, is a ſhort *Demur* in the Sentence, until we regain a *cooler* Temper to
conduct us to the end of our Search, and
to teach us, What *Uſe* is to be made of the
mad mythological Vein? A chief Part of *Ho-*
mer's Works cannot be underſtood without
ſome Knowledge of its Nature and Origin,
nor taſted without a Conſciouſneſs of his Dexterity in the Application. Even the lively
Author of the *Dialogues of the Dead*, with
all his Penetration, has put it as a Maxim
in the Mouth of the Poet, " *That* as it is
" the beſt way to *propheſy* of diſtant things,
" and wait for *Events* to fulfil it; *So* in *Po-*
" *etry*, there is nothing like ſending forth
" a *Fable* into the World, in hopes that ſome
" time or other it may ſtumble upon an
" *Allegory.*"

MYTHOLOGY, taken in the largeſt
Senſe, muſt be diſtinguiſhed into two ſorts:
The one *abſtracted* and *cool*; the Reſult of
great Search and Science: " Being a Com-
" pariſon of the Harmony and Diſcord, the
" Reſemblance and Diſſimilitude of the Powers

M 4   " and

Sect. 10. " and Parts of the *Univerfe*." It often confifts of their fineft *Proportions* and hidden *Ap-
titudes* fet together, and perfonated by a *Being* acting like a *Mortal*. " The other, fud-
" den and flafhy ; rapid Feelings, and Starts
" of a Paffion not in our power." The firft
of thefe may be called *artificial,* and the fecond *natural* Mythology ; the one is a Science,
and may be learned ; the other is the Faculty
that for the moft part, if not always, invents
and expreffes it. This laft cannot be learned ;
but like other natural Powers, admits of *Culture* and *Improvement*. " The Ufe I would
" make of fuch a Divifion is to obferve, That
" *Homer* had the happieft Opportunities the
" World could give, to *acquire* the one, and
" *improve* the other."

IT is but calling to mind his Climate and
Parentage, his Education and Bufinefs, to be
perfuaded of the fair Chance he had for a *noble Capacity* and a proportioned *Culture*. They
confpired to blefs him with fo powerful an
Influence, that the fagacious *Democritus*, ftruck
with admiration of his *Genius,* and its Effects,
faid in a happily invented word, *That it approached to Divinity* ᵃ. And as for *acquired*
Knowledge in the *mythological* way, had he
been to range over the Globe, He could have
pitched upon no Country, in any Age before

or

ᵃ Ὁμηρὸς ΦΥΣΕΩΣ λαχὼν ΘΕΑΖΟΥΣΗΣ.

Διων. Λόγος νϛ

or fince, fo proper for his Inftruction as the Sect. 10. then *Kingdom of* Egypt.

IN EGYPT he might learn their Doctrine concerning the *Origin* of Things; He wou'd be informed of the *Antiquity of* PAN and the *Inventions of* THOTH : He wou'd hear their Statute-Songs and legal Hymns, handed down for thoufands of Years, and containing the Principles of their primitive *Theology :* The Nature of the *Elements,* the Influences of the *Planets,* the Courfe of the *Year,* and Inftincts of *Animals.* How attentively would he liften to the *Songs* of their *Goddefs?* ——the Compofitions of the beneficent ISIS [b]; who, while on Earth, condefcended thus to employ the *Mufes,* and prefcribe the *Form* in which fhe would be worfhipped after fhe was gone? Thefe he would imbibe; and like fome young *Druid* come over from *Gaul* to ftudy under the *Britifh Priefts,* the fenior Doctors of their oral Myfteries, He wou'd return to his Country *fully inftructed,* and a Mafter in their *emblematical Mythology.*

NEVER was there a People fo addicted to *Metaphor* and *Allufion :* Their very *Method of Writing* or *Sacred Sculpture,* was a complete and ftanding Syftem of *natural Simile's.* " It " was an immenfe Collection of all the *Re-* " *lations,* and analogous Circumftances, they " could

---

[b] Ἐμεῖ φασὶ, τὸ τὸν πολὺν ῥύτου σεσωσμένα χρόνον μέλλ, ἧς ἸΣΙΑΟΣ ποιήματα γέγονέναι.　Πλάτων Νόμων. β.

" could find in a long course of Observa-
" tion, between *human* Affairs, and the Na-
" ture and Make of *Birds, Beasts, Fishes, Rep-*
" *tiles, Insects,* or whatever animated or in-
" animated thing they imagined most confo-
" nant in its *Manners* and *Oeconomy* to what
" they wanted to represent."

THUS when they would signify a *dutiful
Child*, they painted a *Stork* ; because that Bird,
as they fancied, being fed by its Dam, and
taught to fly, never afterwards leaves her, but
accompanies and tends her until she die of old
Age. When they had a mind to represent a
Woman that had been *once* with Child, they
painted a *Lioness* ; because they believed that
Animal to conceive but once. When they de-
signed to paint a Man universally *hated* and
shunned, they drew an *Eel*, which is found in
company with no other Fish.

THEY HAD likewise a singular way of
expressing *abstracted* Ideas ; such as *Pleasure*
and *Pain, Impossibility, Antiquity, Happiness,*
and the like. Thus, to express *Pleasure*, they
painted the Number *Sixteen*, which they looked upon as the Year of Life when Mankind is
capable of *mutual Enjoyment*. For an *Impossibility*, they delineated *two Feet* walking upon
Water ; and to denote any thing very ancient,
they painted a Bundle of their *Papyrus*, a
Plant which they thought the *first Food* of
Mortals, before the Invention of Corn, or
eating

eating of Flesh.   Sometimes their Characters Sect.10.
did not only contain a simple Expression of a
Fact, or the Manner of it, but likewise exhi-
bited the *Reasons* and *Cause*; especially if it was
a *natural Appearance* that happened in their
Country, or any thing relating to the Division
of *Time*, or the Revolutions of the *Heavenly
Bodies*.

T H U S, in order to explain the *Overflow-
ing* of the *Nile*, they first painted a *Lion*;
because the Inundation of *Egypt* happens constantly in *June*, when the Sun is in that *Sign*
of the *Zodiack*.   Under him stood three *Water-
Vessels*; and the Figure of a *Heart* with a
Tongue, in the midst of them.   The three
Urns, neither more nor less in number, denoted
the *three Causes*, as they conceived, concurring in the Production of the *Phenomenon*.
One they ascribed to the *Soil* of *Egypt*; of such
a nature, they said, as to generate Moisture in
itself: The second stood for the Influence of
the *Ocean*, whose Waves, according to *Thales*,
were then impelled into the River's Mouth by
the *Etesian* Winds: though that Part assigned
to the Ocean may rather favour the *Opinion* of
Euthymenes, " That the *Nile* takes its rise from
" the *Atlantic*, and yearly overflows *its Banks*,
" at the Season when these Winds beat upon
" the Coast, and drive a greater quantity of
" Water into the mouth of the Cavern that
" feeds

Sect.10. " feeds it [c]." The third *Urn* expressed the true Cause of the annual Deluge; the prodigious *Rains* that fall about that time in the Southern Parts of *Ethiopia*, and are gathered by a large Circuit of Mountains into the Bason or Lake, where the *Nile* has its Origin. These make it swell above its Banks, and lay the *Lower Egypt* under water for three Months in the Year [d].

THE *Heart* was an Emblem of the *Nile* itself, as it gave Life and Motion to *Egypt*, in the same manner as the other does to the *Human Body*: And the annexed Tongue represented *Humidity*, the great Cause of their Happiness; and according to them and their Scholars [e], the *first* constituent Principle of *Being*.

THESE, *My Lord*, are a few Examples of the *enigmatical* Humour of the *Egyptians*. I could with pleasure add to them, both for the Curiosity of what they contain, and because they abound with *Imagery*, and fill the Mind with more Sensations than any other kind of Writing. I could run over the surprising Resemblance they found between the

Sun

[c] Navigavi Atlanticum mare: Inde Nilus fluit, major quamdiu Etesiæ tempus observant : tunc enim ejicitur mare instantibus ventis. Cum resederint, & pelagus conquiescit ; minorque discedenti inde vis Nilo est. Cæterum dulcis maris sapor, & similes *niloticis* Belluæ.

Euthym. Massilienf. apud Senecam. Nat. Quæst. Lib. iv. § 2.

[d] ΩΡΑΠΟΛΛΩΝΟΣ ΝΕΙΛΩΟΥ ΙΕΡΟΓΑΥΦΙΚΑ.
Βιβ. α. κεφ. κ.

[e] *Thales*, and the *Ionick School.*

Sun and a puny *Inſect,* the common BEETLE, Sect.10. in its Generation, Inſtinct, and Parts. I could 〰 relate the Sympathy they obſerved between the *Moon* at her Change, and their *Cynoce-phalus* or APE; an Animal, as they ſaid, de-ſigned by Nature for a *ſacred Symbol,* in ſo far as it comes into the World *circumciſed like an* Egyptian *Prieſt :* And from *theſe* and ſuch like, we might explain a part of the Rea-ſon of their monſtrous Statues, and *Baboon-Worſhip* f. But an Apprehenſion ſtops me, leſt it be ſaid, That all this while I am but indulging a Conjecture, and pleaſing myſelf with an imaginary Scheme; " That *Homer* " never learned the *Egyptian Mythology,* nei-" ther does it appear, that he knew the Grounds " of their Religion."

THE *Argument* of the greateſt weight to prove that He did, is taken firſt from the *Al-legories* that are found in his Writings. They contain the ſame *Doctrine* and *Theogony* as

we

---

f The Opinion which the wiſe and learned *Plutarch* enter-tained of their Rites and religious Ceremonies, is ſomething ſin-gular. Ὀυδὲν ὃ ἄλοϝον, ὀυδὲ μυθῶδες, ὀυδ᾽ ὑπὸ δειϲιδαιμο-ϝίας (ὥσπερ ἔνιοι νομίζυϲι) ἐξηϲπϲοιχειῦτο ΙΕΡΟΥΡΓΙΑΙΣ· ἀλλὰ τὰ μὲν ἠϑικᾶς ἔχοντα ᾗ χρειώδεις αἰτίας, τὰ δ᾽ ἐκ ἄμοιϝα κομ᾽ἐπ᾽ῆϑ Θ ΙΣΤΟΡΙΚΗΣ ἢ ΦΥΣΙΚΗΣ ἐϲὶν : And the very Example he ſubjoins is, διον τὸ περὶ ΚΡΟΜ-ΜΥΟΥ, the Regard they pay to the *Onion.* " The *Egyptians,* " ſays he, have inſerted nothing into their Worſhip with-" out a *Reaſon,* nothing merely *fabulous,* nothing *ſuperſtitious,* " (as many ſuppoſe); but their Inſtitutions have either a Re-" ſpect to *Morals,* or to ſomething *uſeful* in *Life*; and many " of them bear a beautiful Reſemblance of ſome *Fact* in Hiſtory, " or of ſome Appearances in *Nature.*"

ΠΛΥΤ· περὶ ΙΣΙΔΟΣ καὶ ΟΣΙΡΙΔΟΣ.

Sect. 10. we are well affured was delivered by *Orpheus*, and in the fame *veiled* and *myftick* manner: So that with the fame certainty as we can fay, fuch a Man is a *Stoick*, another an *Epicurean*, and another a *Sceptick*, we can affirm that *Homer* is an *Egyptian Mythologift*. We immediately fufpect a Man to be a Difciple of a particular *Sect*, and inftructed in this or the other *School*, from his way of writing, and ufing the Terms peculiar to that Sect. But if we find him building likewife upon the fame *Principles*, and delivering the fame Maxims, we no longer doubt of his *Preceptor*.

THE *Egyptian* Religion and Doctrines, were fettled in the fouthern Parts of *Greece*, by *Danaus* and his Pofterity. Afterwards *Orpheus*, *Mufæus*, *Melampus*, and their Succeffors, fpread them over all the Country. *Homer*, who came after them, made no change upon thofe Rites and Opinions: And yet we find his Writings appealed to, as the Standard of their private *Belief*, and grand Directory of *publick Worfhip*. Is not this the fame as to fay, " *That Homer's* Poetry contains the fame Prin- " ciples and Precepts with thofe of the *Egyp-* " *tian Theologue*, and was the perfecteft Col- " lection of them the *Grecians* had in *Wri-* " *ting?*" Nor are there wanting other Proofs, not only of our Poet's following the general Doctrine of the *Egyptians*, and of the *Grecian*

Law-

Law-giver their Scholar, but plainly borrow-Sect.10.
ing *Images* and *Descriptions* from him, and ∿,
inferting them in his Poetry: Efpecially if
your Lordfhip will take it upon the Word of
the early *Fathers* of our Church, it will be
eafy to make out nothing lefs than downright
Plagiarifm.

"*HOMER*, fays one of them 𝕘, ftretch-
"ing his Privilege as a Poet, and from an
"Emulation of the Glory which *Orpheus* had
"acquired, myftically introduces a *Plurality*
"*of Gods,* that he might not appear to dif-
"fent from the other's Poetry. He has copied
"him fo clofe, that the Refemblance appears
"in the very firft Line of his Works: *Or-*
"*pheus* having begun his Poem with

ΜΗΝΙΝ ΑΕΙΔΕ ΘΕΑ ΔΗΜΗΤΕΡΟΣ ΑΓΛΑΟΚΑΡΠΟΥ;

Homer copies

ΜΗΝΙΝ ΑΕΙΔΕ ΘΕΑ ΠΗΛΗΙΑΔΕΩ ΑΧΙΛΗΟΣ:

"choofing rather to offend in the Meafure of
"his Verfe, than to be the firft that made
"mention of the Name of the GODS."

ANOTHER primitive Writer 𝕙 hath recorded feveral Inftances of his borrowing largely both from *Orpheus* and *Mufæus.* He informs us, that *Orpheus* having faid a very harfh
thing of the *fair Sex,*

'Ωs

𝕘 *Juftin Martyr.* 𝕙 *Clemens Alexandrin.* Stromat. viii.

Sect.10. Ὡς ὲ κύντερον ἦν, ⰺ ῥίγιον ἄλλο γυναικός,

Nothing ſo fierce and impudent as Woman:

Homer had juſt changed a Word, and ſaid,

Ὡς ἐκ αἰνότερον ⰺ κύντερον ἄλλο γυναικός.

Nothing ſo dire and impudent as Woman.

And that as *Muſæus* firſt employed the beautiful and juſt Compariſon of the growth and
decay of the Leaves of Trees, to expreſs the
tranſitory State of Mortals, *Homer* had but
tranſcribed it in the ſixth *Iliad*, " That as
" the Wind ſtrewed the Leaves upon the
" ground, and the ſprouting Wood ſent
" forth others at the approach of Spring; ſo
" one Generation of Men fails, and another
" comes in its room." The Father gives
ſome other Examples of the ſame kind; particularly the noble Deſcription of the *Cyclops
falling aſleep*; which he ſays *Homer* took from
Orpheus's Repreſentation of *Saturn* in the
Theogony :

Κᾶτ' ἀποδοχμώσαι παχὺν αὐχένα, καδδὲ μὶν
ὑπν©,
Ἡρεῖ πανδαμάτωρ ——

———— *Out-ſtretch'd he lay,*
His brawny Neck reclin'd; then ſunk in Sleep,
The all-ſubduing God.

WITH

WITH what views thefe ancient Authors Sect.10. have made fuch Obfervations, or how far they have fucceeded in them, is a Queftion remote from our prefent Subject: Only fo far we may prefume to ufe their Authority in fecular matters, as they firft intended to prove, " That " *Homer* was not himfelf the Author of the " *Polytheifm* which he fung, nor the *Inventer* " of his religious and philofophical Allego- " ries; but had received them, at firft or fe- " cond hand, from the *Egyptians*."

IN this refpect, it would not be difficult for any body who is acquainted with *Homer*'s Writings, and who looks over the few Fragments of *Orpheus*, to make other Remarks to the fame purpofe. As for inftance, that beautiful Defcription of *Heaven*, fo juftly admired, and tranfcribed by *Ariftotle :*

ΟΥΛΥΜΠΟΝΔ' ΟΘΙ ΦΑΣΙ ΘΕΩΝ ΕΔΟΣ.

Radiant from Heaven he came ;—the bleft Abodes,
And Seat unfhaken of th' immortal Gods :
The happy Land, where Tempefts never blow,
Nor chilling Showers defcend, nor fleecy Snow ;
Th' unclouded Sky fmiles with perpetual Day,
And Light eternal darts a gladdening Ray.

This Defcription bears a great Refemblance to thofe Lines of the *Theologue,* (fo the Ancients called *Orpheus*) :

N ——Διώ-

Sect.10. ——Διώριοι δ' ἀνθρώπυς——
         Χωρὶς ἀπ' ἀθανάτων, ναίειν ἴδ῀Θ..

> ———— *Th' Abodes of Men*
> *He fever'd from th' Immortals, to poſſeſs*
> *A blifsful Seat, exempt from all Exceſs;*
> *Where from above no chilling Cold is ſent,*
> *Nor ſcorching Ardour fires the Element;*
> *Where* Phebus' *Axle rowls the middle Road,*
> *And temp'rate Mildneſs dwells beneath the God.*

Here the *Thought* is the ſame, and ſeveral of
the *Names.*

IN THE Fragments that paſs under the
name of the ſame Author, we have Examples
of thoſe hidden pieces of *Art* employed by our
Poet, to give his Work an air of Divinity and
Inſpiration.   Such is the Invocation of his
Muſe at the beginning of his Poem, and his
mentioning the *celeſtial Appellations* of Men and
Things, as if he had underſtood the Language
of the *Gods.*   As to the firſt, beſides what is
told above, there is another Addreſs to his
Genius recorded by *Tzetzes:*

Νῦν δ' ἄʃε μοὶ κούρη Λειβηθριὶς ἔννεπε Μοῦσα,

where the Epithet comes from a Mountain in
Thrace, in the *Odryſian* Country.   For the
ſecond, *Briareus*'s two Names are later than
the *Moon*'s:

Μήσατο

Μήσατο δ' ἄλλην ϳαῖαν ἀπείρατον, lui τε ΣΕΛΗΝΗΝ Sect.10.
Ἀθάνατοι κλήζουσιν Ἐπιχθόνιοι δί τε ΜΗΝΗΝ,
Ἡ πόλλ' εὐρὶ ἔχει, πόλλ' ἄζεα, πολλὰ μέλαθρα.

Another Earth of boundless Size he form'd,
SELENE *call'd in Heaven ; but the Tribes*
Of Men term it the MOON: *She, like this*
     Globe,
Has many Hills, and Towns, and lofty Roofs.

BUT however thefe things may be, whether
Coincidences from Chance, or Imitations arifing from a *Parity of Principles and Manners,*
we may fafely conclude, that *Homer* drew his
Mythology from thefe *three* Sources: Firft, from
the *Form of Worfhip* already eftablifhed in his
Country: Secondly, from the *traditional Doctrines* of *Orpheus* and *Melampus,* who firft formed the *Grecian Ceremonies,* and gave that People a Notion of *Immortality:* And laftly, which
was the Parent of the other two, from the
Egyptian Learning.

I WOULD not be underftood in this, as
if I affirmed that *Homer* had gone through a
Courfe of *Hieroglyphicks* in *Egypt:* Perhaps that
Science was not then brought to fuch Perfection, as it afterwards attained ; tho' their
high Pretenfions to *Antiquity* and *legal Inftitutions* in Religion feem to affure us that it
was.   But the Defign of the Examples in that
way, was to fhew their *Manner of Thinking*

and

Sect.10. *and Writing* upon natural and religious Subjects: From which of confequence we muft
fuppofe, That if *Homer* was among them, as
it appears he was, a *Man* fo capable and inquifitive, could not return without learning fomething of their *Rites*, and the reafons of them;
that is, of their *Mythology*.

WITH refpect to the *traditional* Part of his
Inftruction, it may be afked, How it was preferved in times of fuch Ignorance and Diforder? And thro' what *Channels* it could be conveyed to *Homer?* Tho' this Queftion be upon
the matter anfwered already, and that the Age
in which he lived is too remote, to allow us
to fpeak with certainty of his *Inftructor*; yet
we can give an account of fome *great Men* who
had the honour to pafs for his *Teachers*, and
were named as fuch by the Learned and Wife
among the Ancients.

AND firft, *PRONAPIDES* of *Athens*
is given for his *Mafter* [i]. *Diodorus* the *Sicilian*, whofe Authority is doubly valuable, as
an Hiftorian and a Critick, honours him with
the Appellation of ΜΕΛΟΠΟΙΟΣ ΕΥΦΥΗΣ [k];
and adds, that He had written in the *Pelafgic Character*, in imitation of *Linus* and his
Scholars: That his Subject was likewife the
fame; *The primeval State of Nature*; which
he accordingly infcribed ΠΡΩΤΟΚΟΣΜΟΣ, *The
firft World.*

AFTER

---

[i] Biblioth. Lib. iii.　　[k] A Poet of a fine *Genius.*

AFTER him, *Aristeüs* the famous *Northern* Sect. 10.
Traveller has the fairest Pretensions. He was
a Native of *Proconnesus*, a little Island in the
Propontis near the ancient *Cyzicus*; a delicious
Place, and partaking in the Blessings of that
happy Climate. Invited by his Situation, which
lay just oppofite to *Thrace*, He visited that
Country, wandred a great way up among the
Scythians, and was the first who gave the *Greeks*
any knowledge of the *northern Nations*. He
composed, at his Return, the ΑΡΙΜΑΣΠΕΙΑ
ΕΠΗ, *Arimaspian Poetry*; containing an Account of the several Tribes of the *Barbarians*
he had gone through, and particularly of the
One-eyed Arimaspians, as he calls them, *the
fiercest of Men* [1].

AFTER this, *Aristeüs* made a Voyage *west-
ward*, and viewed *Italy*, at that time almost
as barbarous as the *Scythians* themselves; and
both at home and in his Travels, he seems
to have performed some *Feats* of an extraordinary nature [m], which raised the Wonder of
his Cotemporaries, and made him be looked
upon as a *God*, or at least as a *divine Man*.
This Opinion would not be weakened by
his writing a *Theogony*, like the rest of the
ancient Sages; and exercising himself in a
Field, where anciently Philofophy and Religion

N 3 strove

---

[1] Herodot. Melpomene. Lib. iv.
[m] ἈρισταῖΘ ὁ ποιητὴς ᾶ Ἀριμασπίων καλευμένων ἐπῶν,
ΑΝΗΡ ΓΟΗΣ ὧι τις ἀλλΘ. Στραβ. Βιβ. ιγ.

Sect. 10. strove which should most assist the other, and made an Effort in common for the Good of Mankind.

BETWEEN those two, *Pronapides* and *Aristeüs*, lies the Claim of instructing *Homer*. *Creophilus* too is named as a Competitor; but his Pretensions had better been smothered, as we saw formerly. How to determine between the remaining Pretenders, surpasses my Abilities; and I must in this Particular join with an Author, who, though an Admirer of our Poet, has exercised his Eloquence, in proving him unjust to the *Trojans*, and injurious to the beauteous *Helen*. It is *Dion Chrysostome* I mean, who gives it as his opinion, " *That* " as the precise *Time* and *Place* of his Birth " was not certainly known among the *Greeks*, " so it was likewise a question, *Who had* " *been his Master in Wisdom and Poetry* [n]?"

BUT there is *another* Channel still, thro' which this kind of Science might flow down to *Homer*; not indeed directly from *Egypt*, but from a *Phenician* or *Egyptian Colony*. Your Lordship knows the invidious Story that goes of *Hippocrates* the Father of Medicine: It was a Custom among the Ancients, when any one recovered of a Disease, to write or engrave an account of their Cure upon a *Tablet*, and hang it up in the Temple of *Esculapius*, in sign
of

[n] Ὁμήρȣ μὲν δ, ὥσπερ τὰ ἄλλα τὰ περὶ αὐτὸν, ϗ τȣ̃το ἄδηλον τοῖς Ἕλλησιν.   Διων. Χρυσος.

of Gratitude to the God, who they thought had Sect. 10. directed them to the Remedy. Thefe Tablets, ⌇ they fay, containing the *Hiſtory* of all forts of Diftempers, and their *Method of Cure, Hippocrates* perufed; and having made himfelf Mafter of the Knowledge they afforded, afterwards fet fire to the Temple, that he might enjoy fuch a Treafure without a Rival.

Much of the fame kind is the account we have of *Homer's* Inftruction; only he fpared the *Records* from which he drew it. It was in the firft or fecond Generation after *Oedipus*, fays *Diodorus*, that *Thebes* was fack'd a fecond time by *Alcmæon*. "Among the Captives he carried
" off, was the old blind Prophet *Tireſias*, who
" died by the way: But his Daughter, the ce-
" lebrated *Manto*, was fent to *Delphi* as a part
" of the Spoil. She was no lefs fkilled in *Di-*
" *vination* than her Father; and while fhe
" ftayed in *Apollo's* Temple, made great Im-
" provements in the *Art*. She was favoured
" by the *God*; and having a wonderful Ge-
" nius, compofed *Oracles* of all kinds, and
" in different Forms, *allegorical, prophetical,*
" and *moral*. Thefe were preferved in the
" Temple; and from them, fays the Hifto-
" rian, *Homer borrowed many Verſes, and*
" *inſerted them as Ornaments into his own*
" *Poetry* º."

How imaginary foever this Infinuation may appear, it would be rafh to condemn it as en-

N 4   tirely

º *Diodorus*, Book IV.

Sect.10. tirely groundlefs. It carries indeed in its Face, a certain *air of Fable*; but if narrowly viewed, and the Circumftances weighed, I believe it will be allowed to bear an application of the Proverb, " That if not true, it is at leaft well " contrived." The *Foundation* of the Story, that is, *Alcmæon's* Expedition; the facking of *Thebes*; its Defolation long after, even during the *Trojan War*, are certain and un-doubted *Facts*: The *Neighbourhood* of the *Delphic* Oracle; the fuppofed *Sanctity* of the Place; and the conftant *Cuftom* of the Country to fend a part of the Booty to *Apollo*, make the fub-fequent Parts of it look *probable*.

Bu t when we take in the other Prefump-tions, arifing from the *Oracle* itfelf, and from *Homer's* own *Works*, it becomes difficult for us to refufe our Affent: As firft, That the Places where *Hymns, Songs, Pæans,* and *Poetry* in ge-neral was ufed and known, were anciently no other than the *Temples* and *Altars* of the Gods: The Temple of *Apollo* in particular, which *Homer* in his Hymn to *Diana* calls *the plentiful Habitation of the Delphi*, was the Place where, He fays, " the Sifter of *Phebus* ufed to come, " and celebrate the Meeting of the *Mufes* and " the *Graces* P." Next, That the ΘΕΣΦΑΤΑ

or

P Ἀυ]ὰς ἐπὴν τερφθῆ ᾿Ͻηερσκότ⊙ ΙΟΧΕΑΙΡΑ
Εὐφρήνη δὲ Νοον, χαλάσασ᾿ ἐυχαμπία Τόξα,
Ἔρχεται ἐς μέγα δῶμα κασιγνήοιο φίλοιο,
Φοίβυ Ἀπόλλω.⊙, ΔΕΑΦΩΝ εἰς πίονα δῆμον;
ΜΟΤΣΩΝ κ᾿ ΧΑΡΙΤΩΝ καλὸν Χορὸν ἀρτυνέυσα.
῾Ομηρ. Ῥμν. εἰς ΑΡΤΕΜΙΝ.

or *Sayings* of the God were preferved with a
peculiar Care : They were infcribed fometimes in
Wood, and fometimes in Plates of Metal, and
hung up on the Pillars that enclofed the ᴀᴅʏᴛᴏɴ
or *Sanctuary*. Nay *Plutarch* affures us, That
there was commonly about the Temple at *Del-*
phi, a Set of Men of a *poetical Turn*, whofe
bufinefs it was to fit round the Oracle on
folemn Days, and receive the *Voice* from *Py-*
thia's Mouth, which they were afterwards to
wrap up in a *Vehicle of Words*, in what Phrafe
and Meafure they thought convenient [q].

" For fuch were the Manners, continues
" *the humane Philofopher*, of thefe early Times,
" and fo general was the *Propenfity* to Har-
" mony and Numbers, that every *Science* was
" delivered in *Verfe* : Nothing in Hiftory, no-
" thing in Philofophy, and in a word, no
" Accident or Tranfaction that wanted *Voice*
" and *Defcription*, but what wore the Garb
" of the *Mufes*, and in it was admired. Nor
" for certain, did the *Delphian* God refufe the
" loved Ornament to his *own Art*, or drive
" the *divine Mufe* from the facred *Tripod :* He
" invited her to it, and fanned the poetick
" Fire : He cherifhed the pregnant Breaft, in-
" fpired it with Images, and exalted the myfterious,

---

[q] This is confirmed by *Strabo :* Πυθίαν δεχομένην τὸ πνεῦμα
ἀποθεσπίζειν ἔμμετρα τὲ κ͗ ἄμετρα· Ἐντείνειν δὲ κ͗ ταῦτα εἰς
μέτρον ΠΟΙΗΤΑΣ τινας ὑπηργοῦντας τῷ Ἱερῷ.

Στραβ. Βιβ. θ.

Sect.10. " sterious Sublime of the Soul, until it burst
" forth in Strains befitting his *Shrine.*"

BUT this is not all: We know from *Ho-mer's* own mouth, that *this very Temple* was in high Reputation long before *his* days: That it was honoured by the adjacent Nations, consulted by Princes, and had arrived at an immense pitch of *Wealth* and *Fame.* We find in the *Odyssey*, that *Agamemnon* had consulted it in person, before he undertook the Expedition to *Troy* *ε*: and in the *Iliad, Achilles* tells the Ambassadors, from that *Prince (Agamemnon)* " That
" He would not marry his Daughter, tho'
" she had the Beauty of *Venus*, and the Skill of
" *Minerva*; That he would have no Peace
" with him, nor part in the War; That he
" was resolved to go home to *Phthia*, and
" shun his impending *Fate*; since his Life was
" of more worth to him than all the Wealth
" within the Walls of *Troy*; *and* (to inhance
" the Comparison) more *than all the Treasures*
" *that are preserved within the stone-built* Gate
" *of the rocky* PYTHOS, *the Abode of the*
" soothsaying Apollo *ζ*."

THIS is *Homer's* Description of the *Situation* of the *Oracle:* When we compare it with the accounts left us by *Historians* and *Travellers,*

ε 'Ως γάρ οι χρείων μυθήσατο Φοῖβος Ἀπόλλων
Πυθοῖ ἐν ἠγαθέη, ὅθ ὑπέρβη λάινον Οὐδὸν
Χρησόμενος· Τότε γὸ ῥα κυλίνδετο πήματος ἀρχὴ
Τρωσί τε κὴ Δαναοῖσι.　　　　　　　'Οδυσ. Θ.
ζ Iliad. IX.

lers [t], it appears ſo natural and juſt, that we Sect.10. eaſily believe the Poet muſt have had the *rough* Aſpect of the Mountain in his Eye, and repreſented the Building from a View of the *ſtately Original.* Or if this Belief ſhou'd be thought fond or illuſive, it is not impoſſible to heighten the Evidence: But upon condition, that we remember the Want of Records already mentioned; and that they had in thoſe days no other Method of knowing the Tranſactions of former Ages, than by *Tradition* and Converſe with the *Guardians of Knowledge.*

WITH ſuch Aſſiſtance it is eaſy to make out *Homer's* Acquaintance with *Delphi.* To *him* we owe our Information of the *Antiquity* and *firſt* Settlement of that *ſacred Seat:* From *him* we learn, " *What wiſe Nation* or " *artful People* were then able to project " ſuch an Eſtabliſhment ; or endowed with " the Addreſs neceſſary for executing the " great *Deſign* of explaining the *Purpoſes* " *of Heaven,* and foretelling the *Fortunes of* " *Men.*" A little Reflection will tell us, they could hardly be *Greeks:* The *Grecian Tribes* had not as yet attained the ordinary Arts of Life ; much leſs had they reached this Height of *human Policy* [u]. Or if it was a *Grecian* Settlement, the *Planters* muſt have been ſome *Exception* from the Rule ; ſome privileged Nation, and the *firſt* inſtructed in *Religion* and *Government.*
It

---

[t] Δελφοὶ, πληρῶδες χωείον, θεαλεγεσδὶς, χ' κοινεὴν ἔχον τὸ MANTEION. Στραβ. Βιβ. θ. See alſo *Pauſanias,* Phocis.
[u] See Page 23. and *Section* II. throughout.

Sect.10. IT WAS fo ;————and to make amends
for the Silence or Trifling of fucceeding Hiſtorians, *Homer* hath affured us, That the *Founders* of this *prophetic Colony* were *CRETANS.*
" There were many of them, he fays, and
" *goodly Men*, who came in a Ship from *Cnoſſus*
" the City of *Minos*, and were chofen by
" *Apollo* to offer Sacrifices, and pronounce the
" Oracles of the *God of the Golden Tripod*;
" whatever *Phebus* fhould utter, when he
" prophefied from the *Laurel*, under the *Hol-
" lows* of *Parnaſſus* ᵂ." And that we may
not doubt of the Manner in which this was
done, He tells, That they fung fuch *Pæans* or
Hymns of Praiſe,

ῶΟιοί τε ΚΡΗΤΩΝ ΠΑΙΗΟΝΕΣ, ὅισί τε Μῦσα
Ἐν ςήθεσιν ἔθηκε Θεὰ μελιγήρυν ἀοιδ\ην.

As Cretans *wont to fing* ; *whoſe Breaſt the Muſe
Hath fill'd, divine, with ever-flowing Verſe.*

SUCH WAS the firſt Eſtabliſhment of the
Delphic Oracle. It came to be quickly in repute with its neareſt Neighbours; and in not
a great many Years, *Greece* was full of the
Fame of its Sanctity and Truth. Preſents of
immenſe Value came pouring in, from *Italy*
on one hand, and from *Aſia* on the other.
And

ᵂ Ὁμήρῳ ῞Υμνος εἰς Ἀπόλλ. It is exactly *Strabo*'s Defcription
of the Oracle, Φασὶ δ᾽ ἰῇ τὸ μαντεῖον, ᾽ΑΝΤΡΟΝ ΚΟΙΛΟΝ
χᵀ Βάθυς, ὐ μάλα εὐρύςομον· ἀναφέρεσθαι δ᾽ ἐξ αὐτῆ πνεῦμα
ἐνθεσιαςικ᾽.

And when thefe Treafures were touch'd, or Sect.10. any Indignity was offered the Temple, the ⌇⌇, *Publick* was fure to efpoufe the *Quarrel*, and make a *Holy War* in its Defence. But the greateft honour it had, was to be the Place of Affembly of the AMPHICTYONS, or great Council of *Greece*. They were Deputies fent from the *Sovereign States*, to confult in common the general Welfare of their Country, and determine Differences between the jarring Cities.

WHILE they were affembled, the *Pythian* Games were celebrated in honour of *Apollo*. The reafon why I mention them, is to obferve that it was long before *Horfe-Races* and *Wreftling* came to be a part of the Entertainment. The *firft* and *fole* Actors for many Years, were the ΚΙΘΑΡΩΔΟΙ or *Rhapfodifts* ; and their Trial of Skill was, who fhould fing the fineft *Pæan* in prefence of that auguft Affembly. This Cuftom was eftablifhed before the *Amphictyons* met at *Delphi* : And tho' there were no other Evidence of *Homer*'s having been there, yet I cou'd never bring myfelf to believe, that the fweeteft Singer in *Greece* would foolifhly fhun the Place where the *greateft Honours* were paid to his *Art*.

IT IS plain he was *fond* of the Character; was fenfible to Glory and publick Efteem; and as for his Affection to the *Subject*, the Praife of *Apollo*, befides the firft and longeft

of

Sect.10. of his *Hymns* dedicated to that *Theme*, there goes a *Second* under his Name, where he tells the *God*, " That a fweet-fpoken *Bard*, who " holds in his *Hand* an *harmonious Lyre*, " makes him always the *firft*, and chufes him " as the *laft* Subject of his Song ˟."

AND HERE, a new unbounded Profpect opens full upon us: *Homer* at DELPHI, converfing with the *Priefts*, finging *Pæans* to *Apollo*, and celebrating the Meeting of the Mufes and the Graces! What Advances might he not make in this great School of *Religion* and *Poetry?* The Oracle was the *ftanding Fountain* of their Knowledge : The *facred Spring* that ftood open for their Inftruction in (what they thought) Piety and Learning. Thither they came from every neighbouring Coaft, to learn the Fates of Kingdoms and Common-wealths, and confult the Succefs of their Projects in private Life. Let us think a little, *How it was* poffible to draw fuch Dependence? How to maintain it, in the midft, not only of a *barbarous* People, fuch as the *Greeks* generally were at its Settlement ; But when things were much changed, when they had acquired that Acutenefs and Penetration, for which they were famous fome hundreds of Years before the Oracle ceafed. *Religious Reputation,* we know, is of a ticklifh nature, hard

---

˟ ——— Σὺ δ᾽ ΑΟΙΔΟΣ ἔχων φόρμιγγα λίγειαν
'Ηδυεπὴς, πρῶτόν τε κὴ ὕςαjον ἀιὲν ἀείδει.
　　　　　　Ομήρε ῾Υμν· εἰς Ἀπόλλων· B·

hard to be fupported in a learned inquifitive Sect.10.
Nation; and when once blafted, is irretriev-
able for ever. The *Difficulty* increafes, when
we confider how nicely the *Anfwers* would
be fifted, and their Senfe canvaffed, with more
curious Eyes and anxious Attention, than any
thing in the world befides: And after all, it
feems, " *They flocked to* Delphi, *and believed*
" *the Oracle.*"

As a fort of Apology for a thing incapable
of Defence, we muft fuppofe, that they firmly
believed what many of them have left in Writing, " *That* moft of the Predictions were
" really *accomplifhed.*" Others, they perfuaded themfelves, would ftill come to pafs: For
they reafoned, If *fome* had, *Why not all?* In
the next place, it ufually appeared from the
Anfwer, *That* the *God* was perfectly acquainted
with the Country, Parentage, and Fortunes
of his Suppliant. He commonly addreffed him
with an Appellation taken from the *Founder* of
his Family, or from fome illuftrious *Place* or
Perfon to whom he bore a relation. And indeed through all the Oracles that have reached
us, *We* difcover a wide Knowledge of the
Geography and *Antiquities* of *Greece*; of their
Colonies, ancient *Settlements*, and the various
Turns in their Affairs. Nor is that Knowledge
confined to *Greece*; but *Afia*, *Africk*, and the
Weftern Parts, fall often under the Cognizance
of *Apollo*.

To

Sect.10. To account for this, without suppoſing a *Succeſſion of knowing Men* in the Service of the Temple, and a Stock of Learning unknown to the reſt of *Greece*, would prove a difficult Taſk : And the rather, that there could be no Fallacy deviſed to ſupply the want of it. For the Votaries, however prone to *believe*, and unwilling to *reaſon*, yet could never be deceived as to their *own Country* and *Parentage*. And in this reſpect the Oracle acted in *as fair* a manner as could be wiſhed. It did not, like the *Sibyls*, utter Prophecies at random, upon ſtrange hidden Subjects, without Rule or Choice : But allowed you plainly *to ſtate your Queſtion*, and then, in ſome connexion with it, emitted a Prophecy, or gave the Solution. There ſeems then to be a Neceſſity, either to admit the Knowledge of the Prieſts, or turn *Converts* to the Ancients, and believe in the Omniſcience of *Apollo*, which, in this Age, I know no body in hazard of.

THE *truth* is, ſuch a Settlement could neither have been projected nor executed at that time, by any other than a *wiſe People*, ſkilled in the Arts of Government both religious and civil, and not without ſome Experience in *naval* Affairs. Without this laſt, it was impoſſible to know the *State* of *Greece*; the different Nations that inhabited the ſeveral Coaſts; their Cities, and Product of the

Soil ;

Soil ; the Revolutions in their *Republicks*, and Sect. 10. Origins of their Families.   But a People skil- ~~~ led in Navigation had good Opportunities to know such things ; because, as was already observed, the greater part of *Greece* lay upon the Sea ɣ.   These Qualifications are hard to be found *together*; and when found, they agree to no *Greek* Nation then in being, but to the CRETANS ; the very Men whom our Poet names as the *Founders* of the *Oracle*.   Let us take a View of this ancient Island; and, if possible, trace this *Oracular Science* to its Foun- tain.

IT APPEARS from History, That before the Days of *Minos*, *Crete* lay under the common Calamities of *Greece :* It was afflicted with In- cursions, Devastations, and frequent Removes of its old Inhabitants : But from his time, it became a regular flourishing State ; and by virtue of his Laws, with the assistance of its Situation, had the Happiness *to preserve its Liberty long after the Continent was enslaved.* From such a thorough and sudden Change in their Affairs, it is natural to infer, " *That* the " *Cretan Laws* were not invented by degrees, " like the *Athenian* and *Roman*, or enacted " piece-meal according to the Urgencies of " the State ; but laid down *all at once*; and " resembling, in this respect, the *Spartan* or " *Venetian* Constitution."   And when we con-

O   sider

ɣ See Page 44. Note ᵐ.

Sect. 10. fider it in this Light, we muſt allow ſuch a
Plan of Government to be the Effect of *abſtracted Knowledge*, and of a juſt View of *human Nature*, in its Paſſions and Relations to
outward Objects. But this could hardly come
from a *Barbarian*: It muſt be the Child of
a Man who had either himſelf ſeen, or was
ſoundly inſtructed in the *Arts of Policy*;
who had known a legal civilized Life, and
could provide againſt the Turns of Manners
ariſing in populous Cities and rich Communities, either from inward Luxury or foreign
Violence.

THAT this was done by *Minos* with a
Depth of Wiſdom peculiar to that great Law-
giver, is unanimouſly teſtified by the Ancients: But one Witneſs may ſerve for all
on this Subject; for we may ſafely take
Plato's Word in what belongs to a *Legiſla-
ture*. He ſays *two* things of the *Cretan Laws*:
Firſt, " *That it was with great Reaſon they*
" *were celebrated as the moſt* excellent *in*
" Greece:" And ſecondly, " *That they were*
" *the moſt* ancient *in that ſame Country*."
Let us keep them in view, while we conſider
at the ſame time ſome Particularities in the
Life of the *Law-giver*.

HE IS famous not only in this Capacity,
but as a Founder of Cities, *Cnoſſus, Cydonia*,
and *Phæſtus* [z]; which are two Qualities that
rarely

* Diodor. Sicul. Lib. v.

rarely meet in one Man. He appears to have Sect. 10.
been equally juft in executing his Laws, as he
was wife in contriving them. His two Brothers he made fupreme Judges in the Kingdom. *Talus*, the younger, went a Circuit thrice
a Year thro' the Ifland, to hear Caufes and
give Juftice: The Laws by which he judged
were engraved on Plates of Brafs; and from
the conftant ufe he made of them, he got
the Name of ΧΑΛΚΟΥΣ, or the *Brazen Talus*.
Rhadamanthus, the elder, had the cognizance
of Capital Crimes, and held his Tribunal in
the *Metropolis* [a]. The *Prince* himfelf led his
Armies, and commanded likewife his Fleets in
Perfon; and he is faid to be abfolutely the *firft*
who was *Lord* of the *Ocean* [b]. From this Circumftance in his Life, and the Power of Life
and Death committed to his Brother, they both
feem to have had their Names [c].

BUT the greateft Honour which this Prince
attained to, and what makes moft for our
prefent purpofe, is, that of all the ancient
Heroes, *Minos* alone is celebrated as the *Companion of Jove*, with whom he ufed to con-

O 2   verfe

[a] *Plato* in *Minoe & Epinomide.*

[b] Hanc urbem, ante alios, qui tum florebat in *Armis*,
Fecerat infeftam Populator REMIGE *Minos*.
                              P. Virgil. CEIRIS.

[c] RHADAMANTHUS from *Rhadá* dominari, and *Munoth* Ima-
gines, Umbræ, Phantafmata: Or *Maveth* or *Moth*, Mors, Mor-
tes: As if it were the *Lord* of the *Shades*, or *Prince* of *Death*.
MINOS from *Mi* or *Me*, Aquæ, and *Non*, Filius, Princeps. From
the old Root *Mi* or *Mai*, by a common Tranfpofition, comes *Iam*
the Sea.

Sect.10. verſe as with a Friend [d]. From him, it is ſaid, he had his Laws; and to account for this Familiarity, he was afterwards called his *Son.* Now if to theſe Accounts of this Founder of States, we add another Reflection; " That all " the *Gods* were ſaid to be born in *Crete,* " that there *Jupiter* was nurſed in a Cave, " and the *Curetes,* or *Idæi Dactyli,* danced " about him, leſt old TIME ſhould devour " him, as he had done all the Gods that " had been worſhipped before:" This, I ſay, will carry us a Step further in the Enquiry, and enable us to underſtand what *Ephorus* means, when he tells us, " That *Minos* was " no *Cretan,* but came from *beyond Sea* to " *Crete,* with theſe *Tutors* of *Jove* juſt now " mentioned [e]."

HERE a Light ſtrikes upon us, that ſeems to make ſome amends for the Length of the Deduction. The Oracle of *Apollo* at *Delphi* was a Settlement of *Cretans:* In *Crete Jupiter,* and the other *Gods,* were born; that is, " the " *Cretans* were the firſt *Europeans* who re- " ceived a Form of Worſhip, and learned " the Names and Natures of the Gods; and " from them that Knowledge was propaga- " ted among the *Weſtern* Nations." In this Senſe, *Jupiter* and *Juno, Ceres* and *Neptune,* with

---

[d] *Homer* calls him ΔΙΟΣ ΜΕΓΑΛΟΥ ΟΑΡΙΣΤΥΣ, which *Horace* tranſlates——— *Jovis Arcanis Minos admiſſus,* Lib. i. Ode 28.
[e] Apud Diodor. Lib. v.

with all their Train, were of CRETAN Ex-Sect. 10.
tract as to the *Greeks.* The Inhabitants of〰
Crete, formerly *barbarous,* were inſtructed by
Minos, who came with People already civilized
and inſtructed in civil and manual *Arts,* the
Curetes, Idæi Dactyli, and the *Telchines* from
Rhodes: Which is to ſay in Subſtance, " That
" the Knowledge of the *Gods,* their Tem-
" ples, Prieſts, and Oracles, with the ne-
" ceſſary ſubſervient Arts, were firſt brought
" to *Crete,* by *Phrygians, Phenicians,* and
" *Egyptians.*"

I CANNOT reſolve to lead your Lordſhip
thro' the Labyrinth of Mythology and Hiſtory,
in which a farther Inveſtigation would intan-
gle us : Tho' ſhould we purſue it, and trace
backward the *Delphic* Antiquities, firſt from
Crete, then from *Phenicia* and *Rhodes,* and
thence to *Egypt,* we have every where Veſtiges
that would direct us in the Track. Many of
them have been pointed out already by a *great
Man* [f], tho' with another Deſign : But a Hand
ſo maſterly as his, ſeldom touches a Subject
without ſpreading a Luſtre over every thing
that belongs to it.

CADMUS's Relation to *Egypt,* his Flight from
Phenicia, and founding the *Beotian* THEBES,
are things too notorious to be inſiſted on : Neither is it worth while, to mention many other

O 3　　　　　Facts

[f] Sir *Iſaac Newton,* Chronol. Chap. I.

Sect.10.Facts of the fame nature, which are to be found in every Writer. But I incline to think, that the People laft named, the TELCHINES, came immediately to *Greece* from that Mother-land of Priefts and Superftition.

THE Account *Diodorus* gives of them, is firft, That they were *Children of the Sea;——* or, in plainer Terms, that they came from *beyond Sea* to *Greece* and the Iflands; whofe rude Inhabitants being able to give no other account of their Origin, imagined them (as the *Indians* did the *Spaniards*) to be the Off-fpring of the Element where they firft appear-ed, and therefore called them the *Sons of the Ocean:* For the fame reafon, they had given that fame Name to *Inachus* and his Wife be-fore: They were, for any thing we know, the firft *Egyptians* who came to *Peloponnefus*, and founded the ancient Kingdom of *Argos.* Some faid, that *Inachus* was the God of the *River,* at whofe Mouth he had entered the Country.

IT IS eafy to imagine how prone an igno-rant gazing Race of Mortals would be to entertain *fuch Fancies:* And how great the Barbarity was that prevailed among them, is evident from the Story of *Phoroneus* the Son of *Inachus,* and his Succeffor in the new-formed Kingdom. He is faid to have firft taught the wild Inhabitants to quit the

Caves

Caves ᵍ and Hollows of the *Mountains* in Sect. 10. which they lived ʰ, to build themselves Houses, 〰 and make a sort of *Town* ⁱ. In his Days came the *Telchines*, the second *Egyptian* Colony, and attempted to make a Descent, and settle in the same Place ; but being repulsed by *Phoroneus*, they failed to *Rhodes*, and some of them passed over from thence to *Crete* ᵏ. In both Places they are called the *Inventers* of *Arts* of every kind; as well they might appear to a People so void of Contrivance, and destitute even of the Necessaries of Life ˡ. They were the first of Mankind who reared *Temples*, and made *Images* and *Statues* of Gods. Some of the ancientest Statues in *Greece* bore the *Telchine*

O 4   Name,

ᵍ ———————— ἀυτε πλινθυφεῖς
Δόμους πρεοἔπλες Ίσαν, ὲ ξυλουργίαν·
ΚΑΤΩΡΥΧΕΣ δ᾽ ἔναιον, ὥς ἀήσυερι
Μύρμηκες, ᾽ΑΝΤΡΩΝ ἐν μυχοῖς ἀνηλίοις·
Ἦν δ᾽ οὐδὲν ἀυτοῖς οὔτε χείμαζⓋ τέκμαρ,
Ὄυτ᾽ ἀνθεμώδους ἦρος, οὔτε καρπίμου
Θέρους βέβαιον· ἀλλ᾽ ᾽ΑΤΕΡ ΓΝΩΜΗΣ τὸ πᾶν
Ἔπρασσον·   Αἰσχυλ. ΠΡΟΜΗΘΕΥΣ.

ʰ *Genus et indocile, et dispersum montibus altis.*
                              Virgil. Æneid. Lib. viii.

ⁱ Pausanias Corinth. Lib. ii. ΦΟΡΩΝΕΑ ἐν τῇ ᾗ ταύτῃ γενέσθαι πρῶτον· ᾽ΙΝΑΧΟΝ δὲ ἐκ ἄνδρα, ἀλλὰ τὸν ΠΟΤΑΜΟΝ πατέρα ᾧ ΦΟΡΩΝΕΙ.———Φορωνεὺς δὲ ὁ ᾽Ιάχυ τὰς ἀνθρώπας συνήγαγε πρῶτος ἐς κοινὸν, σποράδην τέως κὴ ἐφ᾽ ἑαυτῶν ἑκάστοτε οἰκοῦντας· κὴ τὸ χωρίον ἐς ὁ πρῶτον ἠθροίσθησαν ᾽ΑΣΤΥ ὠνομάσθη ΦΟΡΩΝΙΚΟΝ.

ᵏ Eusebius. Numb. 229.

ˡ Hanc variæ Gentes, *antiquo* more Sacrorum
IDÆAM vocitant MATREM, *Phrygiasque* Catervas
Dant comites, quia *primùm* ex illis finibus edunt
Per Terrarum Orbem, FRUGES cœpisse creari.
                              LUCRET.

Sect. 10. Name, and preserved the Memory of their Authors: Thus the *Lindians* called theirs, the *Telchinian Apollo:* The old *Camirus* had a *Telchinian Juno :* and in *Iälyssus*, both *Juno* and the *Nymphs* were distinguished by the same *Epithet* [m].

N o w it is generally agreed among the best Judges, that these are all *Egyptian Inventions;* and *the very things* for which that thoughtful People valued themselves above other Nations. The great *Disciple* of their Priests tells us [n],
" That the *Names* of the twelve Gods were
" first settled by the *Egyptians*, and from them
" the *Greeks* had received them: That *They*
" were the People who had raised *Alters,* carved
" *Statues,* and bestowed *Temples* upon the
" Gods, and had first cut the Figure of a living
" Creature in Stone." After this, it is almost needless to add, That the *Telchines* passed for great *Conjurers* and *Magicians;* able to do Wonders with Charms and Drugs, whose Powers they knew, but were extremely *reserved* and *scrupulous* in communicating their Discoveries. Yet these are Characteristicks not only of their being *Egyptians,* but of the *Race* or *Tribe of the Priests,* the old Inventers of the ʹIEPA ΓΡΑΜΜΑΤΑ (*the Holy Characters*) and other

[m] Diodor. Sicul. Lib. v.

[n] Δυώδεχά τε Θεῶν Ἐπωνυμίας ἔλεγον πρώτες Ἀιγυπλίες νομίσαι, ἢ Ἕλληνας περὶ σφίων περαλαϐεῖν. ΒΩΜΟΥΣ τε ἢ ΑΓΑΛΜΑΤΑ ἢ ΝΕΟΥΣ Θεοῖσι ἀπονεῖμαι σφέας ΠΡΩΤΟΥΣ, ἢ ζῶα ἐν λίθοισι ἐγλύψαι.
ʹHερδοτ. Ἐυτέρπη. Βιϐ. β.

other Methods of hiding their Knowledge from Sect.10. the Vulgar ᵒ.

So FAR we are led by the laborious and learned *Diodorus*. From others we learn,
" That the *Curetes*, the *Corybantes*, the *Tel-*
" *chines*, and the *Idæi Dactyli*, were all of
" one and the same Tribe, or with a very
" little Variation : That they were all *en-*
" *thufiastick*, much addicted to *facred Shows*,
" *Bacchic Proceffions*, and *ecstatic* Performan-
" ces : That in confequence of this general
" Character, they chofe to appear as *Servants*
" and *Minifters* of the Gods ; and amazed
" Mankind with the noife of *Cymbals*, *Sif-*
" *trums*, *Pipes*, and the Appearance of the
" *armed Dance* P." In a word, they were a
People come from a *Land of Priefts*, and fond
of propagating their *native Arts* ; thofe Arts
by which they could raife the greateft Admiration

° Τὰς θ' ἱερέας τῶν ΑΙΓΥΠΤΙΩΝ, ᾳ Χαλδαίυς ᾳ Μάγυς σοφία τινὶ διαφέρονζας τῶν ἄλλων, ἡχεμονίας ᾳ τιμᾶς τυγχάνειν παρὰ τοῖς πρὸ ἡμῶν·   ΣΤΡΑΒ ΒΙβ. α.
ᵖ *Strabo*, Lib. x. It is admirably told by the Author : Τὰς αὐτὰς δὲ ταῖς ΚΟΥΡΕΣΙ τὰς ΚΟΡΥΒΑΝΤΑΣ ᾳ ΚΑΒΕΙΡΟΥΣ ᾳ ΙΔΑΙΟΥΣ ΔΑΚΤΥΛΟΥΣ ᾳ ΤΕΛΧΙΝΑΣ ἀποφαίνυσιν. Ὁι δὲ συγγενεῖς ἀλλήλων, ᾳ μικρὰ ζιισας αὐτῶν πρὸς ἀλλήλυς διαφορὰς διασέλλυσιν. Ὡς δὲ τύπῳ εἰπεῖν ᾳ χτ' τὸ πλέον, ἅπανζας ΕΝΘΟΥΣΙΑΣΤΙΚΟΥΣ τινας, ᾳ ΒΑΚΧΙΚΟΥΣ, ᾳ ἐνοπλίῳ κινήσει μῆ θορύβυ καὶ ψόφυ, καὶ κυμβάλων καὶ τυμπάνων καὶ ὅπλων ἔῖι δ' αὐλῦ καὶ βοῆς ἐκπλήῆονζας χτ' τὰς ἱεργγίας, ἐν χήμαπ διακονῦνζων. Καὶ τὰ ἱερὰ τρόπον τινὰ κοινοποιεῖθαι, ταῦτα τε καὶ τ̃ Σαμοθρακῶν, καὶ τὰ ἐν Λήμνῳ καὶ ἄλλα πλέω, διὰ τὸ τὰς Προσπόλυς λέγεθαι τὰς αὐτάς. Ἐςὶ μὲν ἓν ΘΕΟΛΟΓΙΚΟΣ πᾶς ὁ τοιῦτος λόγος τῆς Ἐπισκέψεως, καὶ ἐκ ἀλλότει⊕ τῆς τῦ φιλοσόφυ θεωείας.

Sect.10. tion in Mankind, and gain the moſt Reverence
to themſelves [q].

THAT they came from an *Eaſtern* Country is apparent from the *Order* of their Arrival,
and the *Progreſs* of their Inventions thro' the
weſtern Parts of *Europe*. *Arts*, and *Wealth*,
and political *Inſtitutions* in Religion, for the
greater part, go hand in hand, and can hardly
be diſunited by any human Precautions. They
were inſeparable Companions in the *Progreſſion*
of the *Grecian* Manners formerly mentioned ;
and their real Motions weſtward are accordingly to be gathered from thoſe Paſſages of
Homer's Writings, where he ſpeaks of the Countries then famous for Wealth and Grandeur.
The firſt is *Egypt*; whoſe chief City, THEBES,
bears the Character of that Place in the World

—ʹΟθι ΠΛΕΙΣΤΑ Δόμοις ἐνὶ ΚΤΗΜΑΤΑ κᾶται [r],

" where the Houſes contained the GREATEST
" Wealth :" Next, the Coaſt of *Aſia*, " whoſe
" Inhabitants, ſays the Poet, the ΕΛΚΕΧΙΤΟ-
" ΝΕΣ ΙΑΟΝΕΣ, *Ionians in their flowing Robes*,
" are a delightful Sight to a Man who be-
" holds their fine Appearance, when they
" come to *Delos*, with their Wives and Chil-
　　　　　　　　　　　　　　　　　" dren,

[q] Tympana tenta tonant Palmis, & Cymbala circùm
　　Concava ; raucifonoque minantur Cornua cantû ;
　　Et Phrygio ſtimulat numero cava Tibia menteis ;
　　Telaque præportant, violenti Signa furoris,
　　Ingratos Animos, atque impia pectora Volgi
　　Conterrere Metu quæ poſſint, Numine Divæ.　　LUCRIT.
[r] ʹΟδυσ. Δ.

" dren, ἠδ' αὐτῶν κτηματα πολλα f and Sect.10.
" the GREAT Wealth they poſſeſs :" And
laſtly, the richeſt Man in *Greece*, not in Lands
or Cattle, but in Houſhold Furniture, Plate,
and Apparel, is *Menelaüs*, who

ΚΥΠΡΟΝ, ΦΟΙΝΙΚΗΝ ΤΕ, ΚΑΙ ᾿ΑΙΓΥΠΤΙΟΥΣ ᾿ΕΠΑΛΗΘΕΙΣ,
Had wander'd o'er PHENICIA, CYPRUS, EGYPT t,

and from theſe Countries. had brought home ſo
much Wealth, and ſo many Works of Art,
as to make his Palace ſhine with Gold, Amber, Silver, and Ivory ; and left him without
a Rival in Wealth among the *Greeks*.

EXACTLY agreeable to this, the *Iſlands*
ſaid to be firſt civilized, and brought to live in
a regular manner, were *Cyprus*, *Rhodes*, and
Crete. Your Lordſhip, who knows their Situation, will eaſily perceive, that their Neighbourhood to the *Continent* muſt have procured
them that Precedency ; and for the ſame Reaſon, that *Imbrus* and *Lemnos*, lying ſo near the
Cherſoneſus, became the grand Receptacles of
the *Samothracian* and *Bendidian* Myſteries.
Nine of the *Telchines* are ſaid to have lived in
Rhodes ; and ſome of them went from thence
with *Rhea*, to aſſiſt her to nurſe *Jove* in *Crete*;
that is, " *In a Courſe or Flux of Years, they*
" *went from* Rhodes, *and inſtructed the* Cre-
" tans *in the Worſhip of* Jupiter."

ONE

f ᾿Ομήρε ῾Υμν. ὶις ΑΠΟΛΛΩΝΑ· Α·
t See Page 268.

Sect.10.   ON E of the chief Parts of the Worſhip of the Ancients, was their *Oracles* ᵘ ; and their believing in them was a good proof of their being truly convinced of their *divine Original :* It is not therefore to be ſuppoſed that the *Egyptian Strangers* would neglect a principal Branch of their Religion, or overlook ſo *gainful* an Inſtitution in their new Plantation : But that there may be no uſe for Suppoſition, nor any doubt left of the *Oracular Talents* of this very Tribe, one of the *Telchines,* *LYCUS* by name, leaving their firſt Settlement, went to *Lycia* ʷ, and founded the Oracle of the *Lycian Apollo,* upon the Banks of *Xanthus.* This Temple, the accurate *Strabo* calls ΤΟ ΛΗΤΩΟΝ, *the Temple* of *Latona,* which affords a new proof of its *Egyptian* Origin. The chief *Oracle* in *Egypt* was *Latona's* at *Butoo,* the Mother of *Apollo,* (for the God was of a *ſoothſaying* Family ;) and the *Telchine* who founded this, has probably called it after the honoured Habitation of the Goddeſs in his own Country.

    DELPHI, I take to have been their next Settlement, after they had ſucceeded ſo happily in *Crete,* and eſtabliſhed both their Rites and Laws among the Inhabitants : From it, in a lineal kind of Succeſſion, ſprung the *Oracles*
of

ᵘ Τοῖς ἀρχαίοις μᾶλλον ἦν ἐν πυρῒ, καὶ ἡ ΜΑΝΤΙΚΗ τοθόλυ, καὶ τὰ ΧΡΗΣΤΗΡΙΑ· νυνὶ δ᾽ ὀλιγοεία κατέχει πολλὴ.
Στραϐ. Βιϐ. ιζ.

ʷ See Page 93 of *OLEN* the *Lycian.*

of greateſt fame over *Greece*.   Among the De- Sect.10.
ſcendants of *Machereus* (a *Delphic Prieſt*, famous for killing *Neoptolemus*) was BRANCHUS;
who quitted his paternal Seat, went to *Didymæ*
near *Miletus*, and there ſet up the Oracle of
Apollo, known by the Name of *Branchidæ*.
The Prieſts of this Temple affirmed in the
uſual mythological ſtrain, that *Apollo* was in
love with their *Founder*, and ſo beſtowed upon
him the Gift of *Prophecy*.

A LITTLE before this, the *Clarian* Oracle near *Colophon* was founded by MOPSUS
the Son of the inſpired *Manto*, and Grandſon
of *Tireſias* the *Theban Prophet*.   It ſtood in a
beautiful Grove, as did moſt of the Temples
that were conſecrated to *Apollo* and *Diana*,
and was ſtill in vogue in the days of *Germa-
nicus* the Son of *Druſus*, and *Livia*'s Grand-
child.   There were many of them all along
the *Ionick Coaſt*, which ſeems to have been
anciently a *prophetic Soil:* It came afterwards
to be productive of *Poetry*, and turned at
laſt to *Rhetoric* and *Philoſophy*.   *Apollo* had
Oracles at *Zeleia, Priapus, Lariſſa, Thymbrus,
Cilla, Grynium,* and many other Places.   The
multitude of them ſhews a particular Attachment to his Worſhip; and the reaſon of it is
worthy of our notice, and belongs to our Subject.

THE little Iſland *Delos* is commonly aſſigned, by the *Greek* Hiſtorians, as the Birth-
place

Sect.10. place of *Apollo* and *Diana:* But the *Afiaticks*
have likewise a Claim, and perhaps equally
ancient with the other. " A little up from
" the Sea-fhore, not far from *Ephefus*, there
" ftands a ftately Grove of all forts of Wood,
" but chiefly *Cyprefs:* They call it *Ortygia*,
" and thro' it runs the River *Cenchrius*, in
" which they fay the Goddefs *Latona* bathed
" herfelf after Child-bearing. For here it
" was that her Delivery happened under the
" Care of *Ortygia* the Nurfe; and here they
" fhew the *Recefs* or *Sanctuary* in which fhe
" was brought to bed, and the *Olive Tree*
" on which fhe firft leaned, when her Pangs
" had ceafed. Above the *Grove* ftands *Sol-*
" *miffus*, the Mount where the *Curetes* took
" their Station, and with the Noife of their
" Armour amazed the jealous *Juno*, until
" *Latona* was brought to bed. Many *old*
" *Temples* are to be feen around the Place,
" and fome new built: The firft are adorned
" with *ancient* Statues; fuch as a Statue of
" *Latona* with a Sceptre in her hand, and
" another of *Ortygia* with the *Twin-Gods* in
" her Arms. A grand Affembly is yearly held
" in honour of the *Birth*; the Youth from
" the adjacent parts appear fumptuoufly ha-
" bited, and keep the Feaft with all poffible
" Magnificence; and the ancient *College* of
" the *Curetes* make an Entertainment for
" themfelves, and perform fome *myftick Sa-*
" *crifices,*

" *crifices,* I fuppofe after the manner of their Sect.10.
" *Founders* ˣ."

HERE we have the fame *Rites,* and the fame *Teachers* of them, as we found in *Crete,* the Parent of the *Delphic Oracle:* And it could hardly fall out otherwife, fince the fame Hiftorian who pointed out the Country of *Minos* ʸ, hath alfo told us, " That the CRE-
" TANS under *Sarpedon,* failed to this very
" Coaft, and founded the *old Miletus:* The
" *new* was hard by it; which afterwards fent
" forth Colonies all around it, and on both
" fides the *Helleſpont,* as far as the *Euxine*
" Sea."

WE have the very fame Account from *Virgil,* who is admired and quoted by the later *Roman* Writers, not only as the fineft Poet, but the greateft and exacteft *Antiquarian* of his Country; which, they fay, He has fhow'd wherever the Structure of his Poem did not forbid it. *He* lets us know, That the ancient Inhabitants of the *Trojan* Coaft came from this *Parent-Iſland* under TEUCRUS, and, as all Colonies do, transferred the Names of their old Towns and Mountains into their new Settlements. *Miletus,* or *Milytus,* was a Town in *Crete,* and *Miletus* one in *Aſia* founded by *Sarpedon:* *Ida* was a Mountain in *Crete,* and another of the *fame* Name overlooked *Troy:* The *Dorians, Curetes,* and *Pelaſgi* were *Cretans,*

(fee

ˣ *Strabo,* Lib. xiv.   ʸ *Ephorus* apud *Strabon.* Lib. xiv.

Sect. 10.(fee *Odyff.* XIX.) and the *Dorians, Curetes,* and *Pelafgi* were Inhabitants of the *Leffer Afia*; and alfo brought with them the whole Train of their proceffional Rites, and oracular Worſhip[z].

WITH the *Cretans* came likewiſe theſe *Guardians of young Deities,* the *CURETES*[a], to the maritime Places of *Ionia, Caria,* and *Lycia,* and made *Apollo* be born *here,* as they had made *Jove* be produced in *Crete*; or perhaps, as they or ſome of their Order had made *Apollo* himſelf owe his Birth to *Delos* before.

THAT the *Grecians* were themſelves conſcious of this Genealogy of their God, I gather from the Hymns aſcribed to *Orpheus*; which, tho' not the Work of the great Law-giver, as they now ſtand, are yet the nobleſt and oldeſt *Remain* of the pure *Grecian Liturgy.* They are properly *Invocations* of the ſeveral Deities, and compoſed of the *Diſtinctions, Powers,* and *Attributes* peculiar to each: The *Tuſcan Prieſts* very juſtly called theſe Pieces of Worſhip *Indigitamenta.*

[z] CRETA Jovis magni medio jacet Infula Ponto,
Mons *Idæus ubi,* & Gentis Cunaoula noſtræ.
Centum Urbes habitant magnas, uberrima Regna
Maximus unde Pater, (fi rite audita recordor)
TEUCRUS, *Rhæteas* primum eſt advectus ad Oras;
Optavitque locum Regno: Nondum *Ilium* & Arces
Pergameæ fteterant; habitabant Vallibus imis.
Hinc Mater Cultrix CYBELE *Corybantiaque* Æra
*Idæum*que Nemus: hinc *fida filentia* Sacris,
Et juncti Currum Dominæ iubiêre Leones.
 Æneid. Lib. iii.

[a] Et tandem antiquis CURETUM allabimur Oris.
3 Virgil. Æneid. iii.

Indigitamenta. In the *Address* to *Apollo*, a-Sect.10.
mong the other Qualities, taken from his Nature, as representing the *Sun*; from his Mythology, as vanquishing *Python*; and from his
Effects, as *Health* and *Harmony*, there is *one*
taken from a local Relation; He calls him
MEMΦITHΣ, or the *Memphian Apollo*; an Appellation taken from *Memphis* the Metropolis
of *Egypt*, at the time when these *Hymns* were
composed [b]. It is remarkable as it stands a-
mong the other Epithets; and appearing among
the *first* of them, seems to insinuate an early
Affinity between the *Delphic* and *Egyptian* Prophecy. In these same Hymns, the *Curetes* are
complimented with being

—— *Th' immortal Race*
Who first prescrib'd a Prayer to weak Mankind [c],

And in the Address to *Latona*, it is plain the
Author knew the Pretensions of *Asia* to her
Reception; but he has divided the Honour,
and made her bear *Apollo* in *Delos*, and *Diana*
in *Ortygia* [d].

THERE

[b] *The Hymn begins,*
᾽Ελθὲ μάκαρ ΠΑΙΑΝ, πτνοκ]όρι, Φοῖςε, λυκορεῖ,
ΜΕΜΦΙΤ᾽, ἀγλαόπμα, ἰὼς, ὀλβιοδῶτε, &c.

[c] ᾽Αθάνατι ΚΟΥΡΗΤΕΣ, ἀρήϊα τύχε᾽ ἐχόντις,
Ὑμεῖς καὶ τελετὴν ΠΡΩΤΟΙ μερόπαιιν ἔσειδι.

[d] Γειναμένη Φοῖβον τε καὶ ῎Αρτεμιν ἰωχέαιρα,
Τὴν μὲν ἐν ᾽ΟΡΤΥΓΙΗ, τὸν δὲ κραναῇ ἐνὶ ΔΗΛΩ.

P

Sect.10. THERE is another Connexion ftill remains : To comprehend it in all its Strength and Beauty, requires an Eye like your Lordfhip's, accuftomed to view the various Models of States, and trace the Genius and Refult of different Schemes of Government. I can only pretend to point out the Subftance of it, which ftands thus.

IT IS agreed among the Ancients, That the *Plan* of the *Spartan* Conftitution was taken from the Laws of *Crete*. *Lycurgus*, they fay, made fome ftay in the Ifland, and converfed with the *Cretan* THALES, a Lawgiver and Poet, who informed him, " How " *Minos* and *Rhadamanthus* had framed their " Laws, and publifhed them among the In- " habitants as coming from *Jove*." From thence he went to *Delphi*, and confulted the Oracle concerning the *Plan* he had received ; and it being approved of, he returned to *Lacedemon*, and fettled *it likewife* as the Dictates, not of *Jupiter*, but of the *Delphian God*. It was ftill in vigour when *Herodotus* lived ; who having had occafion to obferve the *Spartan* and *Egyptian* Cuftoms, with more Attention and Underftanding than falls to the fhare of moft Travellers, hath left us a Draught of the *Refemblance* he found in many Particulars, both of their Religion and Government [e]. I will not enter into a *Detail* of

them,

[e] *Herodot.* Erato, Lib. vi.

them, but take notice of an obvious Queſtion; Sect.10.
" How great the Reſemblance muſt have 〰
" been between the Originals (the *Egyptian*
" and *Cretan*) ſince ſo much of it was pre-
" ſerved in the *Copy* at ſecond hand, the *La-*
" *cedemonian* Conſtitution?"

Of all the Inſtitutions of *Crete*, I ſhall
mention but one, to ſhew the diffuſive Influence of the *Egyptian* Cuſtoms. *Muſick* and
Poetry in *Egypt* were circumſcribed by *Law*,
as I obſerved before.; and we learn from the
Sketch of the *Cretan* Common-wealth left by
Strabo, " That their Children were taught
" *Letters*, and the *Songs appointed by Law*,
" and a certain Species of *Muſick*, excluſive
" of all others [f]." In imitation of this, the
Lacedemonian Youth ſung the Hymns of *Ter-*
pander; and to give them the more. Authority, the *Helotes* or Slaves were forbid to ſing
them under ſevere Penalties. Thus theſe three
States, *Egypt*, *Crete*, and *Lacedemon* agreed in
the ſtrange Deſign of ſetting Boundaries to the
two wildeſt things in Life, the Sallies of *Mu-*
ſick and Raptures of *Poetry*. But this, we are
told [g], was the moſt ancient *Philoſophy* in
Greece; and their firſt *Sophiſts*, taught by the
Egyptians, run their Science in this *politick*

P 2

Sttain.

[f] Παῖδας δὲ ϳράμματά τι μανθάνειν, και τὰς ἐκ τ̄ ΝΟΜΩΝ
ἸΩΔΑΣ, και τινα ΕΙΔΗ τῆς Μυσικῆς.   Βίϐ. ί.
[g] ΦΙΛΟΣΟΦΙΑ ἐςὶ παλαιοτάϳη τι καὶ πλείςη τ̄ Ἑλλήνων
ἐν ΚΡΗΤΗ τι καὶ ΛΑΚΕΔΑΙΜΟΝΙ· καὶ σοφιςαὶ πλεῖ-
ςοι ϳῆς ἐκεῖ ἐισίν.   Πλάτων. Πρωταϳόρα.

Sect.10.Strain. They chose, like their Masters, to begin at the Source; and thought it the greatest Wisdom to fashion and regulate the human Passions, by adjusting the *Springs* that set them a going.

AND now we are got upon an *Ascent*, whence we can see to the end of the Disquisition. It now appears *what these* PÆANS *were*, which the *Cretans* were wont to sing:— No other than the *publick Hymns* authorized by *Law*, and appointed to be learned by their noble Youth. It appears in what manner the *Oracle* was erected, and what kind of *Learning* was probably there:——It must have been a *Tradition* of the *Cretan* and *Egyptian Mythology*, involved in Metaphor, and heightened by Enthusiasm. Nor was it solely confined to *religious* matters: All sorts of Subjects came through the hands of *Apollo*; and the Philosopher so often quoted, when he forms a Scheme for improving his Countrymen in Wisdom, and assisting them to make advances in real Knowledge, lays a part of the Stress upon their *Instruction* from the *Oracle* [h].

THITHER our Poet seems to have gone by Sea from *Chios*. For in relating the Voyage of the *Cretan* Vessel that carried the Founders of the Temple of *Delphi*, almost round

the

[h] Παιδίαις τε καὶ ἐν ΔΕΛΦΩΝ Μαντείαις χρωμένας.

Πλάτων. Ἐπινομ.

the *Peloponnesus*, he has described the *Coast* Sect.10.
so minutely as to name *eighteen Promontories*
and Coast-Towns, which they saw one after
another: *He* mentions the distant *Islands*, and
Tops of Mountains, they descried at such and
such Parts of their Navigation; and has not
forgot so much as the *Changes* of the *Wind*
necessary in so indirect a Course. This seems
to be too exact and particular to be received
by *Relation* from another; but looks like the
effect of *personal Observation*, and the exact
Memory our Poet retained of a Voyage *made*
by himself. There let us leave him with his
priestly Instructors, to consider what use he made
of this Stock ' of Knowledge, and *How such*
Materials are to be managed?

So DELICATE is the Nature of *Mytho-*
logy, that it requires not a stronger Head, or
more elevated Fancy, to produce it at first,
than it does a nice Hand to apply it in a
Poem, and interweave it with the Persons and'
Machines concerned in the Action. Of the
two sorts already mentioned, the *last* is apt to
get the upper-hand in the Narration, and con-
found its own Offspring, the *artificial Mytho-*
logy. This produces Inconsistencies sometimes
in Facts, or renders the Meaning of the Allegory impenetrable: But the worst part of its
Influence, when misapplied, is upon *Manners*;
where it destroys the Distinctions of Charac-

ters,

Sect. 10. ters, and often blends Extremes that are incompatible in *Nature*.

There are Circumstances in many of *Homer's* Stories, which have little Connexion with the Transaction where they are employed:
" Some of his Fables, says *Eustathius*, were
" invented by himself for his present purpose ;
" others of them are *purely allegorical :* And
" he has many besides, that were composed
" at first by the *Ancients*, and are inserted
" in their proper places in his Poetry, tho'
" their Allegory does not always respect the
" *Trojan Affairs*, but points at what was in-
" tended by its *first Inventers*."

To shew the Truth and Extent of these Observations throughout *Homer's* Writings, would be, upon the matter, to write a regular Treatise of *Mythology*. It has been done in part by the learned *Proclus* in his Notes upon *Hesiod*, and upon *Plato's Timæus* ; where the Objections raised against our Poet's Representations of the Gods are answered, sometimes with more *Deference* than Judgment. But there are some other Parts of his Management with respect to his *Divinities* ; their ranging themselves on different *Sides* ; and his *Chiefs* being protected by *opposite* Powers, which it will be worth while to examine. They are Beauties in Poetry for the most part but little observed, and give great pleasure, when we

enter

enter into their Meaning, and perceive the Juſt-Sect.10. neſs of their Application.

HOMER's GODS are finely diſtributed between the two Armies, the *Greeks* and *Barbarians*: The *Greeks*, naturally wiſe and brave, and ſo formed by the *Temperature* of their *Climate*, have *Pallas* and *Juno* of their Party. The *Trojans* have *Mars*, or the impetuous *Sally* of War, *Venus* or *Effeminacy*, and *Apollo*, a mixed kind of Divinity; the God of *Heat*, ecſtatick *Muſick*, and *poetick Paſſion*. *Jupiter*, or the *Univerſal Nature*, and particularly the Influences of the *Celeſtial Region*, favours ſometimes the one and ſometimes the other, but generally the *Greeks*. *Neptune* is entirely *Grecian*, as they were Lords of the *Sea*. *Mercury* and *Diana* have little to do in the War, but are mentioned by the *Poet*, the one from the *Egyptian* Tradition as *Latona*'s Oppoſite, and the *Conducter* of departed Souls; and the other, as a *Power*, no Friend to the *Ladies*, whom ſhe kills at pleaſure. Theſe are what we may call the *active Gods*, and this is their general Arrangement. As for *Saturn* or *Time*, *Ceres* or the *Earth*, *Pluto* or *Hell*, they are a kind of *ſtable Deities* that ſupport the *whole* of things, but have but little particular Influence upon any ſingle Action.

IF WE deſcend to their ſeveral Parts, and look nearer ſtill into the Poet's Conduct, we ſhall find every God in his becoming Employ-

ment,

Sect.10. ment, and acting confiftently with the Power
he reprefents. *Phœbus* or the Sun, the God
of Heat and Health, in his Wrath fends a
Plague. *Achilles*, from a Senfation of the Corruption of the *Air* now unwholefome, or in
the Poet's Stile, being warned by *Juno*, calls an
Affembly : Provoked by *Agamemnon,* *Pallas*,
or *Reflexion*, reafons with him, and quiets him.
His Armour is made by *Vulcan*, the God of
Fire; and his vaft Nimblenefs and Humidity
makes him properly the Son of a *Sea-Goddefs.*
The wife and patient *Ulyffes* is favoured by *Mi-*
nerva ; as *Ajax,* rafh, lumpifh, and ftrong, is at
conftant variance with the Goddefs of Wifdom : and it is very remarkable, that *Homer*
never changes this *tutelar Numen* to the Prince
of *Ithaca*, nor reprefents his fubtil *Hero* under
any other Tuition than the blue-ey'd Maid's.
It might have embellifhed his Narration, and
given play to his Fancy ; but he has preferred
the *Truth* of the Character, and ftuck clofe to
his Allegory. The frequent Shipwrecks, and
bad Fortune of the Hero at *Sea*, is, in poetical Language, that *He was hated by* NEPTUNE,
in the fame manner as the Man who committed any Outrage when *drunk,* was under
the difpleafure of *Bacchus.* The other Chiefs
mentioned in the *Iliad* are frequently affifted or
protected by fome *Divine Perfon*, according to
the Nature of the Occafion, the Character of
their Nation, or their perfonal Qualities.

LET

LET us now quit our Bard for a little, Sect. 10. and obferve what Figure this Subject makes in other hands :——The celebrated *Roman* Poet, writing for the Honour of his Country, has been forced to *fhift Sides*, and make the *Tro- jans*, if not the *conquering Party*, at leaft wor- thy to conquer, and only fubdued by Fraud and Stratagem. This, with the received *Tra- dition* concerning the Birth of his *Hero*, has led him into fome Improprieties about his Gods, which he has not failed to cover with his ufual Judgment. For example, that the chief Di- vinity who guides the *holy, wife*, and *brave Eneas*, fhould be VENUS, is fomething un- lucky. She well might tutor *Paris*, and fa- vour all the *Trojans* who had their Seraglio's even then : But it required great Difcretion to make her act in the *Eneid* with any Pro- priety. And after all, however we may be charmed with the Delicacy of her Appearance, and the Pomp of the Defcription, I don't know but fhe is introduced as a *mere Perfon*, divine indeed, and of great Power; but without any regard to her *Character* and *Inclinations*. It was hard to make her appear in a *virtuous Caufe*, or direct the Enterprizes of the pious Hero, in any other Capacity than his *tradi- tional Parent*; except fhe had condefcended to accompany him when he went a hunting, and conducted him into the Cave with *Dido*.

SUCH

Sect.10. Such is the *impatient* Temper of Mythology; and so powerful a thing is *Truth*, that it will not stoop to any other than a *genuine* Representation, nor bear to be disfigured tho' in *Masque*. Perhaps *Homer*'s drawing immediately from the *Fountains*, or having a hand himself in modelling these *divine Phantoms*, was the Cause of his having been so happy and natural in their *Distribution*. Their *Use*, if we may believe the Ancients, was not confined to *Poetry*; nor to raising those high Sensations and magnificent Images of the Universe and of its Parts, for which we admire them: But thro' the channel of *Religion* they reached *Life*, had an influence upon *Morals*, and impressed the Vulgar with that dread of future Punishments, which keeps them in their Duty.

A Person of great Wit, and greater Learning, who has laboured exceedingly to prove, " That Mankind for the most part acts not " from *Principle*," hath at the same time essayed to weaken this Influence [i], and attributes any Good their Religion and its Rites could do, to their filling up that *Time* which must have been otherwise ill employed by a polite and voluptuous People: Yet he allows, that an Apprehension of Punishment from the *Magistrate* restrains from Evil; and why an Apprehension of Vengeance from the *Gods*, if supposed equally certain, should not have the same Effect,

I

[i] Continuation de Pensées diverses par M. *Bayle*, tom. ii. §. 119.

I cannot understand: The former is insuffi- Sect. 10.
cient, in many instances, to prevent Fraud or
Violence, and so no doubt is the latter. And
these Instances, when collected and set together, make a glaring Appearance; but conclude
no more against the Efficacy of Religion, than
against the Necessity of Laws and of Penalties
to inforce them.

THAT the Commonalty of *Greece* and
Rome believed a State of future Rewards and
Punishments; and that *this Belief* kept them
in their duty, is affirmed, as I said, by the
wisest of the Ancients. It is needless to tell
your Lordship, that TIMÆUS LOCRUS was
of the number: The Character he bears of
Plato's Master is sufficient to justify his Claim.
The little Treatise of his, which 'tis thought
his illustrious Scholar purchased at an immense
Price, is no less than a *System of the World* [k].
His Expressions are simple, but his Doctrines
are drawn from deep Observation, and explained in the Harmony and Proportions of the *Py-
thagorick Philosophy*. He begins with *Creation*, which he attributes to a *good Principle*,
whom he calls, " The invisible God, the
" Prince and Parent of all things." Then
he

---

[k] Τιμαίω τῷ Λοκρῳ περὶ ΨΥΧΑΣ ΚΟΣΜΩ καὶ ΦΥ-
ΣΕΩΣ.

Upon this Treatise, these Verses of *Timon* the Satyrist are
preserved:

Πολλῶν δ' ἀργυρέων ὀλίγον ἠλλάξατο βίβλον
Ἔνθεν ἀφορμηθεὶς ΤΙΜΑΙΟΓΡΑΦΕΙΝ ἐπιχύρας.

Sect.10. he goes thro' its *Parts* ; the Nature of the
Elements, the Courfe of the *Planets,* and Periods of the *World,* and concludes with *Man,*
and the Doctrine of *Morals,* in thefe remarkable Words : " The Mind, fays he, that is
" exercifed in fuch Contemplations, and at-
" tains to a *Contentednefs* with the State of
" Humanity, and to a *juft ufe* of the appoint-
" ed Meafure of Life, is undoubtedly happy:
" And whofoever receives this Attainment as
" his Lot from Heaven, is led by *Truth* to
" *Felicity.* But if any Difpofition happens
" to be perverfe and unruly, then *Chaftife-*
" *ment* ought to be applied ; both that which
" is appointed by the *Laws,* and alfo what
" can be drawn from thofe *Traditions* which
" introduce numberlefs Terrors from *Heaven,*
" and Tortures in *Hell*; threatning endlefs
" Punifhments that await the wretched Ghoft
" *below,* with all the Torments which the
" IONICK POET has laudably, and from
" *ancient Tradition,* reprefented the Souls of
" wicked Men to endure *hereafter.* For as
" fometimes, when wholefome Remedies will
" not prevail, we procure Health by admini-
" ftring a fickening Potion; fo we curb the
" Stubborn and Difobedient by *falfe* Rela-
" tions, when the *true* have no Effect. Of ne-
" ceffity therefore THE FOREIGN TOR-
" MENTS muft be inculcated [1]. ——And it
" muft

---

[1] Αἰγυπτῶδ᾽ ἀναγκαίως καὶ ΤΙΜΩΡΙΑΙ ΞΕΝΑΙ

" muſt be told, that *Nemeſis*, the diſtributiveSect.10.
" and avenging *Power*, hath appointed all
" theſe things to happen in the *ſecond Pe-*
" *riod*, and to be executed by fierce infernal
" *Genii*, who witneſſed the Conduct and the
" Crimes of Men. To them the all-govern-
" ing God hath committed the Adminiſtra-
" tion of the World, which conſiſts of Gods
" and Men, and of the other Animals he
" himſelf hath formed, after the perfect Mo-
" del of the *eternal* and *intellectual Idea* m."

IT APPEARS then that Mythology, and
Homer's Mythology in particular, was thought
to be a Cure for a wrong-turn'd Mind, and
a Reſtraint from Immorality and Vice: And
if it was ſo in *Greece*, it was much more ſo
in *Italy*, where *Timæus* was born, and where
long after his days, not only *private Super-*
ſtition prevailed, but the moſt important Steps
of the State were over-ruled by the *Aruſpices*
and *Augurs*; and their Conſuls and Pretors
bowed before a Preſage taken from the Entrails
of *Beaſts*, the Flight of *Birds*, and Signs from
Heaven.

BUT *Timæus*'s Diſciple ſeems to have carried things a little further: He lived in *Athens*
at a time when the Laws had given a Sanction
to *Mythology*; with which, like a good Citizen,

---

m ῞Οις ὁ πάντων Ἀχμῶν Θεὸς ἐπίτρεψε διοίκησιν Κόσμω, συμ-
πεπληρμμένω ἐκ θεῶν τε καὶ ἀνθρώπων, ῆ τε ἄλλων ζώων ὅσα
δεδημιύργηται πετ' ΕΙΚΟΝΑ τὴν ἀείσαν ῎ΕΙΔΕΟΣ ΑΙΩ-
ΝΙΩ καὶ ΝΟΗΤΩ. Τιμαί☉ Λοκρ. περὶ ψυχ. Κ.σμω.

Sect.10. zen, he fo far complies, as to difapprove of a narrow Scrutiny into its *Senfe* and *Origin*. He thinks it beft to *accept* of the literal Meaning, and would have curious inquifitive People rather turn their *Searches* another way.

THERE was a beautiful Spot of Ground a little without the Walls of *Athens*, upon the Banks of *Iliffus*, where it was believed that *Boreas* had run off with the Nymph *Orithya*, while fhe was fporting with one of her Companions upon the Brink of the River. Thither came *Socrates* with a young Gentleman of the Town, in queft of an agreeable Retirement. They were to read a paradoxical Difcourfe of *Lyfias*; the greateft Orator then in *Athens*, proving, " That *Favours* in Love fhould rather " be granted to thofe who never felt the Paf- " fion, than to the real Lover." And having talked a little of the Beauty of the Place, how proper it was *for Girls to fport in*, and mentioned fome other Circumftances of the Story, the Youth very naturally turns to his fmiling Companion, and fays, " But be fincere with " me, *Socrates*; Do you really believe this *Le-* " *gend* to be true ᶰ ?——Why, fays the Philo- " fopher, tho' I did not, (as they fay your " *learned* People do) I fhould not be far in " the wrong ; and then I would go *allegorize*, " and fay, that the real Wind had come in " a

ᶰ 'ΑΛΛ' εἰπὶ μοὶ πρὸς Διὸς, ὦ ΣΩΚΡΑΤΕΣ, καὶ σὺ τῦτο τὸ ΜΥΘΟΛΟΓΗΜΑ πιύθη ἀληθὲς ἔναι.
　　　　　　　　　　ΠΛΑΤ. Φαιδρῖς.

" a Guft, and blown the Nymph off the Sect.10.
" Steep, and fo was reported to have carried
" her away, while fhe and *Pharmacia* were
" intent upon their play. *But* for my own
" fhare, *my Boy*, I look indeed upon thefe
" *moral Meanings* as very pretty and curious;
" but think they belong to a profound *la-*
" *borious Genius*, and are the Work of not a
" very happy Man. My reafon is, (and I
" have no other for it) That after one has
" got thro' this Allegory, he muft next under-
" take the Race of the *Hippocentaurs* ; and
" when he hath adjufted them, then the
" *Chimæra* comes upon him : Next follows a
" Train of *Gorgons* and *Pegafus's*, and other
" unweildy Monfters, inexplicable both for
" their Number and Abfurdity. *Thefe*, fhould
" one go about to explain without *believing*
" them, and attempt to give, according to
" their Texture and Likenefs, but a *homely*
" *Solution* of their Meaning, it would be an
" Undertaking of great Pains and Leifure.
" *But I*, my Friend, can find no Leifure for
" fuch Enquiries; and the reafon of it is,
" That I cannot as yet, in obedience to the
" God of *D E L P H I*, UNDERSTAND MY-
" SELF. Now it appears ridiculous to me,
" to be fearching into *other* Matters while I
" am ignorant of *this*. Wherefore bidding
" thefe Subjects *adieu*; and being perfuaded
" of the Truth of the Opinion fettled con-
" cerning

" cerning them by Law, (as I juſt now told
" you) I fix my Attention upon *myſelf*; and
" confider, not the *Gorgon* or the *Centaur*,
" but *what kind of a Monſter I am*; whether
" more double and ſlippery than *Proteus*, and
" more fiery than *Typhon* : Or perhaps, a *tamer*,
" *milder* Animal, defigned by Nature for a
" *divine Lot*, and a *peaceful Deſtiny*."

Gravelot inv.   Ja. Gacht Sculp.

SECT.

Gravelot inv.   P.Fourdrinier Sul.

SECT. XI.

THERE are few things in the *ancient*
Poetry more moving than the Story of
Orpheus and *Eurydice*. It hath acquired new
Beauties by falling into the hands of the ten-
der and paffionate *Virgil*; and is told by him in
fo melting a ftrain, that fome of the Touches
he hath given it can hardly be read *without*
Tears. When we are wrought up to fuch a
Temper, it naturally leads us to compaffionate

Q   the

Sect.11. the hard Fate of the unhappy Lovers; and we begin to feel some Indignation at the captious Condition, upon which he was to possess his Beauty, or lose her for ever : *Not to look at his loved* Eurydice. Arbitrary and capricious! Unbefitting the just Brother of *Jove*, and unlike the Bounties of a *divine, unenvious Nature* [a] : Unless indeed there be something else understood than appears; some *Truth* in Life or Morals that lies latent under this Circumstance of the *Tale*.

THE great and unhappy Lord *Verulam*, who was sensible of the Incongruity, has given an Explication of the Fable [b]; but seems not to have hit upon the real Meaning. What he says is entertaining and beautiful : for he was a Spirit of that high Order that *go ingeniously wrong*, and who cannot *err* without *instructing*. But I incline to think that the *Moral* of the *Fiction* is rather to be learned at an ordinary *Musick-Meeting*, or an unmeaning *Opera*, than where his Lordship directs us, in the Recesses of an abstruse Philosophy.

ORPHEUS's Mistress was *Musick*. The Powers of it are enchanting. It lulls the Reason, and raises the Fancy in so agreeable a manner, that *we forget ourselves* while it lasts:
The

---

[a] Ἄφθονοι ΟΥΡΑΝΙΔΑΙ, ᾗ ἐν ἀλλήλοις τελέθουσιν·
Ὁυ φθονέει ΜΗΝΗ πολὺ κρείσσονι ΗΑΙΟΥ ἀυγαῖς·
Ὁυ ΧΘΩΝ Ὀυρανίοις ὑψώμασι τέρπεται ἰοῦσιν·
Ὁυ ΠΟΤΑΜΟΙ ΠΕΛΑΓΕΣΣΙΝ ἀεὶ δ' ὁμόνοιαν ἔχουσιν.

[b] F. Bacon, *De Sapientiâ Veterum*. § 11.

The Mind turns diffolute and gay; and hugs Sect. ii.
itfelf in all the deluding Profpects and fond
Wifhes of a *golden* Dream. Whilft every Accent is warbled over by a charming Voice, a
filly Song appears found *Morality*; and the very
Words of the *Opera* pafs for Senfe, in prefence
of their *Accompagnamento.* But no fooner does
the *Mufick* ceafe, than the Charm is undone,
and the Fancies difappear. The firft *fober Look*
we take of it breaks the Spell; and we are hur-
ried back, with fome Regret, to the common
dull Road of Life, when the florid Illufion is
vanifhed.

IN THIS gloomy Temper, *My Lord,* fhould
I be at prefent, had it been my Happinefs to
make one of the *infpired Train:* How unwill-
ingly would a true Son of the *Mufes* part with
his Fictions and Enthufiafm? The myfterious
Egypt! The prophetick *Ifis!* The oracular *Telchines*; thefe nurfing Fathers of the *Grecian Divinities!* To bid farewel to thefe with their
divine Pupils, and travel back with *Homer,*
to Countries of a *cooler Turn,* would be a melancholy Profpect to a *Poet.*

BUT as things are at this time, I find it
poffible to be very chearful under the thoughts
of an Exchange: *Variety* they fay is fweet; and
there is a kind of pleafure in getting rid of the
lymphatick enthufiaftical Tribe, and taking Journey with our Poet, to a Land of Freedom and
Ingenuity: A Land of *Arts* of a different Stamp;

Q 2 not

Sect.11. not fo precife and uniform as the *prieftly* Pre-
fcriptions; but blooming in the native *Grace*
and *Vigour* which is the Gift of Liberty and
unlimited Commerce. Nor will the Change,
I am perfuaded, be difagreeable to *your Lordfhip*, fince it leads to a People and Nation whofe
Memory you are in Gratitude bound to honour.

THE *PHENICIAN* Name is fo famous
in early Antiquity, that the bare mention of it
is fufficient to point out the Source of your
Obligations. It prefents us with the Authors
and Improvers of *Building*, and the nobler kinds
of *Architecture*; with the firft Workers in
Iron, *Wood*, and *Stone*: It makes us think of a
Country, the *Parent* of *Mechanicks*, *Navigation*, and *Aftronomy*; the Inventers of *Glafs*,
and Rivals of *Egypt* for the Invention of *Letters* and *Arithmetick*: In fhort, it reminds us
of the Origin of the *noble* and *ufeful Arts* which
employ many of your Lordfhip's Hours, and
enable you to judge for your Country, in a Capacity not very common among the *Great*.

THIS Happinefs of *Phenicia* in the inventive Genius of its Inhabitants, and its Situation between *Judæa* and the Sea, have made
me often wonder at the Obfervation of an ancient Hiftorian. He is treating of the Rife of
Arts, and what every Nation had found out
for the common Benefit of Mankind; and
concludes his Account with this Remark, *Soli
omnium*

omnium Judæi *nibil in medium contulere. The* Sect.11.
Jews *alone of all the rest have contributed no-*
thing for the publick Good.

I HAVE frequently endeavoured to find a
reaſon for this Diſſimilitude between two
neighbour Nations: Sometimes I have thought,
that the Knowledge of *human Arts* cultivated
in *Phenicia*, was perhaps incompatible with
that *Sacred Science,* for which the other People are ſo juſtly regarded: " Being the only
" *Canton* of the Earth whoſe Inhabitants were
" ſurprizingly illuminated, beyond the reſt of
" the human Race c." At other times I have
imagined, that our Author was *miſtaken* in his
Remark; and he muſt have been ſo in the
groſſeſt manner, according to the Doctrine of
the *Rabbi's.* One of the wiſeſt of them d, makes
no ſcruple to aſſert, " *That* the ſublime and
" profound Parts of all kinds of Knowledge,
" were to be found among the *Jews*; and
" that not only the Principles of *all the Scien-*
" *ces,* but likewiſe the Concluſions which the
" *Greek* Philoſophers, *Pythagoras*, *Plato*, and
" ſuch others, had drawn from them, were

Q 3   " tranſmitted

---

c On eſt ſurpris de voir les Habitans d'un petit Canton de la
Terre, plus eclaires que le reſte du Genre humain.
M Leibnitz Preface à la Theodicée.

d *En nueſtra ley ſe comprehende todo lo ſubtil y profundo de*
las ſciencias; lo que no es anſy en las otras. And afterwards:
Los fundamentos y concluſiones de todas las ſciencias, fueron tran-
ſladados de Noſotros, *à los* Chaldeos *primero, deſpues à los* Perſas
y Medos, *y deſpues à los* Griegos.
R. Yeuda. Cuzary, Diſcurſ. 2do.

" tranfmitted to them from the *Jewifh Sages,*
" thro' the hands, firft of the *Chaldeans,* and
" then of the *Medes* and *Perfians.*" Which
of thefe may have been the Cafe; or whether the Neceffity of *Invention* in *naval Affairs*
may not have produced fome difference be-
twen the bordering Nations, your Lordfhip's
Acquaintance with the *Nature* of thofe Arts,
and the Hiftory of *Men,* will beft enable you
to decide. But our prefent Bufinefs is only
with the *Phenicians.*

THEY were a very ancient Nation; fo ancient, that tho' they are among the firft Countries who make any Figure in Hiftory, and that
Letters were early in ufe among them, yet
their *Origin* is quite uncertain; and in this refpect they are upon a level with their Neighbours the *Egyptians,* or the ancient *Athenians,*
who both called themfelves ΑΥΤΟΧΘΟΝΑΣ[e],
and the *firft of Men*[f]. Some of the old Writers
faid, that they came from about the *Arabian
Gulph,* and fettled upon the *Mediterranean*
Coaft: And others affirmed quite the contrary:
" That fome Merchants of *Sidon* had gone
" from thence, and firft fet on foot a Traffick
" in the *Red-Sea*[g]." However this may have
been,

---

[e] Sprung from the Earth where they lived.

[f] Φασὶ τοίνυν Ἀιγύπλιοι κ' τὴν ἐξ ἀρχῆς τ͂ ὅλων γένεσιν, ΠΡΩ-
ΤΟΥΣ ΑΝΘΡΩΠΟΥΣ γνέωθαι κ' τὴν ᾿ΑΙΓΥΠΤΟΝ.
Διοδωρ. Σικελ. Βιβλ. α.

[g] ᾿Οι μὲν γ' κ' τὰς Φοίνικας κ' τὰς Σιδωνίως τὰς καθ' ἡμᾶς,
ἀποίκως ἐδ τ͂ ἐν τῷ ᾿ΩΚΕΑΝΩ φασι, περιθέντες κ' διὰ τι
ΦΟΙΝΙΚΕΣ ἐκαλῦσθα, ὅτι κ' ἡ θάλαπα ΕΡΥΘΡΑ᾿ ᾿Οι δὲ
ΕΚΕΙΝΟΥΣ ΤΟΥΤΩΝ. Στραβ. Βιβλ. α.

been, we cannot doubt of their retaining much Sect.ii. of the Manners of the *Eaſtern* Nations: Their Language was a Branch of the *Aramean,* and their *Policy* both civil and religious; their *Temples, Records,* and Order of *Prieſts,* exempted from *Taxes,* are very like the Inſtitutions that prevailed over the Eaſt [h].

BUT what diſtinguiſhed them from all the reſt, was their early Application to *Maritime* Affairs, and the noble uſe they made of their Succeſs. They were invited to turn their Thoughts this way by the Commodiouſneſs of their Situation; and purſued it with ſuch ſkilful indefatigable Patience, that they were the firſt Inventers, and continued the ſole Maſters, of the *weſtern Trade,* from the firſt *Hercules* to the time of *Alexander,* for many hundreds of Years. By this means, their Acceſſions of Wealth and People were ſo great, that they grew uneaſy at home, and therefore ſpread themſelves abroad in great Colonies, and filled *Spain* and *Africk* with Cities, little inferior in Power and Splendour to their own [i].

Q 4

THEY

[h] Τὰς τε ἱεροὺς κ[αὶ]αςησαϑαι περαπλησίως τοῖς κ[α]τ' Ἀιζυπ[τ]ον ΑΤΕΛΕΙΣ, καὶ πάσης ΛΕΙΤΟΥΡΓΙΑΣ ἀπολέλυμένυς, ὡς Βαϑυλώνιοι κ[αὶ] ὐπι ΧΑΛΔΑΙΟΥΣ. Διοδωρ. ΒιϹλ. ἀ.

[i] Barcinone (*Barcelona*), Malaca (*Malaga*), Carteia, (*Cartagena*,) with ſeveral others in Spain. In Africk, *Tunis, Tripoli, Leptis, Utica,* and the Rival of Rome, *Carthage: Thebes* alſo in *Beotia.* But their great early Settlement was in GADES (*Cadix*) the little Iſland that lies in the Mouth of the Streights, and commanded all the weſtern Trade of the World. This we can gather even from the divine Prophet, who calls the People of *Cadix,* " *the Inha-* " *bitants of the* ISLE *whom the Merchants of* Sidon *that paſs over* " *the Sea have repleniſhed."* ISAIAH Chap. XXIII. § 2.

Sect. II. THEY WERE bufied about thefe Settlements for fome time *after the Trojan War*[k]:
That is, " While the *Phenicians* were in a
" State of high Profperity, populous and
" powerful, acquainted with foreign Coun-
" tries and ufeful Arts, *then it was*, by a
" ftrange Conftancy of good Fortune, that
" HOMER had Opportunities to know and
" converfe with them."

I MUST acknowledge that fuch a Combination of *lucky Incidents* in the Life of any
one Man, looks fomething fufpicious; and
when I review the Concourfe of them; his
Climate and *Country*, his *Religion* and *Language*, the publick and private *Manners* of
his Age, and his own *Profeffion* and *Travels*,
it ferves but to increafe the Wonder. But
we muft confider, that a thing's being *rare*,
does not prefently conclude it to be falfe or
imaginary; elfe the moft beautiful *Theories* in
Learning, and the higheft *Pitches* of Happinefs in Life, muft be given up as abfurd and
impoffible. Our Bufinefs therefore, is to *tread
cautioufly*, as we have done hitherto, and to
take as little upon *Suppofition*, as the diftance
of Time and Nature of the Subjects will permit.

THAT

[k] Θρυλλᾶται καὶ ἡ ΦΟΙΝΙΚΩΝ ναυ]ιλία· οἱ καὶ τὰ ἔξω
ᾧ 'Ηρακλεῖ·ν σηλῶν ἐπῆλθον, καὶ Πόλεις ἔκ]ισαν κἀκεῖ καὶ
περὶ τὸ μέσα τῆς Λιβύης παραλίας, ΜΙΚΡΟΝ ΤΩΝ ΤΡΟΪ-
ΚΩΝ ΥΣΤΕΡΟΝ.   Στραβ. Βιβλ. α.

THAT *Homer* had the Opportunities men-Sect. II.
tioned, and that he did not neglect to improve them, will beſt appear by conſidering
what he has really learned from the Phenicians: This will be a certain Proof of his
converſing with them, at the ſame time that
it will ſet the Happineſs of this Circumſtance
of his Life in a true Light: And if they are
Leſſons of Importance, it will increaſe at every
Step, as we ſhall find this or the other *Allegory*
or *Tale,* taken from the *Relations* of that ingenious People.

AND FIRST, it may not be amiſs to obſerve in general, That many of the *Egyptian*
Doctrines and Cuſtoms paſſed thro' *Phenicia*
into *Greece:* The *Refugées* from *Egypt* commonly took this Country in their way, and afterwards proceeded to the *Iſlands,* or ſettled
upon ſome part of the *Grecian Coaſt;* Some
of them made a conſiderable Stay in *Phenicia*
before they travelled further Weſt, and therefore carried along with them into their new
Settlements, both the *Phenician Arts,* and the
Egyptian Learning.

THUS *CADMUS,* when he had ſtaid
long in *Phenicia,* went to *Lemnos, Imbrus,*
and *Samothrace,* and is ſaid to have carried
thither the Worſhip and Rites of the *Pheni-*
ian CABEIRI or *Great Gods,* and taught
the Inhabitants their Initiation and Myſteries,
for which they were afterwards ſo famous;
tho'

Sect.11. tho' I rather think the *Telchines*, or the *Idæi Dactyli* were there before him : For why should he not rather have eftablished his favourite Worfhip in *Thebes*, where he finally fettled ?

His Son-in-law *Arifteas* reigned in *Cea* ; his Grandfon *Bacchus* in *Naxos*. *Phalanthus*, another *Phenician*, took up his Habitation in *Rhodes*, and the celebrated *Anceüs* ruled in *Samos*. He was one of the *Argonauts*, and the only Aftronomer among them. His Mother gave her Name to the Ifland *Aftypalea* ; and the greater part of the CYCLADES received Names from the *Phenicians*, which were derived from thofe Accidents and Appearances that occur to a *fea-faring mercantile People*. Their feveral Origins have been nicely inveftigated by the laborious *Bochart*; and they appear to have been given in the fame way as the *Spaniards* and *Portuguefe*, when they difcovered the *Indies*, called their Countries and Rivers, *Tierra de Fuego*, *Tierra de Brea*, Terra dos Papos: *Rio grande*———— *De la Plata*————*De las Concas* ; and fuch others.

But befides this early Intercourfe between the *Greeks* and *Phenicians*, and principally the *Iflanders* [1], (among whom *Homer* lived,)
there

---

[1] There are feveral Proofs of this Commerce in *Holy-Writ*, where *Tyre* and *Sidon*, the chief Towns in *Phenicia*, are commonly joined with the ISLES. Thus " *all the Kings of Tyrus and all*
" *the*

there was another piece of good Fortune Sect. 11.
attended him. In order to converse with the
Egyptian Priests, there was a necessity of
making a Voyage to *Egypt*: But there was
no need of travelling into *Phenicia*, to meet
with a *Phenician Captain*, or the Governour
of a Colony: They themselves went over all,
carrying their Knowledge and Experience a-
long with them. Their manner was, to go
out early in the Spring upon a *Trading Voyage*;
some to the *Bosphorus* and *Euxine*, some to
the *Egean* and *Adriatick*; others passed the
Streights, and steered to the *Gum' Coast* on
one hand, and as far as *Britain* on the other;
and when they had searched thro' all for Mer-
chandise, they returned loaded home late in
the Year.

To THIS intelligent and wide-spread Nation, I am apt to think our Poet stands indebted for *his foreign Geography*.——This is
an uncommon way of speaking; but it will
be

" *the Kings of Zidon*, are joined with *the Kings of the* Isles *which*
" *are beyond the Sea* *." And more particularly by another Prophet, *Tyre* is called " *the City situate at the Entry of the Sea,*
" *which is a Merchant of the People for many* ISLES †: *The Men*
" *of* Dedan *were her Merchants*; MANY ISLES *were the Mer-*
" *chandise of her Hand* ‡." And at her Fall, " *the* ISLES *were*
" *to tremble; the Princes of the Sea to come down from their*
" *Thrones, and lay away their Robes* ‖; *The* ISLES *were to shake*
" *in the Day of her Fall, and the* ISLES *that are in the Sea to be*
" *troubled at her Departure* ‖†. These ISLES were no other than
Cyprus, Rhodes, Crete, and the Islands of the *Archipelago*, where
HOMER lived.

* JEREMIAH XXV. §22.　　† EZEKIEL xxvii. § 3.
‡ Ibid. §. 15.　　‖ xxvi· §15.
‖† Ibid. § 18.

Sect.11. be eafily underftood when we reflect, That Homer was more capable of giving than receiving Inftruction in the *Geography* of *Greece*, the *Leffer Afia*, and perhaps the *Egyptian Coaft*: But what further Knowledge appears in his Writings of the other Tracts of Land in *Europe*, *Afia*, and *Africa*, *That*, I judge, he has received by Information from the *Phenicians*.

MY REASONS for this Opinion are thefe: By ftaying in *Greece*, and making fhort Voyages among the *Iflands*, or even down to *Egypt*, he could never learn that the *Earth* was begirt on all fides with the *Ocean*, as he often fays it is: But the *Phenicians*, who had made long Voyages upon the *Red* and *Mediterranean Seas*, who had paffed thro' the *Streight* of *Gibraltar*, and failed the Coaft on either hand before *Homer*'s days, and were actually making fuch Voyages annually during his Life, *They* might tell him, that where-ever they came, they found the general Barrier was the *Ocean* [m].

FROM the fame *Sea-faring* People, he muft have heard what Countries were the *Boundaries* and *Ends* [n], as he calls them, of the habitable Globe. Some of thefe he plainly names by their *proper* Appellations; others he points out by fuch *Marks* and Peculiarities, as demonftrate that he was not ignorant of their Situation.

To

[m] They named it fo from *this* very Circumftance. See Page 100. in the Notes.

[n] ΠΕΙΡΑΤΑ ΓΑΙΗΣ.   'Οδυσ. Δ.

To the *South*, he directly mentions *Africk*, Sect.11.
Ethiopia, and what we take for *Arabia* º, as
the uttermoſt Parts of the World: To the
North, he deſcribes the Life of the *Hyperbo-
reans*, juſt as we know the *Scythians* and *Tar-
tars* lived, People that inhabit the *Northern*
Continent: To the *Eaſt*, and *Weſt*, he names
no Country, but ſays frequently, *That the Sun
riſes from* P, *and ſets in the Ocean* ꟼ; which can
have no other Meaning, than that the *Aſiatick
Continent* on the *Eaſt*, and the *European* on
the *Weſt*, are bounded by the *Watery Element.* This is the only Senſe the Expreſſion
will bear; and any other put upon it, makes
it a plain Abſurdity.

I T I S the more remarkable, as it comes
from a Man who lived between two great
undiſcovered Lands. *Ionia* had the vaſt Continent of A S I A lying due Eaſt from it; a
very ſmall part of which was known to *Homer* himſelf, or to the *Greeks* long after his
Time. There is no mention made of *Babylon* or *Ecbatana* in all his Writings, which
He, who celebratés the *Wealth* of *Thebes*, and
Arts of *Sidon*, could never have omitted to
do, had he known any thing of the *Aſſyrian*

or

º ΕΡΕΜΒΟΤΣ.

P 'Ηέλιꞷ μὲν ἔπειτα νέον πεοσέβαλλεν ἀϱύϱαις,
'Εξ ἀκαλαῤῥείταο βαθυῤῥόυ 'ΩΚΕΑΝΟΙΟ.
'Οδυσ. Τ.

ꟼ 'Εν δ' ἔπεσ' ΩΚΕΑΝΩ, λαμπϱὸν φάꞷ 'Ηελίοιο,
"Ελκον νύκἸα μέλαιναν.
'Ιλιαδ'. Θ.

Sect.11. or *Median Empire* [r]. Nay so late as the
Reign of *Darius*, the *Lacedemonians* did not
know the distance of *Sufa* or *Babylon* from
the *Sea* [s] : So that I believe *Homer* was acquainted with little more of the *Inland Country*, than what was under *Priam*'s Dominion,
or inhabited by his *Allies*.

ON THE other hand, to the *West* of *Greece*,
lay ITALY, a greater Country, as they imagined, than their own [t], and then undiscovered
by the *Greeks :* Behind it, were the wide and
unknown Tracts of *Gaul, Germany*, and *Spain*,
which were impervious at that time, and had
all the Appearance of an ΗΠΕΙΡΟΣ, or *endless
Continent*. Now, for a Person living betwixt
the two, and knowing little of either (in comparison of the whole) save the nearest Coasts;
for such a Person to say, " That the Sun
" rises and sets in the *Ocean*, That the *Ends*
" of the Earth are upon the *Ocean*, and
" That the *Ethiopians*, the *last* of Men,
" dwell upon the *Ocean*," plainly shews an
Acquaintance with a *Trading Nation*, who
could only discover the Limits of the *habitable* World, and relate them to a *curious*

---

[r] Ὅμηρος γ᾿ ἐν ὅτι τὴν ⟨τ⟩ ΣΥΡΩΝ, ὅτι τὴν ΜΗΔΩΝ
ἀρχὴν ἰδεῖν· Οὐδὲ γ᾿ ἐν ΘΗΒΑΣ ΑΙΓΥΠΤΙΑΣ ὀνομάζει,
καὶ ⟨τ⟩ ἐκεῖ, καὶ ⟨τ⟩ ἐν ΦΟΙΝΙΚΗ πλῦτον, ⟨τ⟩ ἐν ΒΑΒΥΛΩΝΙ
καὶ ΝΙΝΩ, καὶ ΕΚΒΑΤΑΝΟΙΣ παρισσότησι.
               Στραβ. Βιβλ. ιι.

[s] Ἤρετο ὁ Κλεομένης (βασιλεὺς τῆς Λακεδαιμων⊙) ⟨τ⟩ Λει-
σαγόρην, Ὁκοσέων ἡμερέων ἀπὸ ΘΑΛΑΣΣΗΣ ⟨τ⟩ ἐόνων ὁδὸς
ἐιη παρὰ ΒΑΣΙΛΗΑ;   Ἡρόδ. Τερψιχ.

[t] *MAGNA GRÆCIA.*

rious inquisitive Man at his Return. And in-Sect. II.
deed thro' all *Homer's* Works, the *Mention*
of *Coasts,* and *Silence* concerning the *Inland*
Countries (excepting those of *Egypt* and *Greece*)
seems to bespeak that kind of Knowledge
which a Man may learn from the Relations
of a People addicted to *Navigation,* who visit
all *maritime* Places, but never go far into the
Country, from their *Ship.*

As for the Inner-Sea (the *Mediterranean*)
he describes the *Coast quite around it* ; but
with this difference, that he speaks of the
North-East End of it [u], so particularly and
minutely, as to convince his Reader, that he
had visited it *in Person.* He names all the
Towns and Rivers ; he describes their Situations and their Soils: One Country is *rocky*
and *mountainous* ; another *fertile* and *plain* :
One is *dry* and *sandy* ; another *moist* and full
of *Verdure* : This is productive of *Sheep* ;
that abounds with *Horses* ; a third swarms
with *Pidgeons* ; and a fourth is blessed with
beautiful Women. And these Accounts of the
several Places, and their Qualities, are all confirmed by the succeeding *Geographers.*

But when the Poet comes to mention
the Countries and Nations lying round the
West End of the *Mediterranean,* he talks of
them as a Man who had heard of these
Places

[u] Omnis Græciæ fabulositas, sicut et literarum claritas, ex hoc
primum *Sinu* effulsit : Quapropter in eo paululum commorabi-
mur. *Plin.* Lib. iv. § 1.

Sect.11. Places from *Travellers* ; I mean, such Peo‑
ple as are willing to tell *Wonders* of the diftant
Regions they have feen, and take pleafure
in amazing People with Stories of *Giants* and
Monfters, *Witches* and *Wilds*, or of any thing
beyond the common Run of Life, either for
Good or *Ill*. And yet, thefe very Stories,
ftrange as they are, and difguifed with all the
Ornaments of Fiction, bear ftill about them
fome *Marks of Truth :* The Ground-work of
the Wonder is commonly fomething *real*; and
fhews the Juftnefs of our Philologift's Obfervation, " That to frame a *new* Wonder, without
" any previous Foundation from Truth, is
" not in the manner of *Homer* w."

T H U S when we confider his Accounts of
the *northern* Nations, " Who live, fays he,
" upon *Mares-milk*, indigent, haughty, and
" the jufteft of Men x," the Defcription appears at firft fomewhat foolifh : But upon a
nearer view, we difcover the *Truth* of it,
and fee the Beauty that refults from fuch
Variety of Character in a Poem.————We
find there were really fuch People ; *Such* the
Romans

<hr />

w See the Notes, Page 124 P.

x ————Πάλιν τρέπεν ὄσσε φαεινώ
Νόσφεν ἐφ' ἱπποπόλων ΘΡΗΚΩΝ, καθορώμενΘ· ἀιαν·
ΜΥΣΩΝ τ' ἀγχιμάχων, ἠ ἀγαυῶν ἱππομολγῶν,
Γλακ]οφάγων, ἀζίων τε, δικαιοτά]ων ἀνθρώπων.

'Ιλιαδ'. Ν·

Romans found them, when they extended their Sect.11.
Conquests to the North; and we ourselves
find the fame Customs and Manner of Life
prevailing among fome of the *Tartar-Tribes* at
this day.

THE POLISH Hiftorians tell, That after
the Death of *Stephen*, one of the bravest of
their Kings, there came Ambaffadors to *Poland*, from the CHAM of *Tartary*, who was
a Candidate for the Crown y. *They* had Inftructions to reprefent to the *Dyet*, " That
" the *Cham* was a Prince of great Power,
" and could raife *three hundred thoufand*
" *Horfe*, which, if they chofe him King,
" he would either imploy in the Defence
" of *Poland*, or to conquer the neighbour-
" ing Nations, and enlarge its Dominion.
" That as to his perfonal Qualities, he was
" *temperate* and *fober*, caring for no Delicacy
" in his eating, and fatisfying his *Hunger*
" with *Horfe-flefh* only. That being inform-
" ed there were Differences among them a-
" bout *Religion*, he gave them Affurances that
" *their* Pope fhould be *his* Pope, and *their*
" *Luther* fhould be *his* Luther, juft as they
" pleafed to determine." We can trace
this fame kind of *Scythian* or *Tartar Life*,
always among their *Horfes*, unfettled in their
Lands, and free from Avarice, thro' the various
Periods

y Anno 1586.

R

Sect.11. Men toil, in order to support the Luxury of
a *few*: The greater part *muſt* do ſo, for their
own Livelihood; and when they themſelves,
and their Work, become the *Property* of o-
thers, more coercive Methods are applied.

EGYPT was the Country where they had
a peculiar Law, obliging every Man to give an
Account of himſelf once a Year, to the Ma-
giſtrate: He was to tell, "Where he lived?
"How he was ſupported? And what he con-
"tributed to the Publick-weal?" This Law
cou'd be executed with greater eaſe, as the
Lower Egypt, where the Strength of their Government lay, was but a narrow Country, which
made it no difficult matter to keep a ſtrict
Eye over the Subject; and being full of rich
populous Cities, every Inch of Ground in it
became precious, and the People who poſſeſſed and cultivated it were of conſequence
perfectly known. The Policy of the Towns
in *Holland* are no ill Image of theſe ancient Regulations; nor a weak Inſtance of the Influence
of *Situation* and *Government*; ſince it produces ſome Likeneſs between ſuch different Characters, as an *Egyptian* and a *Hollander*.

HOMER's Expreſſion, it is true, hath a
particular reſpect to a ſtate of *Servitude*; and
indeed we know from the beſt Authority, that
the *Egyptians* were *terrible Maſters*: Their
rigid Policy, and immenſe publick Works,
Palaces, Temples, Canals, Lakes, Pyramids, all
things

things of incredible Labour and ſtupendous Sect.11.
Magnificence, might have ſome hand in theſe
Severities; and at the ſame time make them
ſo fond of their *Slaves,* that Signs from Hea-
ven, and what they themſelves took to be the
Finger of G o d, could hardly prevail with
them to ſet a whole Nation of them at li-
berty. But it is certain, that over all the
World there are great Hardſhips and intenſe
Miſeries in the *wealthieſt* Cities : and it was
finely judged of our Poet, to diſtinguiſh this
rich Country by a *Sentiment* which expreſſes an
Effect of their Conſtitution, that hits not the
Eye of every Spectator.

To T H E *North* and *North-eaſt* of *Greece,*
H o m e r mentions the *Thracians, Cimmerians,* and hints at *Colchos* and the *Euxine.*
Theſe People he might know *three* ſeveral
ways: Either from the Relations of *Jaſon* and
his Companions in the *Argonautick* Expedition; or from the *Phenicians,* who were conſtantly paſſing and repaſſing in the *Propontis,*
and ſailing thro' the Iſlands; and moſt certainly, from the *Inroads* that ſome of the
Cimmerian Tribes had made upon *the Leſſer
Aſia* (his own Country) not long before he
was born.

In thoſe *Climates,* the *Winter-days* are ſhorter,
and Sky more cloudy, than in *Egypt* and
Greece : From whence he has taken occaſion
o feign a *ſtrange Nation,* covered with per-

Sect.11. petual Darkneſs, and never viſited by the Beams of the Sun. Their Seats he has not certainly aſſigned ; but leaves them among the *Out o'the World Wonders* which *Ulyſſes* ſaw in his Peregrinations. *Bochart* has ſhewn their Name to be plainly *Phenician* [a], and the Origin of it to be the ſame *dark* Appearance that gave riſe to the *Fable*.

BUT as the *Phenician* Trade lay chiefly up the *Mediterranean*, it is to be *Weſtward* that *Homer*'s Obligations to them lie thickeſt, and the greateſt Preſumptions of his borrowing from them his Accounts of thoſe Countries. Many of his Wonders are to be found in *Greece* ; but his ſtrangeſt Tales, his ΔΕΙΝΑ ΠΕΛΩΡΑ, *horrible Portents*, as he calls them, are in foreign Parts. And firſt, *ITALY* furniſhed him with abundance of Monſters : The *Adriatic* Coaſt, that lies oppoſite to *Epirus*, and the *Gulph* of *Tarentum*, were too well known, and too much frequented by his Countrymen, to produce many Miracles : But the *Weſt-ſide*, whither the *Greeks* had then ſent no Colonies, was only viſited by the *Phenicians* ; and accordingly there are many ſupernatural things told of its *Promontories*, and of the *Iſlands* that lie along that hollow Coaſt.

IN THE Entry of the *Sicilian Streights* (the *Faro* of *Meſſina*) ſtood *two diſmal Rocks*, the

[a] *Cimmir* nigreſcere ; *Cimrir* Tenebrarum atror ; *Cimrire jom* Atrores diei.   *Canaan*, Lib. i. § 33.

the Deſtruction both of Ships and Sailors. At Sect.11.
the foot of the one there was a darkſome
Cavern, the Abode of the *Man-eating* Monſter *Scylla*, and oppoſite to it was the devouring *Charybdis*.   There is but a narrow Paſſage
between them; and if you do not ſail thro'
it, you have no choice, but paſs you muſt between *other two*, the dreadful *Planctæ* : They
were *claſhing Rocks*, that caught and ſhattered
the unwary Ship, and, left the broken Planks,
and mangled Bodies to be toſſed by the Waves,
and *Blaſts of pernicious Fire.*

AFTER you have paſſed them, the *Sirenuſæ*
appear, or *Rocks* inhabited by the enchanting
Syrens, who firſt allured the paſſing Mariner
with their Voice, and, when he approached,
deſtroyed him.   Further up the Coaſt were
the *Leſtrygons*; *Cannibals* likewiſe, who ſlaughtered and fed upon the unhappy Wretches that
were ſhipwreck'd on their Shore ; and beyond
their Country was the ſuppoſed Boundary of
Ulyſſes's earthly Navigation, the Habitation of a
powerful Sorcereſs, the infamous *Circé*. She
dwelt in a *Peninſula* ᵇ.   " Where, ſays *Homer*,
" was the *Abode* of the *Morning*, and Out-
" goings of her Parent *the Sun.*"

ALL *theſe* were in *Italy*, or hard upon the
Shore; and how wild and fabulous ſoever
they may appear, there are few of them, but
upon enquiry, we find to have ſome natural

R 4   Founda-

ᵇ ᾿ΑΙΑΙΑ ΝΗΣΟΣ, A Land-Iſland.

Sect.11. Foundation.　Their *Names* and *Qualities* plainly ſhew their *Phenician* Extract; and that they
were propagated by that induſtrious People,
from the Adventures they met with in the
way of their Trade.

THE *Phenicians*, upon their firſt reſorting
hither, and attempting to land, found the *Natives* of the Country extremely inhuman and
barbarous; and therefore reported in general,
that all the Coaſt, up and down, was full of
Monſters. The Paſſage in the Mouth of the
Faro is but narrow; and as there is often a
great Sea rolling in it, it is probable they have
ſometimes ſmarted for venturing through. On
the one hand is a dangerous *Vortex*; and on
the other ſtands *Scylla's Rock*, a threatning
Precipice, exactly ſuch as *Homer* deſcribes it,
tow'ring, ſteep, and its Top in the Clouds ᶜ. It
is joined to the Land by a *flat Iſthmus*, upon
which, it would ſeem, the inhoſpitable Barbarians
uſed to paſs, and lurking among the *Cliffs*, ſet
upon and murdered the Sea-faring People,
who had taken ſhelter under it, to ſhun the
Whirl-pool on the other ſide. For this reaſon
SCYLLA, or *Deſtruction* ᵈ, a Monſter with
many Heads and Hands, lived at the foot of
it;

ᶜ Ὁι δὶ δύω Σκόπελοι, ὁ μὼ Ὀυρανὸν ἱυρὺν ἱκάνει
Ὀξείη κορυφᾷ· νεφέλη δὲ μιν ἀμφιβέβηκε
Κυανίη.　　　　　　　　　　　　　　　　　Ὀδυσ. Μ.

ᵈ *SCOL*; Exitium, Infortunium lethale.

it ; and opposite to it was CHARYBDIS, or Se&.11.
the *Chafm of Perdition* [e].

THE *PLANCTÆ* have been hitherto
look'd upon as utterly fabulous.   " Two wan-
" dering Rocks that dafhed together, and
" Hurricanes of Fire blowing in the Ocean,"
feem to have exifted no where but in the Brain
of the Poet : And yet, *My Lord*, one of them
is apparently true, the other really fo, and
fometimes both.

I TAKE the Foundation of the Fiction to
have been fome of the *Iflands* that lie in the
Sea, between *Sicily* and the *Circeian Promontory.*   It would be tedious to enumerate them
all, and perhaps too minute and dogmatical,
to fix upon the *two* defcrib'd in the *Odyffey* ;
it is fufficient to know, that all this Coaft, and
the Iflands that lie along it, abound with *burning Mountains,* and are fubject to frequent
Eruptions of Fire.   The moft remarkable of
them lie in a knot together, to the *North* of
Sicily, and are known by the Name of the
Liparean Iflands.   They were anciently *feven*
in number, but now you may count upwards
of a *dozen,* fome of them having been fplit
by Earthquakes, and other new ones caft up
by the Heavings of the fubterraneous Fires,
which undermine that dangerous Shore.   Thefe,
are no more than bare defert Rocks, called
by

[e] *CHOR-OBDAN;* Foramen perditionis.
                     Bochart. Canaan. Lib. i. § 28.

Sect.11. by the *Italians, Parte rotte*, " Parts broken off
" by the Shocks of an Earthquake."

Now the Courfe of a Ship from the *Cir-ceian* PROMONTORY to *Ithaca*, lies directly either thro' the *Faro*, between *Sicily* and *Reggium*; or if you will not hazard that Paffage, there is a neceffity to fail thro' the *Lipareans*, and fo round the *Ifland* [f]. After you have paffed the two neareft of thefe Iflands, if you caft an Eye back upon them, you will find, that they appear to be running together, and in a little time, that they are become *one*, fince you left them. The reafon of it is, the *Current*, which fets in between them, and does not allow you to keep a ftraight Courfe, after you have made good your Paffage : Whereas if you vary but a very little from it, you lofe the *Line* that directs your Eye thro' the Void, and take them up under *one*. Hence the Foundation of the Fable, that they were *floating Rocks*, which run together as a Ship paffed, to catch and crufh her. The fame Appearance will enfue in the Cafe of any two Prominences that are contiguous ; and for the very fame reafon, the *Cyanean Iflands* in the Mouth of the *Bofphorus*, got the Name of *Symplegades*, as if fometimes they had been feparated, and afterwards had clofed and coalefced into one.

BUT

[f] Ἀυ]ὰρ ἐπειδὴ τάς γε παρεξελάσωσιν Ἑταῖροι,
Ἔνθά τοι ἐκ ἔτ' ἔπειτα διηνεκέως ἀγορεύσω
Ὁπποτέρη δή τοι ὁδὸς ἔσεται, ἀλλὰ καὶ αυ]ὸς
Θυμῷ βελεύειν· ἐρέω δέ τοι ἀμφοτερωθεν.

Ὀδυσ. M.

BUT THIS Appearance, tho' it may have Sect.II.
ferved to confirm the Fiction, was not fufficient to raife the *dreadful Idea* that *Homer*
gives of them. I therefore believe the *Phenicians* have happened to pafs, or have been lying at Anchor among thefe Iflands, at the time
of an *Eruption* and *Earthquake.* All over the
Lipareans ᵹ, there are *Clefts* in the Surface of
the Ground, and Vents in the Rocks, that
emit Flame by night and Smoke by day: Some
of them have noted *Volcano's,* which like *Vefu-
vio* or *Mon Gibel,* difgorge with their Flames
immenfe quantities of Afhes, and throw out
Stones of fuch a monftrous Size, that a great
part of the Sea is choaked up, and one of
the Iflands almoft joined to *Sicily* by an
Ifthmus of the Rubbifh. At fuch a Juncture,
the frighted *Mariners* might fee the *Rocks
really clafhing,* and to their dire Experience feel
ΠΥΡΟΣ ΟΛΟΟΙΟ ΘΥΕΛΛΑΣ, *Storms of deftruc-
tive Fire.*

THIS Circumftance alone, were there no
other Signs of Agreement, ties down the
Planctæ either to the *Liparean Iflands,* or to
the *Rocks* that furround *Ifchia,* and participate
of the Difafters of the *Neapolitan Shore:* Here
the

---

§ *Petrarcha,* fpeaking of a *Lover's* Heart, defcribes it thus:

Dentro, confufion turbida, et mifchia
Di doglie certe, et d' allegrezze incerte:
Non bollì mai *Vulcan, Lipari* od *Ifchia,*
Stromboli o *Mongibello* in tanta rabbia.
Poco ama fe, che'n tal giuoco s' arrifchia.

ɪ   *Triomfo d' Amore,* Capitol IV.

Sect.II. the *Phenician* Veſſels that eſcaped, and perhaps ſaw their Companions periſh in the infernal Tempeſt, needed only relate the terrible
Scene, of *Seas*, and *Flames*, and *Rocks* in an
uproar : Their literal Deſcription is the Sum
of the Fable ; and what is added wears the
ſame Appearance of Probability. *Circé*, to ex-
aggerate the danger of coming near theſe Rocks,
ſays, " That the *Birds* of the Air could not
" paſs them." The ſame thing is told of
the *Aörnos*, and other peſtilentious Places,
where yet the Air is not put in ſuch Commotion, as by the Flame and Vapour iſſuing from
a *burning Mountain*. The Storm it raiſes, and
the ſulphureous Steams thrown all around
it, might very readily bring down a flying
Fowl, and give a handle to the beautiful Fable
which *Homer* has grafted upon ſuch an Accident [h].

   " I T I S N O rare thing, ſays *Strabo*, a-
" mong theſe Iſlands, to ſee *Flames* rolling
" upon the Surface of the Deep. They pro-
" ceed from the Caverns of *Fire* below, which
" often find a vent, and force their Paſſage
" up thro' the Waves. *Poſidonius* writes, That
" within his own Memory, one morning
" about the *Vernal Equinox*, the Sea between
" *Hiera* and *Uſtica* appeared to heave, and
                                      " was

[h] Τῇ μὲν τ᾽ ὐδὲ Ποτη|ὰ παρέρχεται, ὐδὲ Πέλειαι
   Τρήρωνες, ταί τ᾽ ἀμϐροσίην Διὶ πατεῖ φέρουσιν.
   Ἀλλά τε κ᾽ τ διαὶ ἀφαιρεῖται λὶς πέτρη·
   Ἀλλ᾽ ἄλλην ἐ.ίησι πατὴρ, ἐναείθμιον ἐD·
                                     Ὀδυσ. Μ.

" was raifed to a ftrange height; that it con-Sect.11.
" tinued for fome time to fwell and to fall
" by turns, and afterwards ceafed. That thofe
" who ventured to fail near it, feeing the
" Fifhes driving *dead* with the Current, and
" being fcorched with Heat themfelves, and
" almoft choaked with a noifome Vapour,
" made what *Speed* they could to the *Shore:*
" Some of the Sailors in the Skiff that went
" neareft expired; the reft, with great diffi-
" culty, got back to *Lipari,* where they fell
" into Fits, like Perfons fubject to the *Epi-*
" *lepfy,* and frequently loft, and then reco-
" vered the ufe of their Reafon. For fome
" time after, there was a kind of Clay and
" Slime found floating upon the Sea; and in
" many places of it, Flames were feen to
" burft forth, and fometimes Clouds of *Smoke*
" and *Afhes:* The floating Matter hardened
" by degrees, and when thrown on fhore,
" grew like Pieces of Milftone. *Titus Fla-*
" *minius* then *Pretor* of *Sicily* gave the *Ro-*
" *man Senate* an account of what had hap-
" pened, and they fent fome of the *College*
" of the *Priefts,* both to *Lipari* and *Uftica,*
" to do *Sacrifice* to the *Sea,* and to the *Sub-*
" *terranean Gods* [i]."

AFTER *Ulyffes* had efcaped the hands of
the *Cyclops,* he left the Coaft of *Sicily,* and
came to the *Eolian* Ifland, where E o l u s lived.

The

---

[i] *Strabo,* Lib. VI.

Sect. 11. The Palace and Oeconomy of this Prince, seem to be purely of the Poet's Invention; tho' *Diodorus* hath given a long and particular Deduction of the *Names* and *Fortunes* of his Children. But *Homer* had some reason to add, in his figurative strain, "That he was beloved "by the immortal Gods; that *Jupiter* had "appointed him to be *Governour of the Winds*, "and given him Power to let them loose or "restrain them at his pleasure." Anciently, the *Liparean* Islands were named from *Eolus*; and the nearest of them to *Italy* [k], was said to be the Place of his Habitation. The Assertion does not want Probability; tho' the rocky Coast of *Lipari* (the largest Island) and great Quantities of *Allum*, found in no place of the World, as they imagined, but in this and another little Isle [l], seem rather to agree with *The brazen Wall*, topped *with a smooth shining Stone*, which run round the ΠΛΩΤΗ ΝΗΣΟΣ, (*floating Island*) where he lived [m].

Betwixt it and *Sicily* lies *Hiera*, a desert Rock consecrated to *Vulcan*, and from thence receiving its Name: Here they fancied he
had

---

[k] *Strongyle*, or the Round Island, now *Stromboli*.

[l] 'Ουδαμοῦ γὰ τῆς 'Οικουμένης τῆς ΣΤΥΠΤΗΡΙΑΣ γινομένης,——'Εν μόνῃ γὰ τῇ νήσῳ ΜΗΛΩ φύεται μικρά τις συνήθεια, μὴ δυναμένη διαρκεῖν πολλαῖς πόλεσιν. Διοδωρ. Σικελ. Βιϐ. Ε.

[m] ————ἔνθα δ' ἔναιεν
"ΑΡΟΛΟΣ 'Ιππολάδης, φίλος ἀθανάτοισι θεοῖσιν,
Πλωτῇ ἐνὶ νήσῳ· Πᾶσαν δὲ τέ μιν περὶ τεῖχος
Χάλκεον ἄρρηκτον, ΛΙΣΣΗ δ' ἀναδέδρομε ΠΕΤΡΗ·
'Οδυσ. Κ.

had a *Forge* as well as in *Etna*, becaufe of Sect.11
three *Volcano's* or *Craters*, at which it frequently difgorges Flame and Sand, and the burning Stones I mentioned before. It is juft
under the Eye of the Inhabitants of *Lipari* [n];
and they fee diftinctly from which of the *Craters* the Flame or Smoke iffues, and in what
degree, whether languid or impetuous. They
likewife hear the uncouth Sounds and hollow
Noifes under ground, which proceed from the
Efforts of the ftruggling Matter in the *fiery
Caverns*, and generally grow louder before a
violent Eruption.

IT *was therefore* the Opinion of the Ancients, " That *Eolus*, from a Courfe of Obfer-
" vations made upon thefe *Volcano's*, and by
" comparing the different Sounds they emit-
" ted, and the various Changes in the Quan-
" tity or Violence of the Smoke or Flame,
" or their fhifting from one Vent to another;
" that by comparing thefe with the enfuing
" *Alterations* of the *Weather*, he had attain-
" ed to a great *Sagacity* in foretelling a Storm,
" and could predict how the Wind would
" blow for a certain number of days after
" he had obferved the Sign." This Skill he
ufed, they fay, with great Condefcenfion and
Goodnefs to the Sea-faring People: He received them into his Harbour, treated them hof-
pitably,

[n] Ταύτης δὲ (τῆς Λιπάρης) μεταξὺ πῶς ἐςὶ κỳ τῆς Σικελίας, ἥν
νῦν ʹΙΕΡΑΝ ʹΗΦΑΙΣΤΟΥ χαλῦσι, πὶζράδης πᾶσα, κỳ ἔρημος
κỳ διάπυρος.   ΣΤΡΑC. Βιϐ λ. ς.

Sect.11. pitably, and directed them when to fail, and what Courfe to fteer upon the dangerous Coaft. For thefe reafons, the *Phenicians* made him *Lord of the Winds*, handed him down as favoured by the *Immortals*, and have given him a Name from the S T O R M S ° he affifted them to fhun.

THIS WAY of accounting for *Eolus's* Knowledge of the Weather, has found credit from *later* Obfervations. There is a Sympathy and Connexion obferved between the Winds and the Agitation of the Fires, both *here* and in *Etna*. They are fierce and violent when the Winds are high, and fubfide when the Air regains a Calm. It is obferved befides, that particular Winds produce different Effects. The accurate *Polybius*, who failed round thefe Coafts with very inquifitive Eyes, affirms, " That before the *South-wind* blow, the Ifland " *Hiera* is covered over with Smoke like " a thick *Fog*, fo that it obftructs the Pro- " fpect of *Sicily* beyond it : That before a " *Northerly-wind*, the Flames arifing from the " *great Crater*, mount with a clearer *Blaze* " than at other times, and greater Noife is " heard from below : That the *Weft-wind* is " preceded by a middle kind of Appearance, " a mixture of *Smoke* and *Flame*, and a fainter " Noife from the *Hollows* of the *Rock*." He concludes

---

° From *A O L* Procella, Turbo: *M E L E C A O L I N* Rex Tempeftatum. Thence the *Greeks* have formed their 'Αἰολία.
Bochart. Canaan. Lib, i. § 33.

concludes his account with what is moft im- Sect.11.
mediately for our purpofe, " That from the
" Diverfity of thefe Sounds, and the various
" Eruptions of the Fire and Vapour, it was
" poffible to know *what Wind* would blow
" for three days to come; and accordingly,
" that there were People in *Lipari* then liv-
" ing, who forewarned the wind-bound Ships
" of an approaching Change, and feldom fail-
" ed in their Prediction ᵖ." In confirmation
of this, we find that the *Lipareans* to this day
are generally *Seamen*, and of fuch Knowledge
in thofe matters, that *Bocaccio* affirms there are
even *few Women* in the *Ifland*, who have not
fome Skill *dell' arte marinarefca* of the Art of
Navigation ᑫ.

THE Connexion between the various Qualities and Changes of the *Air*, and the Force
and Appearances of *Fire*, cannot have efcaped
your Lordfhip's Searches into the feveral Parts
of *natural Knowledge*. It muft be the more
perceptible in thefe *Volcano's*, as the *Fire* is vaft,
and the *Chafms*, at which they belch the Smoke
and Vapour, are widen'd, and laid open to the
Air,

ᵖ Naturalis divinatio aliquando certior eft, aliquando magis in
lubrico prout fubjectum fe habet circa quod verfatur : Quod fi
fuerit naturæ conftantis et regularis, certam efficit prædictionem ;
fi variæ, et compofitæ (tanquam ex naturâ et cafu) fallacem. At-
tamen etiam in fubjecto vario, fi diligenter canonizetur, tenebit
prædictio ut plurimum : Temporis forte momenta non affequetur,
à re non multum errabit.

     Fr. Bacon. de Verulam. *Hiftor. Ventorum.*

ᑫ **Decamerone;** *Giornata* V. *Novella* II.

Sect. 11. Air, by the dreadful Convulſions of the lab'ring
Flames. Nor can they miſs of preſaging a
coming Storm. For if the Openings of the
ſubterraneous Mazes are at any conſiderable
diſtance from the pent-up Fire, which they feed
and keep alive; in that caſe, a *Tempeſt* brood-
ing from that quarter, and beginning to play
upon thoſe Openings, muſt quickly produce an
Alteration at the *Volcano's Head.* But it is
agreed on all hands that *Sicily* and the neighbouring Coaſt is quite *hollow*, and pierced with
many *Croſs-Paſſages* that communicate under
the Bottom of the Sea ʳ. Thus, for inſtance,
there is a Communication believed to run between *Hiera* and *Sicily*; and a Correſpondence
has been obſerved between the Eruptions of
Etna, and of this burning Iſland, both as to
their Quantity and Violence ˢ.

I T   W O U L D   be too great a Digreſſion from
our Subject to purſue this Reaſoning much
farther : But before we venture upon the reſt
of *Homer's Miracles*, it will be pleaſant to obſerve what uſe *Polybius* has made of this very

Story

ʳ ῞Οπ πᾶς ὁ ΠΟΡΟΣ ὕπε ἀπὸ ᵵ Κυμαίας ἀρξάμενᵭ μίχει
ᵵ Σικιλίας, ΔΙΑΠΥΡΟΣ ἐςὶ, κ χᵀ βάθυς ἔχει ΚΟΙΛΙΑΣ
πινὰς εἰς ἓν συναπλύσας, πέᵴς τε Νήσυς, κ πρὸς τὴν ῞Ηπιεον.
Διόπεϱ ἥ τε ῎Αιτνη πιαύτην ἔχειν δείκνυται ευσιν, ὅιαν ἱςορύ-
σιν ἅ ποντις· κ ἀι ᵵ ΛΙΠΑΡΑΙΩΝ ΝΗΣΟΙ, κ τὰ πεϱὶ
τὴν ΔΙΚΑΙΑΡΧΙΑΝ, κ ΝΕΑΠΟΛΙΝ κ ΒΑΙΑΣ χωεία,
κ ἀι ΠΙΘΗΚΟΥΣΑΙ. Στϱαβ. Βιϛ· Ε.

ˢ Λέξυσι γάρ πινες ἐκ τέτων ᵵ Νήσων ῾ΥΠΟΝΟΜΟΥΣ ῎ᵭ
χᵀ γῆς μίχει ᵵ ῎Αιτνης, κ πῖς ἐπ' ἀμφότεϱα ςομίοις συνευ-
μέκς Διὸ κ χᵀ τὸ πλῶᵴον ΕΝΑΛΛΑΞ κϱἰεᵭαι τὰς ἐν πάυ-
ταις ταῖς νήσοις Κϱατῆϱας, ᵵ χᵀ τὴν ῎Αιτνην.
Διοδώϱ. Σικιλ. Βιβλ. Ε.

Story of *Eolus* and his *windy Empire.* He Sect.11.
owns it looks extremely fabulous at firſt telling : *The Winds ſewed up in a Bag, and given
to* Ulyſſes ! And yet here is a Foundation for
it, and ſome Veſtiges of Truth in the Heart
of the Fable : The Poet indeed has uſed his
Privilege ; has told it in his own way, and
dreſſed it up with ſeveral ſtrange Circumſtances, to increaſe our Wonder ᵗ : *Wherefore,*
ſays the Hiſtorian, ſomewhat ſeriouſly, " *This*
" *ſhould* make us believe, that the moſt ex-
" travagant things ſung by *Homer,* are only
" *ſo in appearance :* But that tho' we do not
" comprehend it, there is ſtill ſome Principle
" in Nature, ſome Fact in Hiſtory, or Leſſon
" in Morals, at the bottom of the Tale."

About thirty miles from Shore, directly
off *Naples,* and a Stone's-throw from the South-
fide of the Iſland *Capreæ,* ſtand the Sirenusæ
or Rocks of the *Sirens.* The common Opinion about their Inhabitants, and the moſt
probable, is, " That they were *leud Women,*
" who proſtituted themſelves to the Sailors,
" and, by the Allurements of a lazy voluptu-
" ous Life, made them unmindful of their
" Voyage, and careleſs of returning to their
" native Country." But their Story, as it
is told by *Homer,* lies ſo pat for a *Moral,*
that it is hard to believe it to be any thing
elſe than *pure Fiction :* Their charming Aſpect

S 2   at

ᵗ *Perdona.*——*S' inteſſo Fregi al Ver.*   Taſſo.

Sect.11. at firſt ſight; their beautiful Faces and enſnaring Voice, perfectly repreſent the *fair Appearance* of an Object of Pleaſure; and their falſe deſtructive Nature, their hidden Deformities, and the way to ſhun and deſtroy them, *agree* ſo nicely with the Methods preſcribed by the Moraliſts, for avoiding *a gilded Snare* [u], that it would almoſt be pity to ſpoil the *Allegory*. Nor is there any neceſſity we ſhould: The *Phenician* accounts of theſe enchanting Creatures; their telling how raviſhingly they ſung, and how many Crews had been loſt thro' their means, was ground ſufficient for the Poet: They both gave him a foundation for his Tale, and ſcope to work it up in the *ſymbolical Egyptian* manner, until it loſt its Specialities, and from a private Story, became capable of a general Application.

THERE were ſeveral *Syrens* up and down the Coaſt, who waited for the paſſing Ships, and for that end took their ſtations upon the *Promontories*, or lived in the *Iſlands* neareſt the Shore. One of them ſtaid at *Panormus* [w], another at *Naples*, others at *Surrentum*, and the greateſt number lived in the delightful *Capreæ* in the Mouth of the Bay of *Naples*.
From

---

[u] Ἀινίθεται δὲ ᾗ ταλ· τὸ ἀγαθὸν, τὸ κακὸν, τὸ ὅτε ἀγαθὸν ὅτε κακὸν ἐσιν ἐν τῷ βίῳ· Ταῦτ' ἂν ἐὰν μή τις συνίῃ, ἀπονύται ὑπὸ τ' ΑΦΡΟΣΥΝΗΣ· ἂν δὲ τις ςυῷ, ἀνάπαλιν ἡ μὲν Ἀ-ΦΡΟΣΥΝΗ ΑΠΟΛΛΥΤΑΙ, αὐτὸς δὲ σώζεται, ᾗ μακαριςθ᾽, ᾗ εὐδαίμων γίνεται ἐν πάση τῷ βίῳ.

Κέβη]Θ Θηβαίε ΠΙΝΑΞ

[w] *PALERMO* in *Sicily*.

From thence, it is probable, they paſſed over
to the neighbouring *Rocks* which bear their
Name, to talk with the Seamen from on board,
and perſuade them to moor their Veſſel, and
come on ſhore. *Homer* has retained the *Phe-*
nician Name taken from the moſt obvious
Part of their Character, *their ſinging* [x]; and
Poſterity, by building Temples to them, and
aſſigning the particular Places of their Abode,
and Burial, hath made the Tradition paſs for
a Reality [y].

In the ſame *Claſs* with theſe ſinging Ladies, *Horace* has placed the other *Enchan-*
treſs [z], the powerful CIRCE; and not without reaſon either from the Moral, which he
has had in his Eye, or from their real Story.
As to the Allegory, " She is a Sorcereſs,
" ſkilled in Poiſons, and knowing how to
" mix an intoxicating Draught : She is the
" Child of the *Sun*, whoſe Beams can only
" raiſe a Plant of Virtue, and concoct the

S 3   " Juice

---

[x] From S I R Cantilena: Inde S I R E N Canéns, Canorum.

Bochart. Lib. i. § 33.

[y] Ἀΐκων μακϱὸς ——ἐπὶ θαˊλεϱα μὲν ὁ Ὀϱϖνῆς, τὸ τ᾽ ΣΕΙΡΗ-
ΝΩΝ ΙΕΡΟΝ ἔχων, ἐπὶ θαˊτεϱα δὲ ——νησίδια τεˊια πεϱκείˊ-
μεια, ἔϱημα, πέϱϖδη, ἅ ϰαλῦσι ΣΕΙΡΗΝΟΥΣΑΣ.

Στϱαϐ. βιϐλ. A.

Ὅτι ἐν Νεαπόλει ΠΑΡΘΕΝΟΠΗΣ δίϰνυται μνῆμα, μιᾶς
τ᾽ ΣΕΙΡΗΝΩΝ.   Στϱαϐ. Βιϐλ. A.
Sirenes, ——primò juxta Pelorum, poſt in Capreis inſulâ habi-
tarunt.   *Serv. in Æneid.* V.

[z] Sirenum voces, et Circes pocula noſti ;
    Quæ ſi cum ſociis ſtultus cupiduſque bibiſſet,
    Vixiſſet Canis immundus, aut amica luto Sus.

Horat. Epiſt. ii. *Lib.* 1.

Sect. 11. "Juice of Herbs to a healing or noxious "Quality. With their affiftance, fhe could "change and transform the Mortal that once "tafted of her baneful Cup: She could make "him forget his Refolutions and his Duty; "renounce his Bravery and Manhood; ren- "der him deaf to the Admonitions of his "Friends; and in fine, convert him into fome "Species of a *Brute*, according to the Bent "of his Senfuality."

THE Truth of the matter is, CIRCE was herfelf one of the *Sirens: Like them* fhe fung, and filled her Palace with Melody [a]: *Like them*, fhe lived upon a Promontory that run out into the Sea; *Like them*, fhe waited for the paffing Ships, and *like them* deftroyed the Crews, when fhe had them in her power. Her Name is CIRCE, the *Deftroyer* or *Puller down* [b]; of the fame falfe Nature and deceitful Appearance with her Sifters, and only differing from them as fhe employed other Means

[a] She is ΘΕΟΣ ΑΥΔΗΕΣΣΑ, *The Vocal Goddefs*; and when they approached her Palace,

ΚΙΡΚΗΣ Δ' ΕΝΔΟΝ ΑΚΟΥΟΝ, ΑΕΙΔΟΥΣΗΣ ΟΠΙ ΚΑΛΗ.

And afterwards,

ΚΑΛΟΝ ΑΟΙΔΙΑΕΙ, ΔΑΠΕΔΟΝ Δ' ΑΠΑΝ ΑΜΦΙΜΕΜΥΚΕΝ.
'Οδυσ. Κ.

[b] From *Kirkar*, diruere, perdere, peffundare: Unlefs the *Walls* that inclofed her Palace have got her that Name from *Kir*, a Wall.

Ἕυρον δ' ἐν Βήσσησι τετυγμένα δώματα Κίρκης Ξεστοῖσι λάεσσι, ΠΕΡΙΣΚΕΠΤΩ ἐνὶ χώρῳ. 'Οδυσ. Κ.

Means for obtaining her cruel Purpose besides the Charms of her *Voice.*

IT IS here observable, that the *contiguous Miracles,* or the strange things which the Poet relates of this Coast, are much *of a piece :* His *Monsters,* as well as his Men, are of the same Species, and bear a Likeness in their Manners : The *Cyclops,* the *Lestrygons,* and *Scylla,* are all Men-eaters : And the Female Phantoms, *Circé* and the *Sirens,* first bewitch with a Shew of Pleasure, and then destroy. At first reading, they appear wild and improbable ; but like the other Parts of *Homer's* Poetry, they had a *Foundation* in the Manners of the Times preceding his own.

IT WAS still, in many Places, the Age spoken of by *Orpheus,*

When Men devour'd each other like the Beasts,
Gorging on human Flesh ——

The Subject is dismal, and a particular Description of such horrid Deeds would be odious and shocking : It will be enough to put your Lordship in mind, That our modern *Indians* have not been the only People guilty of the dreadful Act of *feeding upon their Fellow-Creatures.* The same Barbarity is attributed to most Countries, before the *Arts of Life* reached them, and stript them by degrees, of their inhuman Customs. The *East* was

detest-

Sect.11. deteftable for offering Children to their *furious King* [c], and *Egypt* was once infamous for Inhofpitality and Murder [d]. The *Euxine* was glad to change its favage Name [e], and the *Altar* of *Diana*, at the mouth of it, ftood reeking with the Blood of Strangers. The human Sacrifices in *Britain* and *Gaul* remain an indelible Stain upon the Memory. of our Forefathers; and *Greece*, with all its boafted Humanity, was not entirely rid of them at the time of the *Trojan War* [f]. The *Carthaginians* continued them long in *Africk*; and they were not difufed in *Italy*, until the Days of *Numa Pompilius*. Nor did that, religious Law-giver think fit to abolifh them utterly at firft; He chofe to *elude* the cruel Rite, and fubftituted *Images of Straw* in place of the human Creatures, whom they ufed to butcher.

It was upon the *Ides* of *May*, a little after the *Vernal Equinox*, that the *Priefts* of the greateft Dignity, and the *Virgins* who guard the *eternal Fire* [g], accompanied with the *Pretors*, and other Citizens, made a Bridge over the

---

[e] *Moloch,* from *Melech,* a King.

[d]   ——Quis aut Euryfthea durum,
Aut illaudati nefcit Bufiridis aras?   *Virgil.*

[e] ΑΞΕΝΟΣ. *Inhofpitable, Inacceffible to Strangers.*

[f] Tu cum pro vitula ftatuis dulcem Aulide Natam
Ante ARAS; fpargifque MOLA Caput, Improbe, falfa,
Rectum animi fervas?——   *Horat. Lib.* II. *Sat.* V.

[g] Ὁι καλύμενοι ΠΟΝΤΙΦΙΚΕΣ, ἱερέων ὁι διαφερέςαλοι, ꝗ σὺν αὐλοῖς ἀι τὸ ἀθάναλον πῦρ διαφυλάτλουαι παρθένοι.
      ΔΙΟΝΥΣ, ΑΛΙΚΑΡ· ΒΙϚΛ· Ϭ·

the *Tiber* [h], and in a folemn manner, caft Sect.11.
thirty of thefe *Images* into the Stream : In
throwing them over, they called them, by ancient Tradition, ARGIVES [i]; which, as it preferved the Footfteps of this Cruelty in *Italy*,
fo it lets us know what People for the moft
part furnifhed the wretched Victims, and what
reafon the *Phenician*, and afterwards the *Grecian* Sailors had to give out, that this Coaft
was inhabited by *Cannibals*, and *Deftroyers of
Mankind.*

THE oppofite Shore of *Greece*, EPIRUS,
continued long in the fame favage Condition.
The Iflanders even to the Weft, were beginning in *Homer*'s time to unlearn their rude Behaviour to Strangers ; and as confcious of being a civilized People, they threaten their Of-
fenders " with tranfportation to the Continent,
　" to King ECHETUS, the Scourge of all
　" the human Race." So true it is, that the
Iflands were firft brought under Difcipline, and
that Arts and Policy came to *Greece* from beyond Sea.

THEY firft fettled and took root in the
maritime Places, and afterwards fpread by degrees into the Heart of the Country. It was
long before they penetrated to the Weft of
Italy, which we therefore find full of Pro-
digies;

[h] The Rite was fo folemn, and gone about with fo much
Ceremony, that *from it* the Priefts had their *Name*, PONTIFI-
CES, Bridge-makers.
[i] ᾿ΑΡΓΕΙΟΥΣ ἀυΐα᾽ ϰϱλῦῖΙες.　Διονυσ. Αλιϰͷρͷ.ΒιϹλ.Α.

Sect. 11. digies; and the Appellations given them by
Homer, are as *monstrous* as their own Natures,
and found as strangely in a *Grecian* Ear : The
Etymologies of their Names are in vain sought
for in *his* Language, which they only resemble
in their Terminations : But the *Aramean* affords them, and derives them from Words that
shew how these Names have been imposed at
first : They point at the very *Act of Ravening*,
beheld by such *Phenicians* as had the good fortune to escape the merciless Hands of the Barbarians [k]; and have been afterwards fixed as
proper Names, by being often repeated in the
sad Relation of the Fate of their Companions.

But there is too much said of these *Sa-
vages*, and we have dwelt too long upon this
black side of Mankind : Let us quit the Men,
and consider some of the *natural Wonders* of
this fabulous Coast. The City of *Sidon* is situated in thirty-three Degrees twenty Minutes of
Latitude, and the *Circeian Promontory* in forty-
two; and if it be true that the *Phenician* Navigation was first upon the *Red-Sea*, then that
People

---

[k] The *Lestrygons* (Λαιςρυγὰν) from *Laïs-tirgan*, Leo mordax;
their King *Lamus* from *Labam* vorare, deglutire; or *Labm* Caro:
Thence the Goblin's Name, that swallowed Children alive,
Lamia; and the *Greek* word for the Throat, Λαιμῷ. These two,
the *Lestrygons* and *Lamus*, have been observed by *Bochart*. The
King of the Continent's Name likewise points at his Nature. It
comes from *Catath* contundere, cædere, whence *Ecbetath* contu-
surus, contusor erit; and agrees nicely with *Homer's* Epithet :

'Εις 'ΕΧΕΤΟΝ βασιλῆα βροϊῶν ΔΗΛΗΜΟΝΑ πάντων.
'Οдυσ. Σ.

People muſt have been accuſtomed to the near Sect.11.
Equality of Day and Night that happens within the *Tropicks*, and increaſes as you approach
the *Equator*. But when their Trade took another Turn, and they begun to ſail the *Medi-*
terranean, and diſcover the unknown Coaſts
of *Italy*, How would they be ſurprized to
find the Day near two hours longer than at
the Mouth of the *Arabick Gulf*, and one hour
longer than in their own Country? They
would be amazed at the quick Return of the
Morning, and think the Sun was earlier upon
his Road than ever they had obſerved him before. The length of the *Twilights*, longer
too than ever they had ſeen, would contribute
to raiſe their Wonder; and when they com-
pared every thing with their own *Southern*
Climes, and were come to an Anchor under
the *Mons Circeius*, lying *due Eaſt* of them, it
was no wonder, if not knowing how to account for the ſudden Return of Light, they
took it into their Heads, " That *there* was the
" *Abode* of the *Morning*, and the early *Road*
" of the riſing *Sun*."

WHILE the *Phenicians* were making but
annual Voyages, and had not ventured to winter in foreign Ports, they wou'd happen to be
in the *Tyrrhene Sea* and *Gulf of Genoa*, about
the time of the longeſt day. The Diſtance
of theſe Parts from *Sidon*, and the common
Accidents in ſlow coaſting Voyages, (which
the

Sect. 11. the *Phenicians* could only make to unknown
Nations) muſt have employed the Spring-
months, and protracted their Voyage till
that Seaſon. For I make little doubt but this
Fable has been framed, when they were
neither ſuch Geographers, nor Aſtronomers,
as they came to be afterwards : It muſt have
been in the Infancy of their Navigation at
leaſt to the *North Seas*; and ſuch a Tradition,
when once broached, could not fail of being
preſerved, and finding a place in all the future
Relations of that barbarous Coaſt. It is too remarkable a Circumſtance not to have ſtruck
Men, whoſe *Employment* forces them to obſerve the *Weather*, and fixes their chief Attention upon the *Heavens :* To ſuch People
the *Abode of the Morning was in* Circe's *Iſle,*
for the ſame reaſon that we here in *Britain*
are characterized by *Virgil,*

Et minimâ contentos noĉte Britannos.

FROM CIRCE's Iſle, and by her Direc-
tions, *Ulyſſes* ſailed to the *infernal Regions :*
We are told, in the poetical Stile, " That af-
" ter having paſſed the Ocean, he firſt ar-
" rived at a gloomy *Beach* covered with
" Thickets and the Groves of *Proſerpine* ;
" *Poplars* and *Yews* caſting a diſmal Shade.
" Here he drew his Ship on ſhore, and en-
" tered himſelf into the Manſions of *Hell :*
　　　　　　　　　　　　　　　" He

" He trode the Threfhold of the Habitations Sect. II.
" of the *Dead*, and faw within,"

The four infernal Rivers that difgorge
Into the burning Lake their baleful Streams :
Abhorred Styx, *the Flood of deadly Hate,*
Sad Acheron *of Sorrow, black and deep,*
Cocytus *nam'd of Lamentation loud*
Heard on the rueful Stream, fierce Phlegethon,
Whofe Waves of burning Fire inflame with Rage [l].

Upon the Brink, where two of the Rivers met, he was to perform certain Sacrifices to the *infernal Deities,* and pour forth the Blood to the *Ghofts departed.*

T H I S Defcription is partly *real,* and partly *mythological.* The terreftrial part of it feems to agree with the A V E R N U S, a noifome kind of Lake formed by the Sea in the recefs of the *Lucrine Bay,* not far from *Circe*'s Habitation : The reft (too long to be here tranfcribed) is *Egyptian,* and relates to the T I M Ω P I A I Ξ E N A I [m] mentioned above [n]. Next to the B A I Æ, fays *Strabo* [o], lies the *Lucrine Bay,* and within it the Lake *Avernus.* It was *here* the Ancients believed that *Homer* had defcribed *Ulyffes* as converfing with the *Dead,* and confulting *Tirefias*'s Ghoft : for here they faid was the *Oracle* facred to the *Shades,* which *Ulyffes*
came

---

[l] Milton.
[n] p. 220.
[m] Strange foreign Tortures.
[o] Lib. V.

Sect. 11. came and confulted concerning his Return.
The *Avernus* is a deep darkfome Lake, with a
narrow Entry from the outer Bay : It is fur-
rounded with fteep Banks that hang threatning
over it, and is only acceffible by the narrow
Paffage thro' which you fail in. Thefe Banks
were anciently quite over-grown with a wild
Wood, impenetrable by any human Foot. Its
gloomy Shade impreffed an awful Superftition
upon the Minds of the Beholders ; and the
neighbouring People affirmed, That the Birds
P fell into the Water as they flew over it, being·
choaked with the infernal Steam.

HERE therefore they fuppofed was the *Paffage to Hell*, and the Seat of the *Cimmerians*,
who dwelt in *perpetual Night*. Whoever failed hither, firft did facrifice; and endeavoured
to propitiate the infernal Powers with the affiftance of fome Priefts who attended upon the
Place, and directed the *myftick* Performance.
Within, a Fountain of pure Water broke out
juft over the Sea; but no Creature ever tafted
of it, believing it to be a Vein of the River
Styx : Somewhere near this Fountain was the
Oracle ; and the *Hot Waters* frequent in thefe
Parts, made them think they were Branches of
the burning *Phlegethon*.

IN THIS very Bay *Ephorus* places the *Cimmerians :* He fays They lived in fubterraneous
Cells,

P Hence its Name *Aornos* ; and by inferting the *Eolick* F,
Afornos; thence in the *Italick* Pronunciation AVERNUS.

Cells, which they called ARGILLÆ; and that Sect. II.
they had Communication with one another by
means of certain dark Paſſages cut thro' the
Earth, by which they conveyed Strangers down
to the *Oracle of the Dead*. He ſays further,
that they lived upon the Produce of the Metals
which they dug out of the Earth, and upon
the Sacrifices that were offered to the ſubterraneous *Oracle*; whoſe Miniſters had it as a
Cuſtom handed down from Father to Son,
That none of them ſhould ever ſee the Sun, nor
quit their *Grotts, but 'under Covert of the Night.*
This, he gives as the reaſon why the Poet aſſerts, " That *Phebus*, who enlightens the
" World, never looks upon them, nor viſits
" them with his gladdening Beams."

THIS ACCOUNT of the *Cimmerians* is
ingenious, and has ſomething in it both entertaining to the Imagination, and agreeable to
the wond'rous Regulations of the ancient Prieſt-
hood: But as I wou'd be far from rejecting
it, ſo the Poet's deſcribing their Towns and
Tribes in this Part of the Country, is no ſtrict
Proof of their being really *Italians*. *Homer*
often tranſports and mixes his Miracles; eſpecially if they are *of a kind*, and bear any Analogy in their Natures, or Reſembance in their
Manners. *Circe* is of the ſame Blood with
Æetes, and is allied to the Sorcereſs *Medea*,
tho' *ſhe* lived in *Italy*, and *they* in *Colchos* at
the

Sect. 11. the furtheft end of the *Buxine*; feparated by Seas and Continents of immenfe Extent.

THE *Idea* of the *one-ey'd Cyclops*, whom he places in *Sicily*, he is thought to have taken from the *Arimafpians* in *Thrace*; and thefe fame *Cimmerians*, from the long Nights and cloudy Sky, in the fame Country. This laft is the more probable, that the *Phenicians* might be paffing homeward from the *Bofphorus* pretty late in the Year, and might perhaps be tempted to tarry, upon fome Profpects of Gain, until the Winter furprized them in that cold Climate, and froze up their Ship: In that cafe they wou'd literally fee a People ΗΕΡΙ ΚΑΙ ΝΕΦΕΛΗ ΚΕΚΑΛΥΜΜΕΝΟΥΣ, *wrapt up in Darknefs and Clouds*, and might give them a Name, which indeed will agree either with *Thrace* or the *Avernus*.

LET US NOW purfue our Voyage round the *Mediterranean*, and for that reafon leave *Ulyffes* failing back to *Circe*, and affociate our-felves with the other Traveller celebrated by *Homer*, the famous MENELAUS. The South and South-eaft Coaft of this Sea feem to have fallen to his fhare, as the North and North-weft were vifited by *Ulyffes*; tho' I know that the latter is likewife faid to have been driven both to *Spain*, (where there was a Town of his Name, and a Temple of *Minerva*) and to the Coaft of *Africk*, where he faw the *Loto-phagi*. But as the PHENICIAN Accounts

of

of thefe Parts are related by the Poet under
the Perfon of *Menelaus,* it will be proper for
us to follow him.

AFTER the taking of *Troy,* the *Greeks*
found they had purchafed the Victory very
dear: Befides the Men they had loft, there
were few of the furviving Chiefs who had
not fuffered at home, by Diforders in their
Families, or Damage in their Eftates: Nor
was the Spoil that was faved from the Flames,
when the City was burnt, fufficient to enrich
them all. They could not think of ftaying fo
long away, and returning to their empty Habitations with little or nothing, as the Re-
ward of their Toils; and fome chofe rather
to go and feek for Seats in unknown Countries,
than to live in their own Houfes after the
difmal things that had happened in them during their Abfence.

THUS *Diomedes* and *Teucer* went and fettled, the one in *Apulia,* and the other in *Cyprus:* *Menelaus* and *Ulyffes* revived the old
Practice of *Greece,* making Defcents with their
Squadrons upon feveral Coafts, and carrying
what Plunder they met with to their Ships:
And when the Difafters incident to a *piratical*
Life had difabled them from continuing fuch
Violences, they wandred about from place to
place, and fet on foot a kind of *Contribution*
(what the *French* call a *Quête*) where-ever
they came. Their high Reputation procured

T them

Sect.ii. them a kind Reception from all who had heard of the Deſtruction of *Troy*, the greateſt Tranſaction the World had then to talk of: And accordingly they received many ΞΕΙΝΗΙΑ (*Preſents to Strangers*) from the Princes they viſited, and both, tho' late, returned *rich* to their own Countries.

THE ACCOUNT *Menelaus* gives of his own Travels, is in a very plain manner, " That " having ſuffered many things, and wan- " dered far, he had amaſſed much Wealth, " and had come home at the end of eight " years: That having been in *Cyprus*, *Phe-* " *nicia*, and *Egypt*, and having viſited the " *Ethiopians* and *Arabians*, he arrived at laſt " in *Libya*," of which he tells ſeveral Won- ders: But the ſtrangeſt thing that befel him, was in the *Pharos*, a little Iſland in the Mouth of the *Nile*. There he ſurprized and bound *Proteus*, the mutable Prophet of the Sea, and received a Prophecy from him, " That it was " not his (*Menelaus's*) Fate to finiſh his days " in *Argos*, but the Immortals would ſend " him to the ELYSIAN PLAIN, and ENDS " of the Earth, where *yellow Rhadamanthus* " reigns, and where an eaſy affluent Life is " enjoyed by Men; where Snow is never " ſeen nor Rain, and Winter ſhows not his " hoary Face; but ſoft Gales conſtantly blow- " ing from the *Weſtern Ocean*, ſerve to cool

" the

"the Air and fan the Inhabitants of the "happy Shore."

THERE IS no doubt made by the Ancients, but that this Deſcription is taken from the Bay of *Cadix* and the South-weſt Coaſt of *Spain*; and there can be as little, that *Homer* muſt have heard of the Nature and Situation of theſe Parts from the PHENICIANS. It will coſt but a ſingle Thought to recollect, That the *Tyrian Hercules*, long before *Jupiter*'s Affair with *Alcmena*, had made the firſt Diſcovery of theſe Lands, and erected the famous *Pillars* that bore his Name: His Countrymen took care not to loſe ſo ſweet a Commerce; but charmed with the Softneſs and Delicacy of the Climate, and knowing perfectly the Value of the Commodities it produced, they planted it with Colonies, and drew from it the chief Streams that filled *Tyre* and *Sidon* with ſuch immenſe Wealth, and particularly with Coin and Plate [q].

THE Richneſs of the *Spaniſh Mines* afforded ample Materials of *Hyperbole* and *Deſcription* to the ancient Writers [r]; and we find in the

T 2 Poets

[q] TARSHISH was thy Merchant, by reaſon of the Multitude of *all kind* of Riches: With *Silver*, *Iron*, *Tin*, and *Lead* they traded in thy Fairs: ſays *Ezekiel* (Chap. XXVII. § 12.) where the Extent of the Trade of *Tyre*, and the very *Species* of Commodities brought by the ſeveral Nations to that Mart of the World are accurately deſcribed by the eloquent Prophet.

TARSHISH was ſounded *Tartiſh* by the *Phenicians* and *Syrians*, who changed the harſh *Sh* into *T*; whence the *Greeks* formed their ΤΑΡΤΗΣΣΟΣ.

[r] Ποσειδώνιος συνενήνοχε ταῖς ὑπερβολαῖς. Στραβ. Βιβ. γ.

Sect. 11. Poets coming after *Homer*, that the Eafe and
Affluence of their Princes, had paffed into a
Proverb [f]. This cou'd be known to *Homer*
in no other way but by the Report of the
Phenicians; who, when they fpoke of this
happy Country, the chief Source of their
Wealth and Grandeur, called it MECHOS
ELYSOTH, *The Place of Joys* or *Land of
Mirth* [t]. It was the Ships from thence that
" *fung* in the *Phenician* Markets, replenifhed
" their Cities, and made them very glorious
" in the midft of the Seas [u]." From them
therefore our Poet has learned the Nature of
the *Weftern Region*, the Blowing of the *Zephyrs*,
and the Fertility of the *Soil*; and has defcribed his ELYSIUM juft fuch a Place as the
Climate of *Cadix*, and the *Andaluzian Plains* [w].

IT

---

[f] Ἐγώ τ' ἂν οὔτ' ἈΜΑΛΘΙΗΣ βϫλοίμην ΚΕΡΑΣ,
Ὀυτ' ἔτεα πϫνλήκονῖα ϰ ἐνϫτὸν
ΤΑΡΤΗΣΣΟΥ βϫσιλεύσϫι   Ἀναϰρ. Ἀποσ πάσ.
[t] *Bochart*, Canaan.   [u] Ezekiel XXVII. § 25.

[w] Los fertiles Campos de *Andalufia*, tan celebrados de la An-
tiguedad por los *Campos Elifios*, repofo de las Almas bien aventu-
radas——Miré aquel pedaço de tierra, que en fertilidad y in-
fluencia del Cielo, hermofura de tierra y agua, no he vifto cofa
mejor, en toda la Europa——*And fpeaking of the neighbouring
Plain of* Malaga, *he fays*, Fue tan grande el confuelo que recebi
de la vifta della, y fragrancia que traia el *Viento*, regalandofe por
aquellas maravillofas Huertas, llenas de todas efpecies de Na-
ranjos y Limones, llenas de Azahar todo el Anno, que me pa-
reçiò ver un pedaço de Parayfo: Porque no ay en toda la *Re-
dondez* de aquel Orizonte, cofa que no deleyte los cinco Sen-
tidos. Los ojos fe entretienan con la vifta de *Mar y Tierra*,
llena de Arboles hermofiffimos: A los Oydos deleyta con
grande admiracion la abundancia de los Pajarillos, que dia y
noche no ceffan fu dulce Armonia: Los Mantenimientos fon
abundantes y fuftanciofos para el Gufto y la Salud: El Trato de
la Gente muy apazible, afable y cortefano; y *todo* es de manera,
que fe pudiéra hazer un grande Libro de fus excelencias.
Vida de Obregon.

I T gives a particular kind of Pleasure to learn from what *Originals* a celebrated Piece of Painting has been taken, and from what Object the Painter borrowed his *Idea*. We imagine ourselves to be let into a sort.of *Secret*; and discover new Beauties in the Copy, by placing it and the Model together, 'and comparing their mutual Lineaments. The same holds, and perhaps in a greater degree, in *poetical* Representations. An Author to whom our Country owes many a beautiful Treatise, makes not the least question, but that the Gulf thro' which *Virgil's Alecto* shoots into *Hell* is the Cataract of the *Velino*, three Miles from *Terni*. The River falls down a Precipice of an hundred Yards high, and throws itself with such Violence into the Hollow of a Rock, as to raise a continual Mist resembling Clouds, or the Smoke ascending from a vast Furnace ˣ.

B u t *Homer* does not seem to have kept entirely to *one* Model : He has divided his Description of the next World into *three* Parts, and has taken them from three different *Originals*. The first contains an Account of the *Entry* to the Realm of *Pluto*, and is taken from the *Avernus*; the second describes the Passage, and several Stages of the dreary *Progress*, copied from the *Procession* at the Funerals of *Apis* up the *Nile*; the third presents us

T 3   with

ˣ *Addison's* Journey thro' *Italy*.

Sect.11. with the *happy* *Climes* prepared for the Good
and Upright, taken from the *Fortunate Iſlands*
and the neighbouring Coaſt: And all the *three*
are made to coincide in ſeveral Circumſtances,
thro' the Addreſs and good Management of
the Poet.

AFTER this View of the Coaſt of *Italy*
and *Spain*, it wou'd be to little purpoſe to
aſk, How it appears that *Homer* learned theſe
things from the *Phenicians*, or thro' whoſe
Hands he received them? It is ſufficient that
ſuch Knowledge could be drawn from *no*
other Fountain: Tho' at the ſame time, it
will not be unpleaſant to hear that there are
Preſumptions in his Writings, of his having
been *perſonally* acquainted with this induſtrious People.

AND FIRST, He knows their *Character*
perfectly. When he ſpeaks of them in general, they are always ΦΟΙΝΙΚΕΣ, ΝΑΥΣΙΚΑΥ-
ΤΟΙ ΑΝΔΡΕΣ, *The* Phenicians *fam'd for Ship-*
ping, or *renowned at Sea*; " whoſe Merchants
" were Princes, and whoſe Traffickers the
" Honourable of the Earth." This is the
diſtinguiſhing Mark of the Nation. Their
City " was inhabited of *Sea-faring* Men, the
" renowned City, which was ſtrong *in the*
" *Sea*; She and her Inhabitants, who cauſe
" their Terrour to be on all that *haunt it* ꝩ."
Then their ancient Town is ΠΟΛΥΧΑΛΚΟΣ

ΣΙΔΩΝ,

3

ꝩ Ezekiel, Chap. XXVI. § 17.

ΣΙΔΩΝ, Sidòn *abounding with Metals*; and the Sect.11.
Sidonians, ΠΟΛΥΔΑΙΔΑΛΟΙ ΑΝΔΡΕΣ, *ingeni-*
ous artful Men. It is impoffible for any Man,
tho' he had lived a great part of his Life at
Sidon, to give more proper Epithets to the Nation and City, or more expreffive of the Genius
of the Inhabitants. But *Homer* goes further,
and fhews that he has been acquainted with
all Ranks of the *Phenicians.*

THE mean People of a trading Nation
naturally fall into Tricking and low Cozen-
age; and in this refpect the *Phenician* Ped-
lars were the *Jews* of *Antiquity*; and bore fuch
a Character among them as the *Jews* do among
us. Such exactly hath *Homer* painted them.
He calls them ΤΡΩΚΤΑΙ, *Scrapers of Money*
from any thing ᵃ; and to explain how they
did it, he fubjoins, that they were πολυται-
παλοι ἀνδρες, *Men with a thoufand fmall Wiles.*
There was befides a great Intercourfe between
the two Nations: The *Phenician* Ships, our
Poet tells, frequently wintered among the *Gre-*
cian Iflands, and the Prince ᵃ of one of them
had a *Phenician* Miftrefs: She was, according
to his Defcription,

Tall and beautiful, and fkill'd in curious Work ᵇ.

T 4   Homer

ᵃ ΤΡΩΚΤΗΣ· ὁ ἐκ πάντος κερδαίνων, ὅιον ἀπο]ρώγων.
Σχίδα.

ᵃ *Ctefius,* the Son of *Ormenus,* Prince of the rich Ifland
Syria: or, as the later Geographers called it, SYROS.

ᵇ ΚΑΛΗ ΤΕ ΜΕΓΑΛΗ ΤΕ ἡ ΑΓΛΑΑ ΕΡΓ' ΕΙΔΥΙΑ.
Ὀδυσ. Ο.

Sect.11. *Homer* relates her Story so particularly, her
Father's *Phenician* Name [c], his affluent Circumstances, and how she was carried off by
the *Taphian* Pirates as she was returning from
the Country to *Sidon*, that one would almost
think he had heard it from the *Descendents* of
the Family.

TH is Suspicion is confirmed by the Knowledge he discovers of the Produce and Manufacture of the Country. Most of the fine
things he mentions, Gifts to the Gods, or
Presents from great Men, are (he says) of
Sidonian Workmanship. The finest Garment
in the *Trojan* Queen's Wardrobe, was bought,
in *Sidon* by *Paris*, who must no doubt have
been a *Judge* in those Matters [d]; and the
prettiest Utensil in *Menelaus's* Palace was a
Silver Bowl edged with Gold, which he had
received as a Present from the King of *Sidon* ; and it is not improbable that *Homer*
had seen many like it, when in that City
himself [e]. In short, he seldom describes *Toys*
or *Jewels*, or any piece of curious Work,
but he very readily adds, that it was made in
Sidon, or brought over in a *Phenician* Ship:
And herein he hath the Happiness to agree
with our *sacred Chronicle*, where we learn,
that

---

[c] Ἀρύβας: Softened from *Asrubas*, or *Asdrubas*, ASDRUBAL.
                                    Bochart.

[d] *Iliad* VI.   [e] *Odyss.* IV.

that the wife *Solomon* [f], when he was about Sect.11.
to build his magnificent Temple, received a
cunning Man from *Tyre*, " Skilful to work
" in Gold and in Silver; In Brafs, in Iron,
" in Stone, and in Timber; In Purple, in
" Blue, in fine Linen, and in Crimfon ; alfo,
" to grave every manner of Graving, and to
" find out every *Device* which fhould be put
" to him."

BUT we do the *Phenicians* an injury in
making them only *Artificers, Navigators,* and
Merchants. The nobler Sciences were cultivated among them, and they have the Honour
of being the Authors of two famous *Sects* who
gained great Reputation, by Opinions which
the *Grecians* borrowed from them.   We have
                                        it

[f] This Prince had two Fleets, one upon the Red-Sea, at *Ef-
ongaber,* and the other on the *Mediterranean,* perhaps at *Joppa;*
and both of them navigated by *Phenicians.* For Hiram *King of*
Tyre *fent his Servants in the Navy, Shipmen who had Knowledge
of the Sea;* and they traded along the Coaft of *Arabia, and came
to* Ophir (Taprobane or Ceylon) *and fetched from thence four
hundred Talents, of Gold, and brought it to* Solomon [*]. The other
was called the Navy of *Tarfhifh,* which failed in company with
the Navy of *Hiram. Once in three years came the Navy of* Tarfhifh, *bringing Gold, and Silver, and Ivory, and Apes, and Peacocks* [†].
It was fo long before they cou'd accomplifh, in their coafting
Way of failing, a Voyage by *Cadix* to the *Guinea* Coaft, whence
they brought the Commodities abovementioned. They probably
failed as the *Arabs* do at this day : " Comme les *Arabes* ne font
" pas de grands Navigateurs, ils ne voyagent jamais que le jour,
" aiant toujours un Homme fur la Proue, et un autre fur le haut
" du Mât, pour obferver la Mer; Ils mouïllent d'abord que le
" Soleil eft prêt à fe coucher, et ne levent l'Ancre, que lorfqu'ils
" ont le Vent en pouppe; emploiant ainfi deux ou trois Mois
" à une Navigation de fept ou huit jours."
                    VOYAGE du Sr P. Lucas. Liv. VI.

[*] 1 KINGS ix. §27.   [†] 1 KINGS x. §22.

Sect.II. it upon the Authority of *Poſidonius* g, That
what is called the *Atomical* Philoſophy was
firſt advanced by Moschus a *Sidonian,* ſome
time before the *Trojan War :* Of *Atoms,* he
ſaid, the World was made; *Matter,* in its old
primæval State, being in *that form.* For his
Work was *a Hiſtory of the* Creation, or an
Account of the *Riſe of Things,* the common
Theme of the firſt Philoſophers : They always
wrote in an hiſtorical Strain, for the ſake of
the Narrative or *Parable* in which they taught,
and of the Allegories which they interwove as
Epiſodes ; there being nothing then known of
the Manner of our modern Syſtems, which are
built upon metaphyſical Principles and abſtract
Reaſoning.

I am the apter to believe that it was ſo,
becauſe it is certain that *Epicurus* was not the
Inventer of the Doctrine of *Atoms* which he
embraced; but received that Method of accounting for the *Riſe of Things* from *Democritus,*
who had travelled long in the *Eaſt,* and brought
from thence his Learning and Philoſophy. By
this means the Principles which were ſo greedily ſwallowed both in *Greece* and *Rome;* and,
as a witty Writer aſſerts ʰ, were embraced by
all *the fine Gentlemen* of Antiquity, came originally from *Phenicia.* They were preſerved
in

ᵍ 'Ει δ᾽ δῶ ΠΟΣΕΙΔΩΝΙΩ πιϛεύσαι, ᷍ περὶ ϯῶ 'Αϳόμων
δόγμα παλαῖον ἐϛιν ἀνδϛὸς Σιδωνίϗ ΜΟΣΧΟΥ, πϛο τῶν
Τϛωϊκῶν χϛόνων.   Σϳϛαβ. βιβ. ιϛ.
ʰ Monſ. *St. Evremond.*

in that Country by a *prophetical* Sett of Natu- Sect. II.
ral Philofophers, (fo *Jamblichus* [i] calls them)
Mofchus's Defcendants or Succeffors, with whom
Pythagoras is faid to have converfed in his Return from *Egypt.*

I T were eafy to fay a great deal concerning
the *Phenician Theology* tranfcribed by *Eufebius*,
their Records kept in their Temples, and the
Problems that paffed betwixt them and the
knowing and peaceful *Prince* juft now mentioned : But as thefe things belong not immediately to our Subject, nor to the Inftruction
that *Homer* received from this People, I fhall
rather felect a *Grecian* Difciple of theirs, whofe
Works have fome Connexion with our Poet.

A M O N G the earlieft of the *Greek* Philofophers was *Pherecydes*, a Native of that very
Ifland, where we heard that it was cuftomary
for the *Phenician* Ships to winter. He has the
honour to be mentioned as the Mafter of *Pythagoras*, (whom he converted from Wreftling,
to Philofophy) and is famous for introducing
Profe-writing into *Greece*. He had no living
Mafter of his own, to lead him the way in
Science ; but having purchafed from the *Phenicians*, either in his *own* Country, or as is more
probable in *theirs*, fome Volumes of their fublime Philofophy, he drew from thénce his
Knowledge, and acquired a very great Name
among

---

[i] Εν]αῦνα δὲ (Πυθαγόρας) συμϐαλὼν τοῖς τε ΜΟΣΧΟΥ τῦ
ΦΥΣΙΟΛΟΓΟΥ ΠΡΟΦΗΤΑΙΣ ΑΠΟΓΟΝΟΙΣ, κ) τοῖς
ἄλλοις Φοινικικοῖς Ἱεροφάνταις. Ἰαμϐλιχ. Πυθαγ. βίῳ.

Sect. 11. among the *Greeks*. They look'd upon him as the firſt who had ſpoke of the *Tranſmigration* of Souls, a Doctrine much inculcated by the *Pythagoreans* his Succeſſors: and read with admiration his Accounts of the *Birth* and *Succeſſions* of the *Gods*.

His Country is pointed at in *Homer* in a very remarkable manner: " *Above* Ortygia, " *ſays the Poet, there is a certain Iſland called* " Syria, *if ever you heard of it,* ʿοθι τρο- " παι ηελιοιο, *where are the Returns or* " *Tropicks of the Sun*." This, it ſeems, is the *Mark* of the place, which will help us to diſtinguiſh it from the neighb'ring Iſles: But without the aſſiſtance of ſucceeding Hiſtory, and particularly where it relates to *Pherecydes*, we ſhou'd never have known what to have made of it: To have gone in ſearch of ſuch an Iſland under the *Tropicks*, wou'd have been as fooliſh as to think of contriving a *natural Meaning* for the Expreſſion taken in its literal Signification; and in what Senſe *the Returns of the Sun* can be ſaid to be in any one of the *Cyclades*, is a Queſtion that would puzzle our beſt Aſtronomers.

For a *Solution*, the old Scholiaſt upon the Paſſage tells us, that " *In this Iſland there was* " *a* Cave *conſecrated to the Sun, which ſhewed* " *the Time of his Returns*." Theſe are the *very Words* of the Commentary; and they ſeem to ſtand as much in need of an Explication as their Subject. I incline to think, that
the

the *Phenicians* finding the Iſland rich in *Grain*, Sect. II. which they much wanted [k], and accommoda- ～ ted with a fine Harbour, may have endeavoured to fit it in every reſpect for their *Winter Retreat.* With this view it is probable they may have adjuſted a MERIDIAN LINE to ſome Hole or Cleft in the Roof, which admitted a *Ray* of the *Sun* into the conſecrated Cave, and marked the *Solſtices* upon that Line, and what other Subdiviſions they thought fit.

THE *Uſe* of ſuch a thing, for letting them know the *Turns* of the Year, and for point- ing out the Seaſons fit for ſailing, needs no Enlargement; and their Skill in *Aſtronomy* and *Numbers*, leaves as little doubt of their Ability to effect it. The ſame thing was afterwards performed, and perhaps more accurately, by *Pherecydes*; not in the Cave, but by erecting a *Stylus*, whoſe Shadow ſhould mark the Ad- vance and Receſs of the Sun to and from the *Tropicks.* Whether this *Heliotrope* was move- able or not, I cannot tell; but it was long preſerved in *Syros*, many hundred Years after the Author's Death; and from its Duration, I take it to have been ſome *Pyramid of Braſs or Stone*, erected and marked in a level from the Baſe, in the ſame way as the great Obeliſk brought by *Auguſtus* from *Egypt*, and placed in the *Campus Martius* near the City; whoſe Shadow,

[k] HIRAM, Prince of *Tyre*, was to receive from *Judæa* twenty thouſand Meaſures of *beaten Wheat*, and twenty thouſand Mea- ſures of *Barley*, and twenty thouſand Baths of *Wine*, and twenty thouſand Baths of *Oil.*

Sect.11. Shadow, fays *Pliny*, fhewed the Sun's Altitude, and the Increafe and Diminution of the Days and Nights.

HAD *Pherecydes* lived before, or contempo-rary with *Homer*, there wou'd be no doubt but this very Machine was the thing defcribed by the *Poet* ; but being *pofterior*, it is more likely that he himfelf took the Hint from the *Phenicians*, and probably out-did theirs, in the Exactnefs of his Invention.

THERE was nothing like this *Heliotrope* to be feen in any part of *Greece*, fave in this little Ifle, whofe Inhabitants, ignorant like the other *Greeks*, when they came to gaze at the Marks, and afked the ufe of them, could only gather from the *Phenicians* Anfwer (juft what *Homer* has faid) " *That they were the* " Returns *of the Sun* ; or, *that when the Sun* " *had advanced fo far*, He returned *the way* " *he had come.*" *Homer* cou'd not mifs hear-ing of them ; for if he was not himfelf in this Ifland, which he has defcribed fo happy and healthful, he wou'd certainly be informed of every thing concerning it in *Delos*, juft in its Neighbourhood, whither he came every Year to fing at the Feafts of *Apollo*.

HERE, *My Lord*, we will finifh our Voy-age. We fet out from the *Hellefpont*, and taking the Coaft of *Italy* in our way, we have returned by *Spain* and *Africk* to the *Egean Sea*. What we have feen is fufficient to con-

vince

vince us, that *Homer* owed moſt of thoſe Tales Sect.11.
that raiſe our Wonder in the *Odyſſey*, to his 〰
Converſe with the PHENICIANS : And as they
were told from the natural Apprehenſions the
Phenician Seamen and ſimple *Greeks* formed
from the firſt Appearance of the Subjects, that
ſame *Simplicity* has been preſerved in the Relation, and has accommodated them to the
Underſtanding of all Ranks of Men. It was
this happy Circumſtance that directed the Poet
to hit the general Taſte of Nations, and to
touch the *Univerſal Ear* ſo juſt and true, that
no Change of Manners or Politicks [1] can make
his Poems be diſreliſhed where they are but
read and known.

I CANNOT bid them farewel, without re-
flecting with ſome ſurprize on *Homer's Good-
fortune* in this Particular. He was equally
happy in his *Wonders* as in his *Religion.* Too
much Splendour did not glare in his Eyes and
darken his Miracles ; for, if your Lordſhip will
forgive the Oddneſs of the Phraſe, the beſt
Light to place a Wonder in, is a *little Ob-
ſcurity.* His Gods and their Powers were never
ſo much as queſtioned, when he ſung of their
marvelous Alliances and myſtick Generation :
Nor were theſe Countries to the North and
Weſt of *Greece* enough known, to make People doubt of the ſtrange and woeful Stories he
related of them. It was ſo late as the Times
of

[1] See Monſ. *Perrault's Paraleles.*

Sect. 11. of *Auguſtus*, when *Cocceius* and *Agrippa* cut thro' the Mountains, and cleared the *Avernus*, that *Homer's* HELL appeared to be an ordinary BAY; and what he ſaid of it, ΠΑΝΤΑ ΤΑΥΤΑ ΜΥΘΟΣ ΕΙΝΑΙ, *to be all a pure Fable:* But before that, and eſpecially in the Infancy of the *Phenician* Navigation, while the Coaſt lay unexplored, the Miracles would be ſwallowed; and the ſtrangeſt Tale he could tell, would paſs for a certain Truth.

SUCH Reflections as theſe have ſometimes led me to think, that HOMER's *Art* was not ſo great and refined, as we commonly ſuppoſe it to have been : That his *Good Fortune* was far ſuperiour to his *Skill*; ſince he needed but repreſent things both in his own and other Countries, *almoſt as he heard them talked of.* The ordinary Strain in which they were related, was nicely calculated for giving them that air of *natural Wonder*, which affects us ſo ſtrongly in reading them : A thing hardly to be counterfeited! For a man who underſtands any Subject *perfectly*, who knows the Cauſes and Effects of every ſurprizing-like thing about it, of conſequence talks coolly; and having no Admiration himſelf, can with difficulty raiſe it in another. When he attempts it, his Looks and Voice, and laboured Sentences betray him, and ſhew the *Artifice:* But if at any time he can *forget* himſelf, and ſcrew up his Fancy ſo as to *ſmother* his Reaſon, he may then ſucceed; and inſpire

his

his Hearers with a Paſſion he begins to feel: Sᴇᴄᴛ.11.
Yet his Judgment will recur when the *Fit* is
over, and leave him the ſame cool unadmiring
Perſon he was before.

I ʜᴀᴠᴇ heard it declared by thoſe, whoſe
Buſineſs it is to *perſonate* Charaſters and their
peculiar Paſſions, that they never ſucceed ſo
well as when *they forget themſelves moſt*; and
have entered into ſome ſort of Perſuaſion, that
they are indeed the *Perſons* whom they repreſent. But I hardly know, whether I dare apply
their Caſe to our celebrated Poet, and venture to
ſay, " That the more firmly *Homer* believed the
" Wonders he tells, he wou'd tell them the
" better, and paint their moſt moving Circum-
" ſtances with a truer Feeling than if he had
" not been perſuaded of the Truth of the Faſts."

Paulum tu intereſſe cenſes, ex animo omnia
Ut fert natura facias, an de induſtriâ ?

Tʜᴜs, Wᴇ have run over *Homer*'s Advantages from Nature and Education: We have
ſurveyed the *Climate* where he was born : We
have conſidered the *Manners* of his Country,
its *Language* and *Religion*; and have found
from the Nature of things, and their conſtant
Effeſts, that they were *all* in the happieſt temper for Deſcription and Poeſy. We have gone
further, and traced him in his *private Educa-*
tion, his *Employment* and Manner of *Life*, and
found them of the ſame Nature and Tendency :

U   And

Sect.11. And to account for the wide Knowledge of Men and Things that appears throughout his Works, we have look'd abroad, and found *foreign Countries* affording the happiest Opportunities Man's heart cou'd wish, for *poetick* Improvement: Their joint Effects we have found verified in his Descriptions, and in the Numbers of shining Images, natural Allusions, and surprizing Tales that grace his Writings: But take them all together, and they had not been able to raise him to his high Station, if the noblest S u b j e c t that ever fired the Fancy of a Poet had not compleated his Happiness. Let us, *My Lord,* consider it, and conclude the *Enquiry.*

Gravelot inv.   *P.t Gucht Scul.*

S E C T.

Gravelot inv.   P. Fourdrinier Sculp.

S E C T. XII.

OF THE TWO *Heroick Poems* written by
Homer, the *first* contains an Account
of the hotteft Period of a long War between
the confederate Princes of *Greece*, and the
richeft Kingdom of *Afia* with its *Dependen-
cies.* The *fecond* relates the Confequences of
that War, and the Fates of the feveral *Chief-
tains* after the Victory. *Homer* feems to have
been deftin'd for writing the Hiftory of the

U 2   *whole*

Sect.12. *whole Tranſaction,* by being born in *one* Country, reſiding in the *other,* and travelling much
in *both.*

I T   W O U L D be a difficult matter to enumerate the Advantages of ſuch a *Situation.*
It wou'd be to reſume the Conditions in *Manners, Language,* and *Travelling,* we found to
be requiſite in Poetry ; and ſhewing that by
this means they are included in *Homer*'s Fortunes. He appears to be the *only* Bard, who
equally knew the Country of his *Hero,* and
that of his Enemies: And except thoſe Poets
who have ſung of *Civil Wars,* where the con-
tending Parties are of the ſame Country, and,
where, for that reaſon, there can be no Variety,
of Manners; excepting thoſe, I ſay, he ſeems
in *this reſpect* likewiſe to be *ſingular* among
the Poets.

I C A N N O T pretend to determine the preciſe time he tarried in each Country ; how ſoon
he left *Ionia,* or how frequently he returned to
it. A great part of his Life he ſpent in
Chios, whoſe Inhabitants were *Ionians* as well
as thoſe of the other Iſlands in the *Archipelago.* It is accordingly certain, that his Language and Manners are principally *Ionic,* tho'
all the Dialects of *Greece* are employed in his
Poetry, and give proof that he has viſited the
principal Nations, and learned the Peculiarities
of their Speech. His *own,* no doubt, has been
formed, where he ſpent his Youth ; and afterwards,

wards, by wandering up and down in *Afia* Sect.12.
and *Greece*, he hath attained that eafy familiar
manner of fpeaking of them, for which he is
admired. This is a Blefling fo rare in a Poet's
Lot, to be as it were a *Native of both Countries*, that it will be worth while to take a
View of fome of its Confequences.

THE firft which prefents itfelf, is, *That he*
muft have been acquainted with the *Field of
Action*, the PLAINS OF TROY. It was this
enabled him to defcribe it fo minutely; and
give it that Air of Veracity it bears from thofe
natural Incidents he has thrown into his Narration. He had them, not by Reading or Speculation, but from the *Places themfelves*, and
the Profpects that arife from the Culture and
Difpofition of the Grounds. *Who* but the Man
that had wandered over that delightful Plain,
that had viewed the Bendings of the Coaft,
and every Corner of the Fields, could have
defcribed or feigned the genuine *Marks* of it :
The *Tomb* of *Dardanus*, the *Springs* of *Sca-
mander*, the *Banks* of *Simoïs*, the *Beach Tree*,
with many other Circumftances that diftinguifh the *Environs*, and enrich his Landfkip ?
Other Writers, before they relate an Action
that happened in any place, firft *defcribe that
Place*, be it a Grove, or Rock, or River, or
the Declivity of a Mountain. Thefe they
feign according to the ftrength of their Fancy,

U 3   and

Sect. 12. and then they *apply them* [a]. *Homer* mentions his Places with an appearance of Certainty, *as already subsisting*, and already *known* [b]: He does it almost in the manner of an *Historian*, and leaves you to pick up a more particular Knowledge of them from the Circumstances of the Action to which they belong.

IT MAY PERHAPS seem somewhat extraordinary, at this distance of Time, to affirm "That *Homer*'s Accounts of these Places are "not fictitious; that his Battles were given "in no imaginary Spaces, but correspond with "the real state of the Land and Water." Yet a very convincing Proof of it may be drawn from the Nature of a Treatise, of which Time has deprived us.

DEMETRIUS SCEPSIUS was born at a little Village [c], situated upon a Skirt of *Mount Ida*, not many Miles from *Troy*. As he knew every Stream and Brook in the Country, and that there was neither Hill nor Vale, nor hardly a By-way, that had escaped his notice, he wrote a *Commentary* of thirty Books upon few more than *sixty Verses* of *Homer*'s CATALOGUE of the *Trojans*. There he ascertained the *real Places*

[a] Est urbe egressis tumulus, templumque vetustum
Desertæ Cereris; juxtaque antiqua cupressus,
Relligione patrum multos servata per annos; *Says Eneas to his Servants, who must have known those Places as well, or better than himself.* Eneid. II.

[b] ——— *Et in medias res,*
Non secus ac notas auditorem rapit.———
Horat. ad Pison.

[c] *SCEPSIS.*

Places of *Homer*'s Defcriptions, and pointed Sect. 12.
out the Scenes of the remarkable Actions.
He fhewed where the *Greeks* had drawn up
their Ships ; where *Achilles* encamped with
his *Myrmidons* ; where *Hector* drew up the
Trojans ; and from what Countries came the
Auxiliaries : In fhort, he fixed the *Geography*
of the *Trojan* Affairs, and actually performed
what *Virgil* feigns,

—— *Juvat ire et Dorica caftra,*
Defertofque videre locos, littufque relictum.
Hic Dolopum manus ; hic fævus tendebat Achilles ;
Claffibus hic locus ; hic acies certare folebant.

Or, as it is fancied by a fofter Poet :

Hac ibat Simöis ; hic eft Sigëia tellus ;
Hic fteterat Priami regia celfa fenis.
Illic Æacides, illic tendebat Ulyffes ;
Hic lacer admiffos terruit Hector equos.

HERE is the great Witnefs for *Homer :*
He appears to his Character, and attefts his
Veracity after many Searches into the Truth
of his Relations [d]. But tho' there had been
no fuch Teftimony remaining, we might know
he copied from Nature, and defcribed Realities

U 4 from

[d] See STRABO, Book XIII, where he profeffes chiefly to follow
this Author (*Demetrius Scepfius*) his *Commentary upon the Cata-*
logue, in his Defcription of the Dominion of *Troy*, and the adjacent
Countries.

Sect.12. from the *Effects* of his Descriptions upon our own Minds while we read them : It is in this as in other things; no Imagination can supply the want of *Truth* : Flowery Meads and horrid Rocks, dismal Dungeons and enchanted Palaces (things all on *Extremes*) can be easily imagined : But they take only with young raw Fancies, fit to be entertained with Stories of Dwarfs and distress'd Dam'sels. The Traces of *Truth* are only irresistible: the most fanciful *fairy Scene* in the *Argenis*, or the * * * * *, does not please like a View of the *Callicolone*, or a Prospect from the Brow of the *lofty Ide*, because not *real*. In the one, the Harmony established between the human Understanding and *Truth*, commands our Assent: In the other, the Mind doubts and wavers, and views them passing like a *waking Dream*.

SUCH was *Homer*'s Good-fortune with respect to *Places*; and the same Cause has made him equally happy in the Knowledge of the *Persons* whose Actions he sung. A Stranger in ASIA must have been a Stranger to its Inhabitants; but *Homer*, as a Native, had many opportunities to know the *Trojans*, and hear of the Nations and Tribes contiguous to *Troy*. We find him able to recount *Priam's Auxiliaries*, and make up the List of their Leaders, with equal certainty as he had done his BOIᴏTIA or *Catalogue* of the *Grecian* Ships. His
Know-

Knowledge this way will bear the ſtricteſt Scru-　Sect.12.
tiny ; and as we are apt to ſet a high value ⌇⌇
upon thoſe Accounts of Men and Countries,
that are given by People perſonally acquainted
with them, it will not be amiſs to enquire
narrowly into the Poet's Abilities, by dipping
a little into his Subject.

PRIAM's Kingdom, according to *Ho-*
mer, extended from the River E S E P U S, the
Limit of the *Cyzicenian* Territory, all along
the Coaſt of the *Propontis* and *Helleſpont*, until you come to the L E C T I A N Promontory,
over-againſt *Leſbus*, in the *Egean Sea*. This
we learn from *Achilles's* own mouth, who had
ravaged the greateſt part of it. When the
unhappy *Priam* came to him to beg the
Body of his ſlaughtered Son, the fierce *Greek*
began to relent ; and thinking upon the Re-
verſe of Fortune of the aged Prince, he ſays
to him :

Before theſe days, old King, we hear thou ruled'ſt
O'er many Provinces in proſperous State,
From Leſbus *upwards,* Macar's *fertile Seat,*
All between Phrygia *and the* Helleſpont ᵉ.

T H E *Trojan* Dominion, therefore, was
bounded on the Weſt by the *Sea*, and on the
Eaſt by the famed Mount *Ida*, whoſe Skirts
run

ᵉ Καί συ, Γέρον, τὸ πεὶν μὲν, ἀκύομεν ὄλϭιον ἦῦ·
ᵒΟσον Λ Ε Σ Β Ο Σ ἄνω, Μάκαρος ἕδος, ἐντὸς ἐέργει,
Καὶ ΦΡΥΓΙΗ καθύπερθε κ̀ ΕΛΛΗΣΠΟΝΤΟΣ ἀπείρων.
'Ιλιαδ. Ω.

Sect.12. run North to the *Euxine*, and South-east to the Bay over-against *Lesbus*. It comprehended *nine Governments*, or *Provinces*[f], over which it is thought *Priam* reigned before the Arrival of the *Greeks*. Besides these, he drew Auxiliaries from the *high Countries* all around him, as far as from beyond the River *Halys* on the one hand, and the *Old Cilicia* on the other.

WITH THESE, and with their Inhabitants, must *Homer* have been acquainted, to give us such a Plan of the *Trojan Power* as he has done: And in order to fit him for this Task, *some Events* fell out before he was born, which are necessary to be known. As first, " That " this very Country, formerly the Dominion " of ancient *Troy*, reaching from the River " *Esepus* to the *Lectian Promontory*, was, soon " after the Destruction of the City, wholly " occupied by the EOLIANS, a *Grecian* " *Colony*." Next, that within fourscore Years after this Settlement was made, another *Grecian* Tribe, the IONIANS, came and possessed themselves of all the Coast from that Promontory southward, down to the *Cilician Border*.

Not

---

[f] I. From *Esepus* down to *Abydos*, under Adrastus and Amphius the Sons of Merops. II. *Abydos*, with its Territory, under Asius. ' III. The *Lycians* under Pandarus. IV. The *Dardans* under Eneas. V. The *Trojans*, so called from *Troy*, under Hector. VI. The *Leleges* under Altes. VII. and VIII. Two *Lyrnessus's*: One under Eurypylus the Son of Telephus; the *other*, under Myntes, the Country of the beautiful *Briseis*, Achilles's Mistress. IX. *Thebes*, opposite to Lesbus, under Etion, where *Chryseïs* was taken, Agamemnon's loved Captive; and it was also the native City of the faithful *Andromache*.

Not long after this, *Homer* came into the Sect. 12.
World, and had acceſs to hear from his own
Countrymen *their* Exploits, and from his
Neighbours, the Deſcendants of *Priam's* Allies,
the traditional Accounts of what paſſed in the
War.

F ROM ſuch *Remains* of the *Trojans*, as were
left ſcattered up and down in the conquered
Country, he would hear *their Side of the Story:*
What Friends and Anceſtors any of them had
loſt in the *Common Cauſe :* What kind of Men
they were; what Armour they wore; what
Weapons they uſed, and how nobly they
fought before they fell in Battle.   He has deſcribed the Houſes of ſome of the Princes who
lived at a great diſtance from *Troy* ; has given
us an Inventory of their *Armories*, the Number of *Horſes* they kept, and *Chariots* they had
laid up, with all the Circumſtances of a *Family
Story*, ſuch as might be told by one of their
Poſterity.   He appears indeed to have wandered over many of the Places he mentions, and
to have viſited the *native Soils* of the greater
part of his Heroes, where he might hear
their Stories from their Subjects and Deſcendants : They would not fail to tell them with
all the miraculous aggravating Incidents, which
their Love to their Chiefs, and the Warmth
of their Fancies could inſpire : And we all
know how carefully ſuch Traditions are preſerved,

Sect.12. ferved, and faithfully handed down to the young Branches of a warlike Family.

T H E Effect of *this* Good-fortune in *Homer's* Situation is rather ftronger upon our Minds than the other; as we are more apt to be affected with Relations of *Men* and their *Actions*, than of any thing elfe: *Here,* we are Judges, and more ready to feel the Falfehood of a lame Defcription, than where we have nothing that correfponds to it from within. *To perfuade,* upon *this* Subject, muft be a thing very hardly accomplifhed in Verfe. The common *Weak-fide* of Poetry is, that while we read it, we perceive *it is fo:* The Fiction every now and then difcovers its cloven foot, betrays its Diffimilitude to Truth, and tho' never fo willing, we *cannot* believe. How well foever we may be pleafed with the Sweetnefs of the Lines, and the Pomp of the Defcription, the *Mind* is feldom feized, nor do we *enter* into the Subject. The Poet gains no Afcendant over our Opinions, nor puts us in the leaft pain for the Confequences. But when we fit down to H o M E R, and hear him tell over the Number of his *Ships,* recount his *Auxiliaries,* whence they came, how they were armed, what their Fathers and Friends faid to them when they took leave, with what Hopes they fet out, and fo produce, as it were, the *Mufter-Roll* of the two Armies, we can no longer defend ourfelves; and in fpite of all *our*

Precaution,

Precaution, an Opinion creeps upon us, " *That* Sect.12. " *every tittle of what he says is true* [g]."

ANOTHER Confequence of *Homer's* Situation with regard to his *Subject*, is the *Smoothnefs* of his *Language*. I do not mean the Genius of the *Ionic* Dialect, or its general Aptnefs for Poetry; tho' the frequent Return of *Vowels*, and the *fportive Difpofition* of the People, are Circumftances of no fmall Importance, either for *Sound* or *Character*. The Advantage I mention, is the *Softnefs* of the proper Names of *Places* and *Perfons* with which his Poems abound; and their being as it were ready *polifhed* to his hand, and fit to be employed in a Work where Delicacy and Grandeur muft combine to bring it to perfection.

HERE feems to be *another Singularity* in *Homer's* Deftiny, " To fpeak as eafily of a " foreign Country as he does of his own." His Anceftors had come and poffeffed themfelves of all the Dominion of *Troy*; had foftened the Names of the Mountains, the Rivers, and Vales, and given them *Grecian* Terminations: They had familiarized them into their Language before he was born, and he juft came in time to reap the Benefit of it in his Poetry.

WE ARE told that *Virgil*, in his Youth, intended to write a Poem of the *Wars* of *Rome*; but after fome Effays, he was deterred from

the

[g] Denique, Tyndaridem raptam, belloque fubactas
Trojugenas genteis, cum dicunt effe, videndu' ft,
Ne forte haec per fe *cogant nos* effe fateri.　Lucret.

Sect.12. the Undertaking by the Asperity of the old *Roman Names*. That great Master of Verse found it difficult to put such harsh Words as *Vibius Caudex*, *Tanaquil*, *Lucumo*, or *Decius Mus*, into his Poetry. Some of the Names of Towns could absolutely find no place in *Heroic-Measure* [h]. They were almost as frightful as *Boileau's* *WOERDEN* [i], or the hideous *WURTS*, of whose Name he so woefully complains, as quite scaring his Muse [k].

BUT instead of these, *Homer* had the most flowing Names and sonorous Appellations, either imposed by the lately settled Tribes, or softened from their ancient Rudeness into his own *graceful Dialect*. Succeeding Writers have bore testimony to his Excellency in this particular; there being few Parts of his Works from which they have borrowed more largely, than those high-sounding Epithets he every where imposes upon *Persons* and *Places*, and which have been in a manner consecrated to the Poetic Stile, with the unanimous Consent of his Successors.   BUT

[h] Mansuri Oppidulo, quod *Versu* dicere non est.
                              Horat. Lib. I. *Sat.* V.

[i] Des villes que tu prens les noms durs et barbares,
  N' offrent de toutes parts que syllabes bizarres :
  Et qui peut sans fremir aborder *Woerden* ?
  Quel vers ne tomberoit au seul nom de *Hensden* ?
  Quelle Muse a rimer en tous lieux disposée,
  Oseroit approcher des Bords du *Zuiderzée* ?   *Epitr.* 4.

[k] WURTS l' espoir du Païs, et l'Appui des ces Murs ;
  WURTS—Ah quel nom, Grand Roi, quel Hector que ce *Wurts* ?
  Sans ce terrible nom——
  Bientôt—Mais *Worts* s' oppose.   *Epitr.* 4.

Bᴜᴛ tho' we know the Times of the *Eolian* and *Ionian* Migrations, and when they fettled upon the *Afiatic Coaft*, I hardly think that we are got to the bottom of the Affair ; .or that this Knowledge is fufficient *fully* to difcover *Homer*'s Happinefs in being led to the Choice of his Sᴜʙ-ᴊᴇᴄᴛ. I am apt to think that thefe *Colonies* were not the *firft* which croffed the *Hellefpont*, and carried with them fomething of the *Weftern* Language and Manners. I believe there were many Bodies of People from *Thrace* and the *Iflands*, who may have paffed over at different times, and taken poffeffion of fome Parts of the Coaft, and who were afterwards incorporated with the former Inhabitants.

A Pʀᴇsᴜᴍᴘᴛɪᴏɴ of this may be drawn from the *Names* of the *Trojans*, which certainly exifted long before *Homer*'s People came and fettled in their Country. They are for the moft part plainly of *Grecian* Compofition [l] : Nay, even the Names of the *Trojan Auxiliaries* are generally *Grecian* [m], tho' further removed from that Country than the *Afiatic Shore*. Nor is this Obfervation confined to Perfons ; but the Names of many *Hills*, *Rivers*, and *Countries* all around *Troy* are manifeftly *Grecian* [n]. But as thefe may have been impofed by the fubfequent Inhabitants (the new *Greek* Plantation) we could

---

[l] ΔΗΙΦΟΒΟΣ, ΑΛΕΞΑΝΔΡΟΣ, ΠΟΛΥΔΑΜΑΣ, ΑΝΤΗΝΩΡ.

[m] ΑΡΧΙΛΟΧΟΣ, ΑΚΑΜΑΣ, ΛΥΚΑΩΝ, ΙΠΠΟΘΟΟΣ, ΑΜ-ΦΙΜΑΧΟΣ.

[n] ΙΔΗ, ΞΑΝΘΟΣ, ΚΑΛΛΙΚΟΛΩΝΗ, ΑΔΡΗΣΤΕΙΑ, ΠΙΤΥΕΙΑ, ΜΑΙΑΝΔΡΟΣ, ΑΙΓΙΑΛΟΣ, ΓΥΓΑΙΗ, ΡΥΣΟΣ.

Sect. 12. could not build upon this Circumſtance without the Concurrence of other Proofs.

AND FIRST, We are aſſured by a Native
of *Pontus* [o], one of the northern Countries,
formerly in alliance with *Priam*, " *That* the
" *Trojan* Language had many Words and
" Names in common with the *Thracian*."
Of this he gives ſeveral Inſtances, which it
would be to little purpoſe to tranſcribe : But
what appears very remarkable in them is, That
thoſe very Inſtances are generally *Grecian* Terms,
as well as *Trojan* or *Thracian*. There are indeed many reaſons to induce us to believe, that
the difference between the moſt *ancient Greek*,
and the Language of *Thrace*, was not very
conſiderable. The People of *Maçedon* had
many Names in uſe among them, which were
not underſtood by the Inhabitants of *Attica*
and *Peloponneſus*; and the *Thracians* who filled all the Country to the North of *Macedon*,
from *Epirus* and *Illyricum* to the *Strymonic*
Bay, and quite down to the *Helleſpont*, have
no doubt varied yet more from the *Grecian*
Dialect; but ſtill with ſome affinity to the
bordering Language.

TO CONFIRM us in this Opinion, it is
certain that the *Thracians* had anciently great
footing in *Greece* : TEREUS a *Thracian* governed at *Daulis* in the *Phocean* Territory,
where the tragical inhuman Story of *Philomela*
and

[o] *STRABO.*

and *Progne* was acted. From thence a Body Sect.12.
of *Thracians* paſſed over to *Eubœa*, and poſſeſ-
fed themſelves of the Iſland : They are conſtantly called *Abantes*, by *Homer*, from *Abas*,
the Town in *Phocis* whence they came. Of
the ſame Nation were the *Aones, Tembices*, and
Hyantians, who made themſelves Maſters of
the old *Bœotia*; and even the poliſhed *Attica*
itſelf was inhabited by the *Thracians*, under
the Command of the renowned EUMOLPUS.
In a word, the great Tracts of Land occupied
by them, and by the *Egyptian* and *Phrygian*
Colonies, have made the celebrated Geographer aſſert, " *That almoſt all* Greece *was for-*
" *merly poſſeſſed by Barbarians* P."

THIS INTERCOURSE between the Na-
tions, and Affinity of their Dialect, will appear ſtill clearer, if we call to mind *Who*
were the Maſters of the ancient Muſic and
Poetry, and the firſt famed for theſe Arts
among the *Greeks*. It was *Orpheus, Muſæus, Thamyris*, and *Eumolpus*, all THRA-
CIANS; who were not only underſtood by
the then *Greeks*, but capable to charm them
with their Eloquence and Melody, and perſuade them to exchange their Fierceneſs for

a

P ΕΚΑΤΑΙΟΣ μὴν ἓν ὁ Μιλήσι⊙ πεὶ τῆς ΠΕΛΟΠΟΝ-
ΝΗΣΟΥ φησὶν, ὅτι πεὸ τ᷄ Ἑλλήνων ᾤκησαν αὐΐὴν Βάρζαροι.
Σχεδὸν δ᷄ π ἰ ὅ ΣΥΜΠΑΣΑ ΕΛΛΑΣ κά᷄οικια ΒΑΡ-
ΒΑΡΩΝ ὑπῆρξε τὸ παλαιόν. Στεαβ. Βιβλ. ζ.

X

Sect.12. a focial Life and peaceful Manners [q]. No
wonder then if the *Thracian* Tribes which
croffed the *Hellefpont*, and fettled in the Dominion of *Troy*, the *Caucones*, *Treres*, and
Cimmerians, gave Names to their new Habitations, which bear an Analogy to the Language of *Greece*.

BUT BESIDES the *Thracians*, there were
feveral other Tribes, that, in an ambulatory
uncertain kind of Life, ftrayed over *Greece*,
and other Parts of *Europe*, before the *Trojan*
War, whom *Homer* neverthelefs recounts a-
mong the Nations fighting under the Banners
of *Troy*. Thefe came not *from beyond Sea* as
Auxiliaries to *Priam*, he having received no
manner of Affiftance from the *European* Side [r],
and muft therefore have paffed the Sea, and
fettled in *Afia* fome confiderable time before
the Beginning of the War. The moft diftinguifhed of them were the wandering PELASGI,
the great Planters of *Greece* [f], *Italy* [t], and the
Trojan Coaft.   IT

---

[q] Θρᾶκες ἦσαν οἱ ἐπικληθέντες ἧ ἀρχαίας Μυσικῆς, ΟΡΦΕΥΣ ΜΟΥΣΑΙΟΣ κ̀ ΘΑΜΥΡΙΣ. Καὶ ὅτι ἐν τῇ Ἀκλᾷ τῇ πεὶ τὸν Ἄθων ΘΑΜΥΡΙΣ ὁ ΘΡΑΞ ἐϐασίλευσι, ἧ αὐτῶν ἐπιτηδευμάτων γενόμεν, ὧν κ̀ ὁ ΚΙΚΩΝ ΟΡΦΕΥΣ ὃς Ορφεὺς τὰ πρῶτα μὲν ἀγυρεύων δίέζη Ἕϧα κ̀ μειζόνων ἀξιῶν ἑαυτὸν, κ̀ Ὄχλον κ̀ δύναμιν περιποιῦμεν, διφθάρη ἐξ Ἐπιευράπως Ἀνὴρ ΓΟΗΣ ἀπὸ Μυσικῆς τε κ̀ Μαϧικῆς, κ̀ ἧ πεὶ τὰς Τελεϧας ΟΡΓΙΑΣΜΩΝ.

Ἐυσαθ. εἰς Ἰλιάδ. Ῥαψωδ. β.

[r] See Page 22. Note [m] in the end.

[f] ΔΑΝΑΟΣ, ὁ πεντήκοντα θυγατέρων πατὴρ
Ἐλθὼν εἰς ΑΡΓΟΣ, ᾤκισεν Ἰνάχε πόλιν·
ΠΕΛΑΣΓΩΤΑΣ δ' ὀνομασμένες τοπεὶν,
ΔΑΝΑΟΥΣ καλεῖσθαι νόμον ἔθηκαν.   ΕΥΡΙΠΙΔ·

[t] See *Dionyfius Halicarnaff. Antiquit. Rom. Lib.* I.

It wou'd be endleſs to relate their ſe- Sect.12.
veral Settlements up and down thoſe Countries,
and their Expulſions from them: It is ſufficient we know in general, that they were a
great and populous Nation: " Among their
" other Eſtabliſhments, ſays an ancient Hi-
" ſtorian, the *Pelaſgi* were poſſeſſed of the
" whole Sea-Coaſt of *Ionia*, with the neigh-
" bouring *Iſlands:* But being exceedingly given
" to change of Place, and a ſudden Relin-
" quiſhment of their former Seats, they both
" increaſed in an extraordinary manner, and
" were as quickly brought low :" The chief
Blow was given them by the *Eolians* and *Ionians,*
at their Arrival in *Aſia;* who took their Towns,
drove them from their delicious Fields, and
forced thoſe that eſcaped the Sword, to take
ſhelter in the higher Country.

Such Commotions are apt to appear ſomething ſtrange to us now; but very unreaſon-
ably, when we conſider how many *European*
Families are at this day quitting their paternal
Habitations, and croſſing no narrow Arm of
the Sea, to a plentiful Land, like the ancient
Greeks; but traverſing the Ocean in queſt of
uncultivated Grounds, and running to another
World in hopes of bettering their Condition.
This Reflection may ſtop our Wonder: And
when we think of all theſe Removes and in-
terchangeable Seceſſions of Tribes and Nations,
we ſhall not be ſurprized to hear it affirmed

X 2   by

Sect.12. by a Man ſo well verſed in the ancient State
of things as *Strabo*, " That about the time of
" the *Trojan War*, both *Greeks* and *Barba-*
" *rians*, as if ſeized with ſome wandering
" Spirit, or acted by a reſtleſs Impulſe, *de-*
" *ſerted their native Seats*, and *marched in*
." *multitudes* to invade the Poſſeſſions of their
" Neighbours."

I T W A S by this mixture of Tribes, and
Permutation of Places of Abode, that the Coaſt
of *the Leſſer Aſia* was in a manner *naturalized*
to the *Greeks* before the *War of Troy*. Their
Neighbours the *Thracians* had often ſettled in
it ; and the wandering *Pelaſgi*, the *Leleges*, and
the *Caucones*, when driven from the Shore,
had even carried into the upper parts of the
Country, ſome Tincture of the *Grecian* Language, and Knowledge of the Inhabitants of
their Mother-ſoil. Add to this, what has been
already proved, and which renders all other
Arguments needleſs, that the *Trojan* Coaſt was
peopled by *Cretans* under *Sarpedon*, or the
ancient *Teucer* [u] ; and that *Troy* itſelf was a
Grecian City built by *Laomedon*, and governed
by *Capys*, *Tros*, and *Ilus* his *Deſcendants*.

T H E *Language* therefore ſpoken in *Troy*
muſt have been a *Mixture* of the *Thracian*,
Aramean, and *Greek* ; ſo that it is not impoſſible but the People might make ſhift to *un-*
derſtand each other. The *Phrygians*, an inland
Tribe,

[u] See Page 207.

Tribe, were not underſtood by the People of Sect. 12. *Troy* [w] ; the *Carians*, Inhabitants of the Eaſt, ∿ were likewiſe ΒΑΡΒΑΡΟΦΟΝΟΙ *of a barbarous Speech* [x], and the Auxiliaries from the ſeveral Countries had

'Ἄλλη δ' ἄλλων ΓΛΩΣΣΗ πολυσπερέων ἀνθρώπων [y].

But the *Greeks* and *Trojans*, originally from the ſame Country, ſeem to have ſtood in no need of an Interpreter to go between them. *Paris* therefore might be capable to court a *Grecian* Dame in an intelligible Stile; or, if it ſhould be maliciouſly ſaid, that *this* may be done without much Language, *Homer* him-ſelf without much difficulty might learn from the Deſcendants of the *Trojan* and *Lycian* Fa-milies, the mighty Deeds of their *warlike Pro-genitors.*

THIS will appear ſtill the more probable, if we conſider that few of the *Genealogies* of the *Trojan* or *Dardan* Chiefs reach above three or four Generations: So far they can

X 3 trace

---

[w] 'Οἴρευς δ' ὅςι πατὴρ, ὄνομα κλυ]ὸς, εἴπου ἀκόυεις,
   Ὅς πάσης ΦΡΥΓΙΗΣ ἐυτειχήτοιο ἀνάσσει·
   Γλῶσαν δ' ΥΜΕΤΕΡΗΝ, καὶ ΗΜΕΤΕΡΗΝ σάφα ὅιδα.
   ΤΡΩΟΣ γὸ μεγάρῳ με]εφὸς τρέφεν, ἡ δὲ διατρὸ
   Σμικρὺ παῖδ' ἀπ]αλλε, φίλης ἀπὸ μητὲρὸς ἐλῦσα.
   ΩΣ δὴ τοι ΓΛΩΣΣΗΝ τε καὶ ΥΜΕΤΕΡΗΝ ἐυ ὅιδα.
Says *Venus* to *Anchiſes*, when ſhe appears to him alone upon Mount *Ida*, and perſonates a *Phrygian* Girl wandered from home.   'Ομηρε 'Υμν· εἰς 'ΑΦΡΟΔΙΤΗΝ.

[x] 'Ιλιάδ. Β.   [y] 'Ιλιάδ. Β.

Sect. 12. trace their Defcent, and no farther. A great
Proof of the *late peopling* the Country. Any
of the Races that go higher, run into Mythology, and derive their Pedigree from *Heaven*;
that is, they are the Offspring of fome ftroling
Man, or ftroling God, who came into their
Country three or four Generations ago, (they
cannot tell from whence) and left them behind him, as his Pofterity.

I T W A S a common Phrafe among the
Ancients, when they addreffed a Man whofe
Appearance and Converfation befpoke him to
be of a noble Family, *That he was not fprung
from the Rock, nor dropt from an aged Oak:*
Upon this Suppofition, when they found themfelves at a lofs for a *flefhly Father* as the
Stock of their Race, they took care to give
themfelves fuch an *Original* as they were fure
would never try to difprove their Claim.
But this *very Want* fhews a recent Settlement ; and a mixture of *Strangers* lately come
into the Country, who muft either impofe
new Names upon things, or pronounce the
old with the Accent and Tone peculiar to the
Genius of their native Tongue. In any cafe,
Homer's Writings muft have felt the foften-
ing Influence, and been exempted from that
Harfhnefs and Diffonancy, which a number of
foreign Names unavoidably introduce into *narrative Poefy.*

THESE

THESE are beautiful Circumſtances in the Sect.12. Poetic Deſtiny of our Bard: and it might give great diſtaſte, if a Compoſition was deprived of the Graces that attend them. For is it not here as in *Life?* That we too frequently overlook our Enjoyments, and are ignorant of their real Value, until ſome cruel Accident ſnatch them from us, and make us ſenſible of their Worth by their *Abſence.* But *Homer*'s Good-fortune, almoſt in every Circumſtance of his Fate, makes him, methinks, appear like ſome *exquiſite Statue,* the Work of *his Country,* and placed with Judgment in a well-regulated Garden: There, Pieces perhaps of *ordinary* Workmanſhip grace this or the other Parterre; but all the Openings terminate upon this *favourite Figure,* and at every different Turn you diſcover a new Beauty, and think it more graceful than before.

YET among all theſe there is generally a chief *point of view*; ſome advantageous *Stand,* which gives the ſweeteſt Attitude, and moſt amiable appearance of the Figure. This, *My Lord,* is ſtill before us: It may open upon us at the next Turn, and has perhaps been luckily reſerved for the *laſt Look,* that we may retire full of the *Idea,* and with a higher Taſte of the Beauty of the Original.

THE GREAT Good-fortune that attended *Homer,* I take to have been what we may call the *material Part* of his Subject. " It

X 4 " was

Sect. 12. " was a prodigious Rendezvous of the bra-
" vest Inhabitants, and Sons of the noblest
" Families of a free Country, wide and war-
" like ; and engaged in a violent struggle of
" Paſſions and Arms, with another of more
" effeminate Manners. The Effect was, that
" it afforded him *real, hiſtoric Characters* for
" his MODEL."

To ſet this matter in a juſt Light, and
ſhew the extent of its Influence, we need
make but this Reflection ; " That ſuch an
" Aſſembly of the Chiefs of two great Na-
" tions, diſplaying their Virtues and Vices
" upon the greateſt and moſt intereſting Sub-
" jects, *muſt include the prime Characters* of
" MANKIND ; and of conſequence preſent
" a Poet with the moſt *genuine* and *faireſt*
" Materials that can beautify a human Com-
" poſition."

LET US remember what it is that gives
us ſuch perpetual Pleaſure in reading the *Iliad.*
That makes us ſtart at the Turns in the Speeches,
and fills us with Anxiety and Wonder. It
is not the beautiful Deſcriptions of *Places,* nor
even the Rage and Ardour of the *Battles.*
But thoſe *high ſtrokes of Character* that every
where occur, and are conſtantly preſenting
us with new Sentiments of the human Heart,
ſuch as we expect, and from our own Experience feel to be *true.* Theſe can never miſs
their Aim : They at once charm the Fancy
with

with Images, and fill the Underftanding with
Reflection: They intereft every thing that is
human about us, and go near to agitate us
with the fame Paffions as we fee reprefented
in the moving Story.

TH IS Reflection will bear to be turned on
every fide, and dreads no Search be it ever fo
fevere.　In the choice we make of any *Meafure* in the conduct of our Bufinefs or Plea-
fures, we examine its Juftnefs and Expediency,
not only by confidering what good end it
ferves ;　but likewife, what *Inconveniences* are
avoided, what Pains or Trouble fpared, or what
Mifcarriages prevented, to which *another Method* might be liable.　Take *Homer*'s Subject
in the fame Light, and it will appear with a
Pre-eminency hardly to be expreffed.　*Such a
Convention of Princes*, from different Countries
and Soils, but all fpeaking the fame Language,
furnifhed him with *great Materials*, and hin-
dered him from attempting an *Impoffibility* ;
　" I mean the feigning or forming new ima-
　" ginary Characters, without Originals from
　" which he might copy them."　The flourifhing Condition of *Greece* at that time ; the
great number of Principalities, free Cities, and
growing Republicks, fent forth an Affembly
of Heroes, the World could hardly match ever
fince.　The *Grecians* themfelves confeffed, that
their Country, when much more polifhed and
improved, had never produced fo many *free*
natural

Sect.12. *natural* Characters, not tainted with *Politicks*, not moulded by *Laws*, nor effeminated with *Pleasures*; and for that reason, *half-deified* those very Persons, whom they knew at the same time to be but the *Sons of Men*.

His *Subject* therefore, saved him from a *desperate* Enterprize ; and prevented him from falling into those Errors and Absurdities which deprive many a lively Poet of his Reputation. *To it* he owed the Statelines and Dignity with which *Idomeneus* the *Cretan* King appears on all occasions. *To it* he owed the beautiful and unwarlike *Nireus*, the faithless *Pandarus*, and the amiable humane *Patroclus*. And above all the rest, *to this* he was indebted for the noble CONTRAST *of Characters* that adorn his Poems. There we see the ancient *Nestor*, mild, and calm, and talkative, opposed to the young fiery *Thessalian*, the intractable *Achilles*: The too indulgent *Priam* stands by the prudent *Polydamas*, and the wise *Antenor* : The Hardines of the noble *Hector*, and Debauchery of the luxurious *Paris*, serve but to illustrate one another, and come all originally from the *same Fountain*.

The *Detail* of this part of his Happines would prove tedious in any other Hand than his own : But there are two remarkable Circumstances in *Homer*'s Writings, which have been generally look'd upon as *Strokes of Art*, where I am apt to think the Nature and Situation

of

of his Subject bore a confiderable Sway. It Sect.12. has been obferv'd to his Honour, " That the 〰 " *Characters* of his *Heroes*, tho' of the *fame* " *kind*, and excelling in one and the fame " thing, are yet all diverfified, and mark'd " with fome Peculiarities which diftinguifh " them, and make a Separation." Thus, for inftance, both *Achilles* and *Ajax*, *Diomedes* and *Hector*, *Ulyffes* and *Merion*, are all *brave* ; but it is in a different manner. *Achilles* is fierce and impetuous, *Ajax* fteady and firm, *Diomedes* gallant and open, *Ulyffes* cautious and bold; and both *Agamemnon* and *Hector* are mark'd with that *princely Courage* which becomes the GENERALS of two great Nations. *This, My Lord*, I hardly think could ever have been feigned ; it was Truth and Nature alone that could form thofe Differences, fo real and yet fo delicate, and afterwards offer them to a Reprefentation.

To DESCRIBE fo many *Men*; to point out their *Manners*; to paint their *Perfons*, relate their *Adventures*, and make a long Recital of their *Families*, feems to be beyond the Power of Fiction. The *making* or *feigning Faculty*, be it ever fo rich and inventive, after an Effort or two, recoils upon itfelf ; and if it finds no ftore of Originals *within*, either falls a repeating the fame Characters with a tedious uniformity, or contrives *falfe* ones, that glare and make a Show, but by
                                                    fome

Sect.12. fome *wry Feature* certainly betray their Un-
likeneſs to Truth.

HOMER has kept true even to the Fortunes and Eſtates of his *Heroes : Agamemnon*
and *Achilles* were the two richeſt Men in
Greece : The firſt, by reaſon of his large Do-
minions and the Sovereignty of the Iſles ᶻ :
And accordingly we find him lending ſixty
Ships to the *Arcadians*, and inland People ;
and promiſing many *Towns* and *Lands* in
Dow'ry with his Daughter.   The other, *Achilles*, was Lord of the rich *Theſſalian Plains*,
early famed all over *Greece*, for Wealth and
Horſemanſhip ª.   He had likewiſe taken and
plunder'd three and twenty Towns lying round
Troy, and was enriched by his Share in the
Spoil. ··We are not therefore ſurprized at the
Treaſure he throws away with ſuch Profuſion
at the Funerals of *Patroclus* ; nor to find him
renowned for his *Horſes* and *Chariot-racing*,
beyond the reſt of the *Greeks*.   He was ſo
remarkable for it, that when *Ulyſſes* meets his
Shade in the infernal Regions, the firſt Circumſtance which occurs to him is, *That now
alas! he was there,* ΛΕΛΑΣΜΕΝΟΣ 'ΙΠΠΟΣΥ-
ΝΑΩΝ, *unmindful of his Horſes and Chi-
valry.*

THE

ᶻ 'Αυ]ὰρ ὁ αῦτε Θύες· 'Αγαμέμνονι λεῖπε φορῆναι,
Πολλῆσι ΝΗΣΟΙΣΙ καὶ 'ΑΡΓΕΙ παν]ὶ ἀνάσσειν. 'Ιλιάδ'. Β.

a Ω Μένων, πραῖ]ὸν μὲν ΘΕΤΤΑΛΟΙ εὐδόκιμοι ῆσαν ἐν
τοῖς 'Ελλησι, καὶ ἐθαυμάζον]ο ἐφ' 'ΙΠΠΙΚΗ τε καὶ ΠΛΟΥ-
ΤΩ.   Πλα]ων. ΜΕΝΩΝ·

THE *Second* thing which has been look'd Sect.12. upon as a noble Proof of his Judgment, is the Period of Time he has chosen for the Beginning of his Poem. He has not, they say, set out with the *first* Campaign; nor attempted to deduce the *Trojan* Story from the miraculous Birth of *Helen* [b], or her Brothers: He has confined himself to the *last Year* of the War, and by that means filled his Poem with *History and Action.*

BUT here too, he was happy in his Subject, which directed him of its *own accord* to make the Choice. There were *two* distinct *Periods* in the War. The first was long and tedious, while *Achilles* and his Myrmidons were fighting on the side of the *Greeks,* and ravaging the Country around *Troy.* During all that time, the *Trojans* kept within their Walls, and durst not meet this dreaded Warrior in the open Field: So that there was but little to be described, except these Excursions to pillage, which are occasionally inserted in the Dialogues of the *Iliad.*

BUT the *second Period* was *short* and full of *Action:* For no sooner was the disobliged inraged Hero retired to his Ship, and had withdrawn his Troops, than the Face of the War was wholly changed: The *Greeks* were now no longer supported by his tremendous *Arm;* and the

[b] *Nec reditum Diomedis ab interitu Meleagri,*
Nec gemino bellum Trojanum orditur ob ovo.
Horat. ad Pison.

the *Trojans* ventured to quit their Town, and face the Enemy. Battles, and Truces, and Perjuries, enfued: Fear, and Terror, and Defpair, took their turns in the Camps, and filled every anxious Hour with Paffion and Amazement. The W R A T H of the Hero was the Spring of all this Mifery; and therefore a *happy Theme* for an Epic or Narrative Poet.

I T W A S S O, in many refpects. The Wrath of *Achilles* was in reality the *Hinge of the War*, and *that* upon which the whole of the great Tranfaction turned. The *Time* of Action; the Defigns of the Leaders; the Difpofition and *Temper* of the Armies, all depended upon it, and were directed by it. This made it a kind of *Rule* for the Conduct and Difpofition of his Poem: and if he kept it in his Eye, (as we fee he has certainly done) it would naturally lay out his general *Plan*, and influence the Proportions of the fubfervient Parts. It has befides, the peculiar Excellency of fhewing and exercifing more *Paffions*, and of more *oppofite* Natures, than any other Period of the War. It was raifed by Love and Ambition, inflamed by Pride, foftened by Friendfhip, kept up by Glory and confcious Virtue, and only vanquifhed by a fuperior Paffion, *Revenge*.

M A N Y O T H E R Parts, and *Epifodes*, if I may fay fo, of the *Grecian Expedition*, furnifhed Materials for Epic Poems. *Demodocus* fung the A M B U S H of the *Trojan* Horfe; *Phemius*, the

R E-

RETURN of the *Greeks* with *Agamemnon*; Sect.12. and the LITTLE ILIAD (a Poem fo called) con-tained both thofe Subjects, and the occafional Adventures that had followed upon the War; the adjudging the *Arms* of *Achilles*, —— *Phi-loctetes*, —— *Neoptolemus*, —— *Sinon*, with fome others [c]. But it is worth our notice, what Judgment the Father of Criticifm has paffed upon thefe Pieces: He fays, " That whereas " the *Iliad* and *Odyffey* could furnifh but two, " or at moft but four, regular and entire " *Actions*, the *Little Iliad* could afford double " the number; fo that you might compofe " *eight* different Poems of the Materials it " contained :" So fimple and connected a Sub-ject was the Wrath of *Achilles*, and the Wan-dering of *Ulyffes!*

IT WAS, at the fame time, not only rich in *Action*, but in *fuch Action* as is capable of being defcribed, and *admits* of a *Recital*. When a great Town is taken fword in hand, the Car-nage and Fury exercifed in it can hardly be *told:* That horrid Face of Mifery is, in the real meaning of the Phrafe, *beyond Expreffion :* The Intenfenefs of the Ill *tranfcends* all Lan-guage, and *mocks* the Words we ufe in the Defcription. Much lefs can we collect from
every

[c] Τ̔Οιον Ὁ ΠΛΩΝ ΚΡΙΣΙΣ, ΦΙΛΟΚΤΗΤΗΣ, ΝΕ-ΟΠΤΟΛΕΜΟΣ, ΕΥΡΥΠΥΛΟΣ, ΠΤΩΧΕΙΑ, ΛΑΚΑΙ-ΝΑΙ, ΙΛΙΟΥ ΠΕΡΣΙΣ, καὶ ᾿ΑΠΟΠΛΟΥΣ, καὶ ΣΙ-ΝΩΝ, καὶ ΤΡΩΑΔΕΣ.
VIRGIL has been deeply indebted to this Performance.

Sect.12. every quarter, the various Scenes of Woe, and
represent them *together*. But the Action that
has fallen to the share of our Poet, is generally of such a nature as to give play to the
Imagination : We can follow it step by step,
observe its Progress, and lose but little of the
whole. We can accompany *Diomedes* and
Ulysses in every Motion of their nocturnal Expedition [d]; and can walk up and down the
Grecian Camp, and visit the Watch, with
Agamemnon and *Nestor*, as if present upon the
Place [e].

IT IS TRUE, we cannot comprehend the
Shock of a general Engagement, nor describe
what is doing in all the Parts of a Battle :
But the ancient manner of fighting made a
compensation for this to the Poet. Their Battles were, for the most part, so many *Duels*,
or single Combats of Chief against Chief, and
Man against Man : Hardly was there a *random* Blow given, or a Javelin let fly, without
being aimed at a particular Person. The Warriors had time to know one another, and to
throw Reproaches and Threats, as well as
Spears, at their insulting Adversary. This manner of fighting is finely fitted for *Description*;
and tho' we cannot be in all parts at once, yet
we

---

[d] Ιλιαδ'. Κ.

[e] Δεῦρ' ἐς τὺς Φύλακας κ]αβείομεν, ὄφρα ἴδωμεν
  Μὴ τοὶ μὲν καμάτῳ ἀδδηκότες, ἠδὲ καὶ ὕπνῳ
  Κοιμήσων]αι, ἀτὰρ φυλακῆς ἐπὶ πάγχυ λάθων]αι.

                                    'Ιλιαδ'. Κ.

we can attend upon any fingle Hero, hear him Sect. 12. threatning, and view him performing, in the Rage of the Field.

I should tranfcribe a great part of his Poems, if I intended to point out every particular Advantage which *Homer* reap'd from this *happy Change*. But there is *one famous Doubt* concerning his Works, which deferves our Attention. It is pleafant to obferve how ferioufly the Ancients propofe it, and it cannot be difagreeable to find his *Subject* affording an Anfwer.

They feem inclin'd to believe " that the " *Principles* of all the Sciences are to be " found in his Works : No Species or Kind " of Writing for which he has not fet an " Example ; nor almoft any *Art*, whofe Pre- " cepts may not be deduced from his *Poe-* " *try*." They went further, and enter'd into a *Detail* of his Knowledge. General Affertions did not content them ; but fuch wife Men as *Dionyfius* the *Halicarnaffean*, and the ingenious *Plutarch*, thought themfelves judicioufly employed, in *collecting* the feveral Branches, and fetting them together. They have attempted to fhew, that Poetry in all its Forms, *Tragedy*, *Comedy*, *Ode*, and *Epitaph*, are included in his Works ; That *Oratory*, *Politicks*, *Oeconomy*, and *War*, are bound to acknowledge him as their Mafter. The *laft* we fhould not fo much wonder at, fince the great *Mace-*

Y   *donian*

Sect.12. *donian Conqueror*, among other Honours done to his Works, profeffed himfelf his *Scholar* in this *Kingly Science :* But fome went ftill further, and found the greateft Secrets of *Nature*, and hidden *Myfteries* of the Univerfe, revealed or fhadowed out by this wonderful Poet. Hardly a depth in *Aftronomy*, or latent Principle in *Heaven* or *Earth*, which they have not dif-cover'd him to be acquainted with, and to have hinted at its Powers in fome *Allufion* or *Me-taphor*.

THESE are indeed very ftrange Affertions; and it feems ftranger ftill, that the *fevereft* Reafoners in the World, the Men leaft ob-noxious to Illufion or poetic Enthufiafm, fhould adopt and defend them. The famed *Antifthenes* had begun a Treatife to prove ὅτι τὰ μὲν ΔΟΞΗ, τὰ δὲ ΑΛΗΘΕΙΑ εἴρηῖαι ΤΩ ΠΟΙΗΤΗ; *That the Poet fpoke fometimes according to* TRUTH; *and fometimes according to Appearance :* But not living to finifh it, no lefs a Man than ZENO, the Parent of the *Stoic Philofophy*, took up the Defign : He fhewed, that *Homer* no where contradicted himfelf, pointed out the latent Meaning of his Allegories, and the *natural* Senfe in which they were to be taken [f]. The learned CRATES *Mallotes*, contemporary with *Ariftarchus*, and *Panetius*'s Mafter, took a ftep ftill beyond them : He thought it not enough, that what *Homer* himfelf had touched upon should

[f] Διατ. Χρυσῖς. εἰς ῾ΟΜΗΡΟΝ

should be demonstrated to be *true*; but he Sect.12.
actually applied his *Hypotheses* to the *Phenomena*
of things, and, by their assistance, endeavoured
to solve those Difficulties in *natural Philosophy*,
which had not been directly explained by the
Poet ᵍ.

T H E Y D I D indeed imagine, that there was
nothing in the World but what he understood:
And being struck with *what they saw*, they
gave into the common weakness of Mankind,
and made large Allowances for *what they saw
not*. They came at last to persuade themselves,
that a Mind so vast cou'd not belong to a *Man*;
that so much Knowledge cou'd only flow from
a *heavenly* Source; and having once firmly settled his A P O T H E O S I S ʰ in their own Minds,
they wanted next, that every thing about him
should appear *supernatural* and *divine*. The
Uncertainty about the Place of his Birth, they
improved into a *celestial Lineage*; and because
they knew not the name of his Father, they
called him the Son of *Apollo*.

A P P I O N the celebrated Grammarian
writes, " That the Herb *Cynocephale*, the Egy-
" ptian *Osirites*, has a miraculous Virtue : that
" it is a sovereign Remedy against Witchcraft,
" and commands the *infernal* Powers: that
                    Y 2   " the

ᵍ Τίνας ᾗ πρὸς ΕΠΙΣΤΗΜΟΝΙΚΑΣ ῾ΥΠΟΘΕΣΕΙΣ
Ἔτρεψαν τὴν ῾Ομήρε ποίησιν.   Σιεφε Βιϐ γ.
ʰ *Deification.*

Sect. 12. " the Perſon who digs for it, immediately
" dies; but that he himſelf having procured
" it from *another*, had charm'd up the Shades,
" and enquir'd into *Homer*'s Country and Pa-
" rentage: That he had received an Anſwer,
" but durſt never publiſh what he had learn'd
" upon that Subject [i]." To ſuch Extrava-
gancies does *fond Opinion* lead us! It was not
impoſſible, among the Ancients, to improve a
common Accident into a ground of *Admiration*; and the loweſt Circumſtance in Life, into
a Proof of their imaginary *Divinity* [k].

BUT, the plain Account, which *Homer*'s
Subject makes of theſe ſuſpected Sciences, is
this: NATURE *includes them all*: Her *Proportions* are juſt and invariable: Whoever
paints her *true*, or any part of her that is full
of Action; and applies that Action to *Times*,
Places, *Perſons*, and their *Signs*, will include
theſe *Proportions*, and their *Meaſures*, without
intending it, almoſt without knowing it, but
never without ſome Perception of their Propriety and Truth.

IT WOU'D be ridiculous to imagine, that
Homer firſt learned the Sciences and their Rules
abſtractedly; that then he applied them to proper *Objects*, and theſe again to the *Subject* of
his Work: That by this means he had converted the Principles of all the Sciences, natural
and moral, into *human* or *divine* Perſons, and
then

[i] *Plinii* Hiſt. Nat. Lib. XXX. § 2.
[k] See Note ſ Page 5.

then wrought them into the under-parts of his Sect.12.
Poem. This is beginning at the wrong end; 〰
and however proper the Method may be, or
rather neceffary in *Philofophy*, it wou'd fpoil all
in the hands of the *Mufes*.

HOMER took his Plan from *Nature*: He
has followed her clofely in every ftep: He
has related Actions and Paffions of every kind:
He has painted *Places, Perfons, Animals,* and
Seafons, with their proper *Marks* and Qualities.
He has done this with a conftant view to the
Effects which thefe things produce; both as they
ftrike upon the human *Mind*, and do good or
ill in human *Affairs* [1]. By this means he gives
us back our own Sentiments on every Accident
in Life, and paints the Impreffions we receive
from the other Parts of the Univerfe. He becomes an allowed Mafter in *Morals* [m], and is

Y. 3 fufpected

[1] Τὸν ΟΜΗΡΟΝ, καθάπερ ἐν ἁρμονίᾳ μουσικῇ πάντας ζῆλαι
τοὺς ποιητικοὺς ἢ Τρόπων· Καὶ Τὰς Ποιητὰς ἐφ' ὅις ἐγίνετο ὑπερ-
Cεβλῆσθαι πάντας, ἐν ὅτῳ ἑκάστῳ αὐτῶν ἦν κράτισον. Μεγαλοφ-
ρημοσύνην τε ὑπὲρ τὸν ΟΡΦΕΑ ἀσκῆσαι· ἐδόνη τε ὑπερ-
Cαλέσθαι τὸν ΗΣΙΟΔΟΝ, καὶ ἄλλῳ ἄλλον. Καὶ ΛΟΓΟΝ
μὲν ὑποθέσθαι τὸν Τρωϊκόν, ἐς ὃν ἡ ΤΥΧΗ τὰς πάντων Ἑλλήνων τε καὶ Βαρβάρων ΑΡΕΤΑΣ ξυνήνεγκεν. Ἐσαγαγέσθαι δὲ
ἐς αὐτὸν ΠΟΛΕΜΟΥΣ, τὰς μὲν περὶ Ἄνδρας, τὰς δὲ
περὶ Ἵππους, καὶ Τείχη, τὰς δὲ περὶ Πόλαμὰς, τὰς δὲ περὶ
Θεοὺς τε καὶ Θεάς· Καὶ ὁπότε κατ' ΕΙΡΗΝΗΝ εἰσὶν καὶ Χο-
ρὸς, καὶ Ἡδὰς, καὶ Ἔρωτας, καὶ Δαῖτας· Ἔργα τε ἂν ΓΕΩΡ-
ΓΙΑ ἀπέπαις· καὶ ΩΡΑΣ δὲ σημαίνωσιν ὁπόσα χρὴ ἐς τὴν
ΓΗΝ πράττειν· καὶ Ναυτιλίας, καὶ Ὁπλοποιίας τὴν ἐπ' Ηφαίσω·
ΕΙΔΗ τε Ἀνδρῶν, καὶ ΗΘΗ ποικίλα. Ταῦτα πάντα τὸν
ΟΜΗΡΟΝ ΔΑΙΜΟΝΙΩΣ ΕΞΕΙΡΓΑΣΘΑΙ, καὶ τοὺς
μὴ ἐρῶντας αὐτῷ ΜΑΙΝΕΣΘΑΙ. Φιλόστρατ. ΗΡΩΙΚΑ. § II.

[m] Trojani Belli fcriptorem, maxime Lolli,
Dum tu declamas Romæ, Prænefte relegi:
Qui quid fit pulcrum, quid turpe; quid utile, quid non;
Plenius ac melius CHRYSIPPO et CRANTORE dicit.
Horat. Lib. I. *Epiff.* II.

Sect.12. suspected of Mystery and hidden Meanings in
the several Branches of *natural* Knowledge.

I T I S, I think, generally allowed, that a
Poet's *Plan* is much wider than an Historian's.
The Writer of History represents but one single
Portion of *Nature*; and for the most part, only
that *side* of it which is connected with Politicks
and Government: But the Poet, tho' confin'd
to a single Action, takes *Mankind* for his *Rule*
in the Execution. He has an *Universal Idea*
for his Model, all the Passions to fill the Under-parts, and the whole Train of Accidents
and Adventures in War, Dangers, and Death,
to make out his Narration. He takes them
originally from real Life and a *single Part*; but
he is not tied down to the Circumstances of
the Fact. The Image turns *general* in his
hands; and the more his *Subject* is varied, the
richer and truer will be his *Imitation*.

T H E *Veil of Fable* is of such surprising
Virtue, that it *magnifies* the Objects which it
covers: It shows them in a grander Light, and
invites the Eye to contemplate them more ea-
gerly than if they were open and undisguised.
To *Vulgar* Eyes it is dark and impenetrable,
while it speaks plainly to the *Wife*, yet some-
t'mes amends is made even where it *hides*; for
if you see not the real Object, it presents you
with some *Species* or *Appearance* in its stead,
which, tho' not so instructive, is perhaps as entertaining as the Reality. HOMER came into

the World at a proper *distance of Time*, after Sect. 12.
the Expedition which he fung; not too near
it, when *naked Truth*, and the fevere Appearance of known Facts, might quafh Enthufiafm, and render Ornaments ridiculous; but
when the Circumftances of the Story had fufficient time to *ripen into Fable*, or at leaft be
fufceptible of it, from a fkilful hand.

H I s *Manner* of writing muft therefore be
taken into the Account. A *Metaphor* is a *general Pattern*, which may be applied to many
Particulars: It is fufceptible of an infinite number of Meanings; and reaches far, becaufe of its
Ambiguity. It leads, as we found before, even
to *Madnefs*; and wantonly ranges the Corners
of the World for Comparifons to fit its fancied
Properties. This way of treating a Subject
muft render it ftill more general, and when
joined with the TRUTH of *Defcription*, will
account for the MYSTERIES in *Homer*'s Writings.

BUT how wonderful a thing is it to be
able to *join* thefe Extremes? To fpeak in
the *fimpleft* and moft *comprehenfive* manner:
To foar fo high, and ftoop fo low, as to
follow Nature minutely, and at the fame time
fill the Images with *Expreffion* and *Majefty*.
And yet the greateft Objections againft our
Poet, arife from the *too great Truth* of his
Defcriptions; and from his reprefenting his
Heroes in thofe *natural Lights* which we think
Y 4 below

Sect.12. below the Politeneſs of our Manners. They have been frequently anſwered ; and here, their very *Foundation* turns out to the Honour of the Poet, and proves the grand Ornament of his Performance.

It could, in reality, enter into no Man's mind, to have given ſuch an Epithet, for example to a *Prince*, as ΒΟΗΝ ΑΓΑΘΟΣ ΜΕΝΕΛΑΟΣ, *The loud-voic'd Menelaus* ; had not the Exigences of War rendered this a very eminent and uſeful Quality. Before the Invention of Trumpets or Drums, the Leaders of Armies were often at a loſs how to make a general *Signal* ; eſpecially by night, or in thick weather, when a viſible Sign could be of no ſervice. In the famous *Scythian* Expedition, undertaken long after *Homer's* time, by *Darius* the Father of *Xerxes*, we find a Man of ſtrong Lungs the moſt neceſſary Perſon in the Camp. This Epithet then was taken from the *real ſtate* of things : And indeed it ſeems impoſſible, that either the Poet's Deſcriptions, or the Actions deſcribed, ſhould be ſo *different*, and yet ſo *true*, had he followed any other Guide.

The particular Circumſtances of the ſeveral Encounters could never have been ſo *variouſly* imagined in the road of *Fiction* only : Neither the ſingle Combat between *Menelaus* and *Paris*, nor that between *Ajax* and *Hector*, where every thing is managed in a very

I　　　　　　　　　　　　　different

different manner, and yet with the higheſt Sect.12.
Próbability in both. In the firſt, the Prayer ∿
of the *Grecian* Hero to *Jupiter*,——the ſhiver-
ing of his Sword,——the Fury he feels at the
Diſappointment,——and breaking the *Lace* that
bound on the Helmet of the effeminate *Trojan*, are delicate Circumſtances, and nicely
adapted to the *Temper* of the Warriors, and
Inequality of the Match. In the other, where
the Heroes were more upon the level, and
without *perſonal* Enmity, how exactly do things
fall out in proportion to this Equality? The
Gallantry of *Hector*,——the Bluntneſs of *Ajax*,
——the Effects of their Spears,——and their
betaking themſelves to ſuch rough Weapons as
pond'rous Stones, are agreeable to the Strength
of the Combatants, and the manner of fighting then in uſe.

 I ᴀᴍ not in hazard, with *your Lordſhip*,
of being underſtood as if I aſſerted, that *Homer's* Accounts of Facts, even excluding his
Allegories, are *literally* true: That, for example, the Lot of *Ajax* ſprung firſt out of
the *Urn*, juſt as the *Greeks* themſelves could
have wiſhed; or that *Hector's* Spear pierced
exactly thro' *ſix* of the ſeven Folds of his
maſſy Shield, and ſtuck in the *laſt*. This
would lead into a peeviſh Diſquiſition of the
Truth of Circumſtances which Poetry will
never bear, and is againſt its Laws: It is
        ſufficient,

Sect.12. sufficient, if the *Gross* of the History and chief Characters are true.

AND HERE we find the Poet copying *Nature* so close, as to connect the Manners of his Heroes with the *Make* and *Cast* of their *Persons*. Their Stature and Aspect is constantly suited to their Temper and Disposition. His Poem is like the first View we take of an unknown Face, which prejudices in its favour, or creates a Dislike: In the same manner, we no sooner see the *Form* of a Man delineated by *Homer*, than we expect from him such *Passions* and *Manners*, and such a kind of Conduct, as we find ascribed to him in the Poem. *Ulysses's* Picture is almost inimitable wherever he mentions him [n]: But it cannot be juster than his *Herald's*, the trusty *Eurybates*. This ancient Person served as a Counsellor to the Prince of *Ithaca*; he accompanied him to the Siege of *Troy*, and held the chief place in his Confidence and Esteem: His *round compacted* Shoulders, his *swarthy* Face, and *short curling* Hair, promise that kind of Perception, and Aptness for Toil and Business, which is necessary in a *second part* in Life; and make us think of a Man who knows how to resign his Passions and Appetites to those of his *Master* [o].

THE

---

[n] See Ἰλιαδ. ζ. line 192, and compare it with Ὀδυσ. Z. Θ, Σ.

[o] ——Κῆρυξ ὀλίγον προγενέςερος αὐτᾶ,
Γυρὸς ἐν Ὤμοισι, μελανόχροϊσ᾽, οὐλοκάρηνος. Ὀδυσ. Τ.

THE *Characters* of many other Perfons in Sect.12.
Homer are fo beautiful, that it wou'd be worth
while to collect the Accounts we have of their
Lives and Fortunes from other Writers, and
compare them with the *Poet's:* But thefe hi-
ftorical Scraps are very imperfect, and often
contradictory to one another. For after all
HOMER is the beft *Hiftorian* [p] : And it is to
be prefumed, that the faint Tradition concerning the Adventures of thefe *Heroes,* was rather
ingrafted upon the Characters they bear in his
Poetry, than that they arofe from a nearer
Acquaintance with them, or better Opportunities to hear of them, than were enjoyed by
the Poet. The prettieft thing of this kind
is a fanciful Piece of the elegant *Philoftratus,*
which he calls his *Heroics.* His Favourite a-
mong them all, is the unfortunate *Palamedes,*
whom he endeavours to raife upon the Ruins
of *Ulyffes;* and fpeaks much of the Injuftice
done him in the *Iliad.*

PHI-

[p] Καὶ γὰ κ) ὅπως πρὸς τὰ τῦ Ὁμήρȣ Ποιήματα διαλέθεμαι,
ὡς ΘΕΙΑ π ἀνῆ ἡγέμμον, κ) πόρα ΑΝΘΡΩΠΟΥ δέξαι.
Καὶ νῦν ἐκπέπληγμαι μᾶλλον ἐκ ἐπὶ Τῇ Ἐποποιίᾳ μόνον, ἐφ'
ᾗ πὴ Ἡδονὴ Δίκαι σφῶν ἀλλὰ πολλῷ μᾶλλον ἐπὶ τε τοῖς
ΟΝΟΜΑΣΙ Τ ΗΡΩΩΝ, ἐπὶ τε τοῖς ΓΕΝΕΣΙ Καὶ νὴ τὸν
Δί, ὡς ἕκας Θ αὐτῶν ἔλαχε τῦ κλέϊναι τινα, ἢ ἀποθανεῖν ὑφ'
ἑτέρȣ. Πόθεν γὰ αὐτῷ ΕΥΦΟΡΒΟΙ; πόθεν δὲ ΕΛΕΝΟΙ τε
κ) ΔΗΙΦΟΒΟΙ; Καὶ τὸ δὲ ἐκ τῆς ἀνλικειμένης Στρατιᾶς, οἱ
ΠΟΛΛΟΙ ΑΝΔΡΕΣ, ὧς ἐν Καταλόγῳ φράζει· Τὸ γὰ μὴ
ΥΠΟΤΕΘΕΙΣΘΑΙ ΤΑΥΤΑ τὸν ΟΜΗΡΟΝ (ὥσπερ)·
ἀλλὰ ΓΕΓΟΝΟΤΩΝ τε κ) ΑΛΗΘΙΝΩΝ ΕΡΓΩΝ ἀπαγ-
ϳελίαν ποιᾶται, πλὴν ὀλίγων, ἃ δοκεῖ μᾶλλον ἐκὼν μεϳασ-
κευάσαι, ἐπὶ τῇ ποικιλίᾳ τε κ) ἡδῖω ἀποφῆναι τὴν Πόιησιν.
Φιλοςρῶτ. ΗΡΩΙΚΑ. §XVIII.

Sect.12. *PHILOSTRATUS* manages the Cause of his neglected Hero, with the Humanity and Good-nature which is remarkable thro' all his Writings. He mixes every where high Praises of *Homer*, and, in order to excuse him, contrives a strange enthusiastick Story of an Agreement or Compact between him and the Ghost of *Ulysses*. He supposes it impossible for any Person to have come at the knowledge of so many Particulars concerning the *Trojan* War in a *natural* way, and therefore feigns that *Homer* conjured up *Ulysses*'s Ghost, who revealed them to him, upon this condition;

" That the Poet would palliate his Faults,
" and raise his Character in his Writings, by
" giving him the Honour of the Actions of
" *Palamedes*."

BUT a later Author [a], zealous and grave, and a great Enemy to the *Grecian* Superstition, has put the matter upon a different foot: He affirms, " that it was *Palamedes* who wrote
" the Poem of the *Trojan War*; that *Ho-*
" *mer* had received it from *Agamemnon*'s Po-
" sterity, and was bribed by them to omit
" the Passages that did honour to the Author,
" or reflected upon their Parent. The Poet
" complied, and suppressed the Name of *Pa-*
" *lamedes* thro' Envy, a Passion, says he, that
" taints the greatest Minds."

THIS

[a] ΣΟΥΙΔΑΣ, ἐν Παλαμηδ'.

THIS STORY, the *only* bad one I ever read of our Poet, as it is told by *Suidas*, contradicts itself, and therefore requires no Refutation. I wou'd only take occasion from it to remark, That one of the greatest Changes which *Science* has undergone, and one little obferv'd, first took birth when thefe Authors wrote. *Philofophy* was putting on a new Face about the Age of *Philoftratus*: It was beginning to forfake the natural Precepts of *Life* and *Morals*; to neglect that noble Connexion, which the first Mafters had eftablifhed, between *Phyfical Contemplations* and this prime Science of *Manners* and *Actions*. A Connexion never to be overlook'd; and which we have the Satisfaction to fee revived [r], fince the Sciences have gained a new Luftre; and by the happy Application of *Geometry* and *Numbers*, to the Appearances of Nature, have loft that Uncertainty which was long their Reproach, and the Caufe of their Decay.

BUT inftead of this, in *Philoftratus*'s Age, the Knowledge of *Secrets* was coming in vogue. *Unnatural* Virtues, and marvellous *Feats*, were affected by the vain-glorious Leaders of the feveral Sects: They found it eafier to diftinguifh themfelves by *high Pretenfions*, than by laborious Study, and a Conduct, unfhaken by the Frowns of

[r] See *Philofoph. Natur. Principia, Scholium ult. of* Sir Ifaac Newton. *Chronology, Chap.* 2, *and* 3, of the fame Author. Cumberland *de Legibus Nat.* Characterift. *Vol.* II. *Treat.* V. *Theodicte* de Leibnitz. Derham*'s Aftro and Phyfico-Theology, and* Woolafton*'s Religion of Nature delineated.*

Sect.12. of Fortune, and humble under her Smile. *Slavery* was growing intenfe : Not only *Virtue* felt its Sting, but whatever belonged to Greatnefs of Mind, or had any relation to *Freedom* of Thought, was a fufpicious Quality : Learning in general fell under the difpleafure of tyrannical Power; and the *Superiority* and *Firmnefs* which the Knowledge of Men and Things infpires, grew dangerous amidft a Croud of Slaves.

S u c h a Preffure upon the Minds of learned Men made them look out for *uncommon* Relief : Either they ftretched the Powers of the human Mind to an impoffible Pitch of *Infenfibility*, which was the Revival of high *Stoicifm* ; or they attempted to bring new Supports from *Heaven*, when they could find no Refource upon Earth : Some Reigns afterwards, about the time of *Suidas*, when the Philofophers came to be haraffed likewife on *another* fcore, they unanimoufly gave into this latter Folly : They were all agog after *Miracles* ; and a general Affectation of a fupernatural Intercourfe between the *Gods* and *them*, like a *Phrenzy* had feized the *perfecuted Sages*.

I t i s in this very Tafte that *Philoftratus* relates the Story of *Palamedes*, in a Converfation with a *philofophical Hermit*, who had retired from the World, and lived in a Vineyard : He fays, that the young and amorous *Protefilaus*

laus ufed to appear to him once a week in a favourite Walk, teach him fome divine Secrets, and
then complain of the hard ufage that *Palamedes,*
and fome of his Brother Heroes had received
from the *Grecian* Bard. The whole Relation
is extremely fanciful and amufing, and adorned
with all the fweet elegant Circumftances which
you might expect from a Philofopher loved by
a Princefs: But is not of weight to alter the
received Opinion, " That *Palamedes* died be-
" fore he had done any thing very con-
" fiderable in the War; and that what he
" did, fell not within the bufy Period chofen
" by our Poet for his Subject."

The faint Accounts of the *other* Princes,
and the wandering Reports concerning their
Lives, are not worthy of greater Regard.
They are mentioned by the old Hiftorians of
Greece, whofe Writings we have now loft:
But tho' they had efcaped the hand of Time,
we fhould have reaped but little advantage:
For *Homer* has obtained credit fo far above
them, even in refpect of their Veracity, that
Strabo, who had ftudied them carefully, declares " he wou'd rather believe him and *He-*
" *fiod,* and the *Tragedians* who have copied
" their *Heroic-Hiftory,* than follow *Hellani-*
" *cus,* or *Theopompus,* or *Ctefias,* or even *He-*
" *rodotus* himfelf ᶠ."

His

ᶠ 'Ράλλον δ' ἄν τις ΗΣΙΟΔΩ κỳ 'ΟΜΗΡΩ πιςεύσιιεν ἠ-
ϱιολογύσι, κỳ τοῖς τϱαγικοῖς Ποιηλαῖς, ἢ Κτησία τε κỳ 'Ηϱοδότῳ
καὶ 'Ελλανίκῳ, καὶ ἄλλοις τοιέτοις. Στϱαβ. Βιβλ. ιᶜ.

Sect.12. H*is Subject* therefore still comes upper-
most, and appears with greater Excellency the
more it is canvassed. It is this that distin-
guishes *him* amidst the *poetic Tribe*, and joined with his Language, Manners, and Religion, has left him without a *Rival*. The great
Difference between him and *Virgil* has been
already pointed out in a lively elegant Essay
upon the Life of our Poet: It comes originally
from a hand already said to be happy in painting *modern Life*; and who, at the same time,
has taught *Homer* to speak *English* incompa-
rably better than any Language but his *own* t.
It was his INVENTION that made him the *First*
of *Poets*; whose Sources and Opportunities
have been the principal Object of this *Enquiry*.

BUT if your Lordship will indulge me in
the Liberty taken by *Juvenal's She-Critick* u, I
would further observe, that *Virgil* had been accustomed to the *Splendour* of a *Court*, the
Magnificence of a Palace, and the Grandeur of
a Royal Equipage; Accordingly his Representations of *that* Part of Life, are more *august*
and *stately* than *Homer's*. He has a greater Regard to *Decency*, and those polished Manners
which render Men so much of a piece, and
make them all resemble one another in their
Conduct and Behaviour. His *State-designs* and
political Managements, are finely laid, and
carried

---

t *Homer's Iliad*, translated by Mr. POPE.
u *Juvenal*, Satyr. 6.

carried on much in the Spirit of a Courtier. Sect.12.
The *Eternity* of a Government, the Forms of 〰
Magistrature, and *Plan* of *Dominion* (Ideas to
which *Homer* was a Stranger) are familiar with
the *Roman Poet.* But the *Grecian's* Wiles
are plain and natural; either Stratagems in
War, or such Designs in Peace as depend not
upon forming a *Party* for their execution. He
excels in the simple instructive parts of Life;
the Play of the *Passions*, the Prowess of *Bodies*,
and those *single Views* of Persons and Characters, that arise from untaught, undisguised
Nature.

THIS *Difference* appears no where more
strongly than in the *Chiefs* of the *Armies.* The
Characteristick of *Homer's* Hero is *violent Paffion*; his *honoratus Achilles* must be

   Impiger, iracundus, inexorabilis, acer:

   Paint him, says *Horace,*

  Forward, and fierce, of unrelenting Wrath.

Nay so great was his *Impotence* of Mind, that
when the young *Antilochus* brought him the
dismal News of *Patroclus's* Death, he was forced
to hold the Hands of the distracted Hero, lest
he should have attempted to cut his own Throat [u].

                            It

[u] Δείδιε γὸ μὴ ΛΑΙΜΟΝ ἀπιτμήξειε σιδήρω.   Ἰλιαδ. Σ.

Z

Sect.12.It is true, we are apt to make *allowances* for
this Excefs of Paffion : We think of the *ill
Ufage* he met with : Our *eye* is turned upon
his unbounded *Courage* and fuperior Strength,
and we are willing to *bear* with his haughty
Spirit : But what fhall we fay to the Prince
of the *Grecian* Powers, who was to think
for them all, and lead their Armies ; their
Stay and Confidence, the ftately *Agamemnon?*
How is he toffed and agitated between *Anger*,
Love, and *Dread* of a Mifcarriage? He is not
afhamed to own his Paffion for a *Captive Maid*,
in face of the whole Army : He tells them
plainly " that he likes her much better than
" his Lady, the beautiful *Clytemneftra*, of the
" prime *Grecian* Nobility." He is befides,
now and then, a little *covetous* ; and tortur'd
with *Fear* to fuch a degree, that his Teeth
chatter, and his Knees ftrike one againft another ; He groans and weeps, and rends his
Hair ; and is in fuch *piteous plight*, that if
we were not well affured of his perfonal Bravery, we fhould take him for a downright
Coward.

But Virgil durft make no fuch Condefcenfion to Nature, nor reprefent the *human
Frailties* in their genuine Light. His Characters are all *formed* and *regulated* ; and except that his *Hero* is fometimes, as Don *Quixote*
fays of his Amadis, *algo lloron, a little apt to
weep* ; excepting *that*, and the Cave-Adventure,

he

he behaves in every other refpect with all theSect. 12.
Dignity and Referve of a *Roman Senator*.

Here the Force of the *Model* appears, and
the Power of *publick Manners*: Virgil's
Poem was to be read by a People deeply dif-
ciplin'd ; whofe early Neceffities had taught
them *political Forms*, and from being a Company of *Banditti*, had *forced* them into publick
Virtue: Thefe Forms had time to take root
in the Minds and Manners of the Nation ; and
Conftancy, *Severity*, and *Truth*, was become a
Roman Character: Even when the Subftance
was gone; when Luxury and high Ambition
had ftript them of their original Integrity, they
were ftill forced to feign and diffemble : They
put on a *Shew* of Virtue ; and tho' they were
really vicious, and knew themfelves to be fo,
yet they could not bear a *profeffed Ruffian*, nor
an *avowed Profligate* : They became nicely
fenfible of Reputation; and what they called
a Man's *Fortune*; not in our Senfe of the
Word, but that *Fate*, which as they imagin'd,
attends every Man, and over-rules all human
Enterprizes. For this reafon they did not love
that any *Accident*, which had frighted or put
them in diforder, fhould be known: They
thought it diminifhed their Authority, and
made them *look little* in the Eyes of the People ; and therefore concealed their Paffions,
and the Events that raifed them. Thus they

Z 4 *dif-*

Sect. 12. *difunited* things from their Appearances, and by
that means difguifed their *Humanity.*

But the *natural Greek*, in *Homer's* days,
covered none of his Sentiments. He frankly
owned the Pleafures of *Love* and *Wine* ; he
told how voracioufly he *eat* when he was hun-
gry, and how horribly he was *frighted* when
he faw an approaching Danger: He look'd
upon no means as bafe to efcape it ; and was
not at all afhamed to relate the *Trick* or *Fetch*
that had brought him off: While the *haughty*
Roman, who fcorn'd to owe his Life to any
thing but his Virtue and Fortitude, defpifed accidental Efcapes, and fortuitous Relief in Perils ;
and fnuffed at the *Suppleness* and *Levity of Mind*
neceffary to put them in practice.

After the *Heroes*, the Difference appears
moft confpicuous in the *female Characters* of
the two Poems. The *Ladies* make but an in-
confiderable figure in the Eneid ; and excepting a *Queen*, who raifes Horror by the fatal
Cataftrophe of her Death, the *reft* are feeble
languifhing Shadows, who feldom fpeak or act
throughout the Piece. *Lavinia* herfelf, who
fhou'd be the moft amiable and important Character, is an obfcure retired Perfon, whom we
hardly know. She is juft like a *Senator's*
Daughter, kept from fight ; and, according to
the Rules of a wholefome Oeconomy, without
a Will or Paffion of her own. The *Italian*
Referve appears in her Manners, and that *paf-*

I   *five*

five Tameness with which our *gay People* find Sect.12. such fault in the *virtuous* Characters of the an- cient Plays.

BUT the *Heroines* of the *Grecian Poet* are among the striking Figures of his Subject. His *Captive-Beauties* are indeed in a state that draws Compassion ; they are too much upon the *eastern* Establishment, to be look'd on without *Pain*, by one accustomed to *European*, and particularly to *British* Manners. To think of a fine Woman, dragged away from an indulgent Father, or a fond Husband, and left at the mercy of a brutal Conqueror, bathed in the Blood of all she loved, is a most shocking Circumstance: It is not to be palliated, even tho' they are represented in a little time, as *pretty easy* under the Dispensation, and unwilling to part with their new Acquaintance w.

BUT HOMER's *Ladies of Quality* are all remarkable for great Good, or great Ill, and make their appearance accordingly. The too lovely *Helen* is not more distinguished by the Gracefulness of her *Person*, the Charms of her *Face*, and that Air of Grandeur which accompanied her motions, than by a *Mind* capable to *please*. She is not only fitted for the

Z 3 softer

---

w Ἐκ δ' ἄγαγε Κλισίης ΒΡΙΣΗΙΔΑ καλλιπάρηον ·
Δῶκε δ' ἄγειν· τὼ δ' ἀΰτις ἴτην παρὰ νῆας Ἀχαιῶν
Ἡ δ' ΑΕΚΟΥΣ' ἅμα τοῖσι ΓΥΝΗ κίεν.——Ἰλιαδ. α.
ΔΜΩΑΙ δ' ἃς Ἀχιλεὺς ληΐσατο Πάτροκλός τε,
Θυμὸν ἀκαχμέναι, μεγάλ' ἴαχον· ἐκ δὲ θύραζε
Ἔδραμον ἀμφ' Ἀχιλῆα δαΐφρονα· χερσὶ δὲ πᾶσαι
Στήθεα πεπλήγοντο· λύθεν δ' ὑπὸ γυῖα ἑκάστης.

Ἰλιαδ. Σ.

fofter Hours of Life, but anſwers *Priam* the old *Trojan* King, with all the Diſcretion of a *Privy-Counſellor*. She appears at times with a high Senſe of *Honour*; and in the end laments ſo feelingly the *Slip* ſhe had made thro' the wrath of *Venus*, calls herſelf ſo many hard Names, and touches upon a *tender point* (her former Lover) with ſuch Delicacy, that I make no doubt but many a good-natur'd Huſband, to ſee her *look*, and hear her *talk*, wou'd approve of *Menelaus*'s taking her home, after ſhe had lived ten Years with another.

THE ancient *Hecuba*, and the young *Andromache*, are the livelieſt Characters of a tender Mother, and a more tender Wife, that ever were painted. All their Speeches, and Sentiments, are ſo natural and juſt, that it is impoſſible to read them without emotion. *They*, and *old Priam*, are the only Perſons who ſpeak long; both as they are moſt ſuſceptible of Fear, and the apteſt to complain under a Calamity.

THE aged venerable *King*, when he wou'd perſuade his daring Son to re-enter the Town, and ſhelter himſelf from the Spear of *Achilles*, uſhers in his Speech with a *moving Action*. He acknowledges the Superiority of the dreadful *Hero*, and then falls into a natural *Wiſh*, " That the Gods had no greater regard for him " than he:" He calls to mind the Miſeries which he had brought upon him; and they are

are fo diftracting, as to make him forget *Hector* Sect.12.
for a little, and talk of *Laothoe* and her *Chil-*
dren, whom *Achilles* had flain.——But foon returning to the *prefent* Object of his Care, he
again begs him to come within the Walls; not
fo much to fave himfelf, but left *Achilles*
fhould triumph, and to defend from *Slavery*
and *Death* the Men and Women of wretched
Troy: Then rememb'ring his own feeble and
deftitute Condition, if *Hector* is killed, he *raifes*
his Voice, and calls upon him to return, at leaft
to keep his aged Father from beholding thofe
Miferies that ftare him in the face: He bids
him do it, Ἔτι φρονέοντα, *while he is yet in his*
Senfes, which has a peculiar Beauty, and is
ftrangely moving; It fignifies either *as yet alive,*
or rather, *before he begins to doat*; when he
fhou'd be infenfible of his Fate, and like a *Cap-*
tive Infant, not know whether he was happy
or miferable.

THE RECITAL which *Andromache* makes
of her *own Life*, when fhe wou'd diffuade her
loved *Hector* from going to Battle; the lofs of
her *Father*, her *Mother* and *Brothers*; her
own forlorn ftate if fhe lofes *him too*, are all
the Dictates of Nature itfelf. But what fhe
adds, when her Tears begin to flow; *the ufe*
fhe makes of her *Orphan Circumftance*, is melting beyond Expreffion. She ftops a little,——
looks at him,——and then burfts forth,

Hector!

Sect.12. *Hector! now thou'rt my All: my Father first,*
My tender Mother, Brother, and my Husband.

THE remaining Characters, *Hecuba, Penelope, Nausicaa,* and *Calypso,* act and speak with the same Propriety: They serve but to lead us back to *Homer's* SUBJECT. They shew its Fitness for Poetry in every respect we can consider it, and by every Comparison we can make with it. It is so rich and luxuriant, that the Poet seems almost overwhelm'd with the flow of *Passion* and Sentiments which croud upon him, and offer themselves to Description. He has seldom room to appear himself; and as *Strada* says elegantly of *Lucretius,* that he is frequently covered with the Machinery and Majesty of his Subject [x], so *Homer* is perpetually *personating,* and says little or nothing as immediately from himself.

IT here appears, that NATURE is the surest Rule, and *real Characters* the best ground of Fiction: The Passions of the human Mind, if truly awak'd, and kept up by Objects fitted to them, dictate a Language peculiar to themselves. *Homer* has copied it, and done Justice to Nature. We see her *Image* in his Draught, and receive our own Perceptions of Men and Things reflected back under different Forms. By this means he fixes our Attention, commands our Admiration, and enchants our Fancy
at

[x] *Prolusiones Poetic.*

at his pleasure: He plays with our Passions; Sect.12.
raises our Joys; fills us with Wonder, or damps
us with Fears: Like some powerful Magician,
he *points his Rod*, and Spectres rise to obey his
Call: Nay so potent is his *Spell*, that hardly
does the Enchantment vanish; it is built upon
Truth, and made so like it, that we cannot
bear to think the delightful Story shou'd ever
prove untrue. His Work is the *great Drama
of Life* acting in our View. There we see
Virtue and *Piety* praised; *publick Religion* pro-
moted; *Temperance, Forgiveness,* and *Fortitude,*
extolled and rewarded; *Truth* and *Character*
follow'd; and accordingly find it standing at
the head of *human Writings.*

By THESE Steps, then, *Homer* is become
the Parent of Poetry, and his Works have
reached their exalted Station: By the *united*
Influence of the happiest CLIMATE, the most
natural MANNERS, the boldest LANGUAGE,
and most expressive RELIGION: When *these*
were applied to so rich a Subject as the War
between *Greece* and *Troy*, they produced the
ILIAD and the *ODYSSEY.* Their conjunct
Powers will afford your Lordship the wish'd-
for Solution; and a proper Answer to the Question, " *By what Fate or Disposition of things it*
" *has happen'd, that no Poet has equalled him*
" *for upwards of two thousand Years, nor*
" *any, that we know, ever surpassed him be-*
" *fore?*" SINCE IT IS NO WONDER, if a
Pre-

Sect.12. *Production* which requires the *Concourse* of fo
many diffimilar Causes, fo many rare Chan-
ces, and uncommon Ingredients, to make
it excel; (the Abfence or Alteration of any *one*
of which would fpoil it) That *fuch* a Production
fhould appear but *once* in three or four thoufand Years; and that the Imitations which refemble it moft, with due regard to the Manners of the *Times,* fhould be next in Efteem
and Value.

Gravelot inv.

INDE X.

INDEX.

Acquain-

INDEX.

ALCMÆON

INDEX.

INDEX.

ARISTA-

INDEX.

INDEX.

INDEX.

INDEX.

INDEX.

INDEX.

CHALDEANS,

INDEX.

CHOR-

INDEX.

INDEX.

Courtier

INDEX.

INDEX.

INDEX.

INDEX.

INDEX.

4

INDEX.

INDEX.

INDEX.

INDEX.

Feelings,

INDEX.

Friend-

INDEX.

Ghost

INDEX.

INDEX.

INDEX.

Hector,

INDEX.

INDEX.

INDEX.

HOMER, *Prince of the Poets*, 2 : *Prophet of the* Gods, 3, 132 : *deified by Kings*, 2 n (ᵃ) (ᵇ) *by Posterity*, 149, 321, 322 : *his Birth*, 5 : *his Country*, ibid. 182, 291, 296, 298 : *his Mother*, 5 n (ᶜ), 82 : *his Father*, 105 : *his Language and Manners*, 15, 16, 17, —— *throughout the* Section, 291, 302, 308, 309 : *State of the World when he was born*, 22, 149, 232, 263, 287, 298, 325 : *not engaged in Affairs*, 23, 115, 116, 127 : *his* First *Happiness*, 34 : *his* Second, 46 : *when he wrote*, 65 : *an* Egyptian *Adept*, 50 : *his* Third *Happiness*, 51 : *Religion of his Age*, 52 : *Laws*, 54 : *Manners*, 55 : *exempted him from Vice*, ibid. *his Education*, 82 : *chief Part of it*, 127 : *his Masters*, 82, 180, 181, 182 : *his Rivals*, 92, 111 n (ˢ) : *his Enemies*, 92 n (ˣ): *a publick Singer*, 93 : *digested the* Grecian *Theology*, 100 : *did not invent it*, 101, 102, 103, 177, 178, 277 : *his* Fourth *Happiness*, 102, 103 : *his* Fifth *and greatest*, 105 : *lived stroling and indigent*, ibid. 109, 110, 125, 126, 127 : *in the House with his Master*, 105 : *succeeded him*, ibid. *turns* ΑΟΙΔΟΣ *or Bard*, 106, 110 : *blind*, ibid. *his usual Residence*, 111, 112, 113, 212, 234 : *begins his Travels*, 116, 124, 128 : *breathed nothing but Verse*, 123 : *his Fortitude*, 125 : *his Friends*, 126 : *has no active Character*, 127 : *Fund of his Learning*, 128 : *extols his Profession*, 129—*throughout the* Section : *a Geographer and Historian*, 135, 235, 331, ibid. n (ᵖ) : *goes to* Egypt, 135 : *a Plagiary*, 73, 89, 135, 175, *to* 184 : *suspected to be an* Egyptian, 135 : *sailed with* Mentes, 145 : *his* Sixth *Happiness*, 146 : *his Mythology perfected*, 147 : *little understood*, 148 : *happy in it*, 169, 170, 190, 212 : *and in his*

INDEX.

his Wonders, 149, 287, 326 : *his own Belief,* 150, 289 : *wisely fabulous,* 153 : *inquisitive,* 147, 182, 238 : *instructed by Tradition,* 182, 190, 212, 298, 299 : *fond of Honour,* 189 : *sails round the* Peloponnesus, 213 : *visits* Delphi, ib. 190 : *hears the Priests,* ibid. *Distribution of his Gods,* 215 : *Use of his Mythology,* 218 : *its Influence on Life,* 219, 220, 221 : *hard to adjust and explain,* 223, 224 : *his* SEVENTH *Happiness,* 232 : *converses with the* Phenicians, 233 : *learns their Geography,* 238 : *knows only the Coasts,* 239, 240 : *tells nothing purely fictitious,* 242, 243, 259 : *instructs in two different Methods,* 242 : *his Veracity,* ibid. *Witness for it,* 259 : *another,* 295 : *a third,* 322 : *a fourth and fifth,* ibid. *a sixth,* 331 n (P) : *where he places the Tropicks,* 284 : *was in* Syros *himself,* 286 : *went yearly to* Delos, ibid. *whence he had his Wonders,* 287, 288 : *his* EIGHTH *Happiness,* 291 : *destined to sing the War of* Troy, ibid. *singular among the Poets,* 292 : *enjoyed the Advantages of a Native of* two *Countries,* ibid. *happy in the Knowledge of* Places, 293 : *of* Persons, 296, *to* 300 : *narrates like an Historian,* 294 : *heard both Sides of the Story,* 299 : *his Information, whence,* 299, 300 : *his* NINTH *Happiness,* 301 : *his Language softened,* ibid. 302, 309, 310 : *consecrated to Poetry,* 302 : *might understand the* Trojans *and their Allies,* 309 : *his* Poetick Destiny, 311 : *like the* Vista's *of a Statue,* ibid. *his* LAST *and chief Happiness, as to his Subject,* 311, 312 : *had Kings for his Pupils,* 321 : *never inconsistent,* 324 : *believed to understand every thing,* ibid. *why,* 325, *to* 328 : *learned no Science abstractedly,* 324 : *follows Nature,* ibid. *a Master in Morals,* 325 n (l) : *like a Musician in Poetry,* ibid. n (m) : *surpassed all before and after him,* ibid.

INDEX.

ibid. *calumniated by* Suidas, 332 : *his Veracity admired by* Philoſtratus, 331 n (ᴾ) : *by* Strabo, 335 : *Difference between him and* Virgil, 336, *to* 341 : *taught to ſpeak* Engliſh, 336 : *excels in Female Characters,* 340 : *is perpetually perſonating,* 344 : *has done juſtice to Nature,* 345 : *plays with our Paſſions,* ibid. *a Painter from Life,* ibid. *Author of the Iliad and* Odyſſey,   ibid.

Homer's GENIUS, *naturally formed,* 4 : *where,* 5 : *comprehenſive,* 10 : *cultivated by Practice,* 123 : *by an* Egyptian *Education,* 135 : *approached to Divinity,* 168 : *but a part of his Happineſs,*   345

Homer's MODEL, *ancient Manners,* 14, 15, 16 : *unaffected and ſimple,* 34 : *warlike and ingenuous,* 54, 55 : *wide and unconfined,* 118, 119 : *real Characters,* 312. *See* Character, Manners.

Homer's SUBJECT, *a noble Field,* 4 : *compleated his Happineſs,* 390 : *what it was,* 391 : *material part of it,* 311, 312 : *includes the prime Characters of Mankind,* ibid. *ſaved him from Abſurdities,* 313, 314 : *directed him where to begin,* 317 : *full of Hiſtory and Action,* 318 : *ſhows Paſſions,* 317 : *comprehends all Sciences,* 323, 324, 325 : *left him without a Rival,* 336 : *rich and luxuriant,* 344 : *its Effects,*   345

Homer's WORKS, *of human Compoſition,* 4 : *inſpired by what,* ibid. *Manners in them,* 17 : *reſemble* Orpheus, *and the Oracles,* 72 : *not written at firſt,* 217, 218 : *their Strain,* 122 : *not underſtood,* 148, 167 : *the Standard of Religion,* 174 : *falſe Meaſure in the firſt Line,* 175 : *a famous Doubt concerning them,* 321 : *contain all manner of Knowledge,* ibid. *why,* 326 : *a Ground of Phyſiognomy,* 331 : *beyond the Power of a Man,* 322, 331 n (ᴾ) : *ſtand at the Head of human Writings,*   345

HOMERIDÆ,

INDEX.

INDEX.

INDEX.

INDEX.

INDEX.

C c

L.

INDEX.

MAGI,

INDEX.

INDEX.

C c 4 MENELAUS

INDEX.

INDEX.

Mountains,

INDEX.

N.

N.

NAMES, *how invented*, 38 : *proper, how imposed*, 234 : *how softened in* Hómer, 302 : Roman *Names, harsh*, ibid. *impossible to insert in Verse*, ibid. *proper Names stiffen Poetry*, 310 : *polished and prepared for* Homer, ibid.

NAPLES, *Coast of*, 251 : *Bay of*, 260,261

National *Character*, 13 : *Rites, necessary*, 79

Nations *expelling one another*, 15, 16, 21 : *Northern, when known to the* Greeks, 181, 287 : Homer's *Account of them*, 240 : *covered with Darkness*, 245, 271, 272 : *Nations relinquishing their Seats*, 302, *to* 308

Nature, *finest Perception of*, 5, 6, 116, 126, 157 : *Aspects of*, 10, 88, 160 : *Powers*, 88, 102, 148, 166, 167 : *Universal Nature*, 215 : *alone forms Characters*, 315 : *followed*, 324, 327 : *the best Rule*, 70, 344 : *her Image in* Homer, ibid.

NAUSICA'A, 344

Navigation, *Grecian*, 15 : *Phenician*, 231, 235, 266, 268, 287 : Homer's, 145, 212 : Ulysses's, 247 : Menelaus's, 272 : *Navigation described by* Homer, 325 n

NAXOS, 234

Necessity, *Parent of Invention*, 19, 23, 230

NEMESIS, *a powerful Goddess*, 221

NEOPTOLEMUS, *killed by a Priest*, 205 : *a Tragedy*, 319

NEPTUNE, 148, 152, 156, 196, 215, 216

NESTOR, 18, 28 : *his Character*, 314

NEWTON, *Sir* Isaac, 197, 333 n

NILE,

INDEX.

INDEX.

D d Piracy,

INDEX.

INDEX.

INDEX.

PROTE-

INDEX.

REDUAN,

INDEX.

INDEX.

S.

INDEX

INDEX.

INDEX.

INDEX.

INDEX.

Superftition,

INDEX.

2

INDEX.

Thucydides,

INDEX.

E e Travellers,

INDEX.

INDEX.

INDEX.

INDEX.

INDEX.

INDEX.

Writing,

INDEX.

FINIS.

Lightning Source UK Ltd.
Milton Keynes UK
UKHW021524090219
336936UK00007B/779/P